67.

Edexcel

foundation

GCSE Modular Mathematics

unit 2

Keith Pledger

Gareth Cole

Peter Jolly

Graham Newman

Joe Petran

www.heinemann.co.uk

✓ Free online support
✓ Useful weblinks
✓ 24 hour online ordering

01865 888058

Heinemann

Inspiring generations

Heinemann Educational Publishers
Halley Court, Jordan Hill, Oxford OX2 8EJ
Part of Harcourt Education

Heinneman is the registered trademark of Harcourt Education Limited

First published 2006

10 09 08 07 06
10 9 8 7 6 5 4 3 2 1

British Library Cataloguing in Publication Data is available from the British Library on request.

10-digit ISBN: 0 435 53382 7
13-digit ISBN: 978 0 435533 82 3

Typeset by Tech-Set Ltd, Gateshead, Tyne and Wear
Original illustrations © Harcourt Education Limited, 2006
Cover design by mccdesign
Printed and bound at Scotprint
Cover photo: Photolibrary.com

Acknowledgements
This high quality material is endorsed by Edexcel and has been through a rigorous quality assurance programme to ensure that it is a suitable companion to the specification for both learners and teachers. This does not mean that its contents will be used verbatim when setting examinations nor is it to be read as being the official specification – a copy of which is available at www.edexcel.org.uk.

The publisher's and authors' thanks are due to Edexcel Limited for permission to reproduce questions from past examination papers. These are marked with an [E]. The answers have been provided by the authors and are not the responsibility of Edexcel Limited.

The authors and publishers would like to thank the following individuals and organisations for permission to reproduce photographs: Getty Images/PhotoDisc pp**1**, **2**, **3**, **7**, **13**, **20**, **27**, **34** bottom, **41**, **45**, **53**, **66**, **71**; Corbis pp**5** top, **6**, **23**, **42**, **43** top, **47**, **50**, **85** top, **85** bottom; Harcourt Education Ltd/Debbie Rowe pp**5** bottom, **52**; MorgueFile/Cahilus p**10**; Nature Picture Library/Doug Wechsler p**19**; Empics p**21**; Photos.com pp**24**, **43** bottom, **60**; Harcourt Education/Tudor Photograph p**34** top; Harcourt Education/Mark Boulton p**38**; iStockPhoto/Ian Francis p**40**; Getty Images/Stone p**65**; Harcourt Education Ltd/Jules Selmes p**73**; Harcourt Education Ltd/Malcolm Harris p**76**; Digital Vision p**86**

Every effort has been made to contact copyright holders of material reproduced in this book. Any omissions will be rectified in subsequent printings if notice is given to the publishers.

Publishing team

Editorial	Katherine Pate, Jim Newall, James Orr, Evan Curnow, Lindsey Besley, Lyn Imeson, and Elizabeth Bowden
Design	Christopher Howson
Production	Helen McCreath
Picture research	Chrissie Martin

Websites
There are links to relevant websites in this book. In order to ensure that the links are up-to-date, that the links work, and that the sites aren't inadvertently linked to sites that could be considered offensive, we have made the links available on the Heinemann website at www.heinemann.co.uk/hotlinks. When you access the site, the express code is **3827P**.

Tel: 01865 888058 www.harcourt.co.uk

Quick reference to chapters

1 Collecting Data 1

2 Representing and processing data 13

3 Averages and spread 27

4 Interpreting data 40

5 Scatter graphs, correlation and time series 51

6 Probability 66

Examination practice paper 88

Answers 92

Contents

1 Collecting data

1.1 Introduction	1–2	Types of sample; sources of data	HD1a/2c/5k
1.2 Designing questions	2–4	Writing questions for questionnaires, minimising bias	HD2c/d/e
1.3 Tally charts	4–7	Designing and using data capture sheets	HD3a
1.4 Two-way tables	7–10	Designing and using two-way tables for data capture	HD3c
Mixed exercise 1	10–11		
Summary of key points	12		

2 Representing and processing data

2.1 Bar charts and pictograms	13–16	Drawing and interpreting bar charts and pictograms	HD4a/5b
2.2 Pie charts and line graphs	16–19	Drawing and interpreting pie charts and line graphs	HD4a/5b
2.3 Stem and leaf diagrams	20–21	Drawing and interpreting stem and leaf diagrams	HD4a/5b
2.4 Frequency polygons	21–23	Drawing and interpreting frequency polygons	HD4a/5b
Mixed exercise 2	23–26		
Summary of key points	26		

3 Averages and spread

3.1 Ungrouped data	27–29	Calculating statistics for small data sets	HD4b/j
3.2 Frequency distributions	29–31	Calculating statistics for discrete frequency distributions	HD4b/g
3.3 Grouped frequency distributions	32–35	Calculating statistics for continuous grouped data	HD4b/g
Mixed exercise 3	36–39		
Summary of key points	39		

4 Interpreting data

4.1 Information from tables	40–42	Interpreting databases, tables and mileage charts	HD3b
4.2 Information from graphs and charts	42–45	Interpreting line graphs and bar charts	HD5a/b/c/d

4.3 Comparing data sets	45–47	Comparing distributions using measures of average and spread	HD5a/d
Mixed exercise 4	47–50		
Summary of key points	50		

5 Scatter graphs, correlation and time series

5.1 Scatter graphs and correlation	51–54	Investigating the relationship between two sets of data; correlation and lines of best fit	HD4a/h/5b/c/f
5.2 Time series	54–58	Drawing and interpreting time series	HD4a/5b/j/k
5.3 Retail Price Index	58–61	Interpreting social statistics; calculating prices in line with RPI	HD5k
Mixed exercise 5	61–65		
Summary of key points	65		

6 Probability

6.1 Probability scales	66–69	Representing probabilities on scales labelled in words and numbers; equally likely outcomes	HD4c/5g
6.2 Mutually exclusive outcomes	69–71	Identifying mutually exclusive outcomes; adding simple probabilities	HD4c/d
6.3 Listing outcomes	71–74	Systematic listing and sample space diagrams	HD4e
6.4 Probability of an event not happening	74–76	P(event does not happen) = 1 − P(event happens)	HD4c
6.5 Estimating likely outcomes	77–78	Predicting results, based on theoretical probability	HD4d/5g
6.6 Estimating probability	78–82	Relative frequency, experimental probability	HD4d/5g
Mixed exercise 6	83–87		
Summary of key points	87		

Examination practice paper Section A (calculator)	88–89
Section B (non-calculator)	90–91
Answers	92–102

About this book

This book has been carefully matched to the new two-tier modular specification for Edexcel GCSE Maths. It covers everything you need to know to achieve success in Unit 2. The author team is made up of the Chief Examiner, the Chair of Examiners, Principal Examiners and Senior Moderators, all experienced teachers with an excellent understanding of the Edexcel specification.

Key features

Chapters are divided into **sections**. In each section you will find:

- **key points**, highlighted throughout like this

> • A **histogram** is used to display continuous grouped data.

- **examples** that show you how to tackle questions
- an **exercise** to help develop your understanding.

Each chapter ends with a **mixed exercise** and a **summary of key points**. Mixed exercises, which include past exam questions marked with an [E], are designed to test your understanding across the chapter.

Hint boxes are used to make explanations clearer. They may also remind you of previously learned facts or tell you where in the book to find more information.

> A census is usually only practical for small populations.

An **examination practice paper** is included to help you prepare for the exam at the end of the unit.

Answers are provided at the back of the book to use as your teacher directs.

Quick reference and detailed Contents pages

Use the thumb spots on the **Quick reference page** to turn to the right chapter quickly.

Use the detailed **Contents** to help you find a section on a particular topic. The summary and reference codes on the right show your teacher the part(s) of the specification covered by each section of the book. (For example, HD3b refers to Handling data, section 3 Collecting data, subsection b.)

Teaching and learning software

References to the *Heinemann* Edexcel GCSE Mathematics **Teaching and learning software** are included for you and your teacher. (The number refers to the relevant chapter from the linear course on which the software is based.)

> **5** Data collection sheets

1 Collecting data

1.1 Introduction

10 How to collect data

- You can collect data:
  - by using a questionnaire
  - by making observations and recording the results
  - by carrying out an experiment
  - from records or a database
  - from the internet.
- Data you collect yourself is called **primary data**. Data that has been collected by other people is called **secondary data**.
- A **census** collects information from every member of a population.
- A **sample** collects information from only part of a population. The larger the sample, the more reliable the results will be.
- When you carry out a survey, select a **random sample** to avoid **bias**.

The National Census collects information for every household in the UK. The information is collected every ten years. The next Census will be in 2011.

In a random sample, every member of the population has an equal chance of being chosen.

Example 1

Brian wants to find out what people think about Heavy Metal music.

He considers asking three different groups of people.

Group A: The people in his class
Group B: The people at a Heavy Metal concert
Group C: The people at a school fete

Which group of people should he ask?

Group C

There is likely to be a mix of ages and views in this group.

In group A, Brian would be finding out what people in his own age group think about Heavy Metal music. The people in this group are unlikely to be representative of people in general. In group B the people like Heavy Metal music! They are not representative of people in general.

Exercise 1A

For questions 1–4 select the most appropriate group of people to ask: A, B or C.

1 What people think about snooker
A: The people in a shopping centre
B: The people in a youth club
C: Snooker players

2 What people think about Chinese food
A: People in a Chinese restaurant
B: People in a supermarket
C: Men in a football club

3 If people are in favour of the new road
A: Car drivers using the road
B: People without a car
C: People at the local cinema

4 What people think about the cost of dental care
A: People in a library B: Dentists C: Students

5 Hal is doing a survey of the people in his school.
(a) Who will he choose if he takes a census?
(b) Write down one advantage of taking a census.
(c) Write down one disadvantage of taking a census.

6 Here are some sets of data.
Decide whether each is primary or secondary data.
(a) Prices of MP3 players in a catalogue
(b) Ages of people in your family
(c) Numbers of households with a PC
(d) Favourite bands of people in your class
(e) Local people's views on sports facilities
(f) GCSE results for a school

1.2 Designing questions

10 Designing questionnaires and surveys

- In a survey **bias** can result from:
  - leading questions, which invite a particular answer
  - unclear or ambiguous questions
  - people not answering every question.
- When you are writing questions for a **questionnaire**:
  - be clear what you want to find out and what data you need
  - ask short, simple questions
  - provide tick boxes with possible answers
  - avoid questions which are vague, too personal or may influence the answer.

Example 2

Tony conducts a survey into people's TV viewing habits.
In his questionnaire he asks the question
'You enjoy watching soap operas, don't you?'

(a) Explain why this is not a good question to ask.
(b) Write three suitable questions which invite people to provide reasonable information about soap operas.

(a) The question is a poor one because it is leading; it invites a person to answer YES.
(b) Three suitable questions might be:

1. Tick the box which shows most accurately the number of hours (t) you spend each week watching soap operas on TV:

Do not watch	$0 < t \leqslant 1$	$1 < t \leqslant 2$	$2 < t \leqslant 3$
☐	☐	☐	☐
$3 < t \leqslant 4$	$4 < t \leqslant 5$	More than 5	
☐	☐	☐	

2. In this list of soap operas, write the numbers 1, 2 and 3 in the boxes to show your 1st, 2nd and 3rd favourite.

Next Door to You	☐	For and Against	☐
Abdication Road	☐	Junction Road	☐
Riverside	☐	Other	☐
Westsiders	☐		

3. If you have written a 1, 2 or 3 in the box next to 'Other' in question 2, please write the name of this soap opera here:
Other is ________________________

Exercise 1B

1 Shani and Erica carry out a survey on the sweets people eat in the office canteen.
Shani writes the question 'Which sweets do you eat?'
Erica says that this question is too vague.
Write down two ways in which the question could be improved.

2 Jack is designing a survey to find out about people who use an internet cafe near his home. One of the things he wants to find out is how far people have travelled to get to the cafe.

(a) Decide which question below is best to ask. Give two reasons for your decision.
A How far have you travelled to get here today?
B Where do you live?
C Do you live far from here?
D Please show me on the map where you have travelled from.

Jack decides to do the survey one Friday evening outside the internet cafe.

(b) Give one reason why this could give a biased sample.

3 Petros wants to find out how teenagers communicate with each other.
He designs a questionnaire.
Here are two of his questions.
The questions are **not** suitable.
For each question, write down a reason why.

(a) Do you prefer to communicate with your best friend by mobile or by email?
Yes ☐ No ☐

(b) How many email addresses do you have?
1 ☐ 2 ☐ 3 ☐ 4 ☐

4 Daniel is conducting a survey into the amount of money that teenagers spend on magazines.
He uses this question on a questionnaire.

How much money do you spend on magazines?
£1 ☐ £2 ☐ £3 ☐

Write down **two** things that are wrong with this question.

Activity – Pastimes
- Design a questionnaire to find out about people's pastimes.
- Test your questions by asking some of your friends.

1.3 Tally charts

10 Data collection sheets
12 Discrete and continuous data
12 Frequency tables

- When you carry out a survey or an experiment you can use a **data capture sheet** to record your results.
- Data that can be counted is called **discrete data**.
- Data which is measured is called **continuous data**.
- A **tally chart** is a way of recording and displaying data.

Example 3

Hitesh did a survey of the numbers of calls to the emergency services in his town in one month. Here are his results:

3	9	13	2	7	3
5	1	10	16	3	1
6	8	8	10	11	7
4	1	8	4	11	12

Design a data capture sheet on which this data can be collected.
Record the data on the data capture sheet.

The numbers of calls are discrete data. A suitable data capture sheet is a tally chart with numbers of calls in groups of four.

This gives four groups:
1–4
5–8
9–12
13–16

Numbers of calls	Tally	Frequency
1–4	𝍸 𝍷𝍷𝍷𝍷	9
5–8	𝍸 𝍷𝍷	7
9–12	𝍸 𝍷	6
13–16	𝍷𝍷	2

Remember:
Use 𝍸 to represent 5.

Example 4

The weights in grams of 30 humming-birds are:

6.7	4.2	5.8	6.2	7.1	9.2	3.8	6.7	6.1	5.2
6.8	4.4	6.1	6.5	4.3	5.5	6.9	8.0	7.1	6.6
5.4	7.3	7.7	8.8	6.6	6.0	5.5	6.1	9.3	4.2

Design a data capture sheet and use it to record the data above.

A suitable data capture sheet is a tally chart with weights in groups of 10 g.

The smallest weight is 3.8 g.
Start the groups at 3.0 g.

$3.0 \leqslant w < 4.0$ includes weights of 3.0 g and over, up to but not including 4.0 g.

Weight, w (kg)	Tally	Frequency
$3.0 \leqslant w < 4.0$	𝍷	1
$4.0 \leqslant w < 5.0$	𝍷𝍷𝍷𝍷	4
$5.0 \leqslant w < 6.0$	𝍸	5
$6.0 \leqslant w < 7.0$	𝍸 𝍸 𝍷𝍷	12
$7.0 \leqslant w < 8.0$	𝍷𝍷𝍷𝍷	4
$8.0 \leqslant w < 9.0$	𝍷𝍷	2
$9.0 \leqslant w < 10.0$	𝍷𝍷	2

The largest weight is 9.3 g.
End the groups at 10.0 g.

Exercise 1C

1 Which of the following are discrete data and which are continuous?

(a) The time taken to eat breakfast
(b) The number of songs on a CD
(c) The number of bees in a beehive
(d) The weight of an elephant
(e) The temperature of a cup of tea

2 David sold 24 DVDs on ebay ~~an internet auction site~~. He recorded the number of bids for each DVD. Here are his results:

9	15	8	7	9	2
10	5	7	12	8	11
13	6	4	3	19	3
6	17	16	7	9	5

Copy and complete the tally chart for this data.

Number of bids	Tally	Frequency
1–5		
6–10		
11–15		
16–20		

3 The heights of 30 trees, in metres, in a park are recorded:

13.1	8.7	6.8	4.3	5.6	18.1	8.3	14.0	10.8	21.7
22.2	6.0	13.6	3.1	11.5	10.8	15.7	3.7	9.4	8.0
6.4	17.0	7.3	12.8	13.5	12.9	10.0	4.2	16.0	11.5

Copy and complete the frequency table below, using intervals of 5 metres.

Height, h (m)	Tally	Frequency
$0 \leqslant h < 5$		

Make sure your groups don't overlap.

4 30 people used an off-licence one evening. They bought:

Beer	Wine	Spirits	Wine	Sherry	Wine
Sherry	Sherry	Sherry	Beer	Sherry	Beer
Beer	Beer	Spirits	Spirits	Beer	Spirits
Beer	Beer	Beer	Sherry	Sherry	Spirits
Beer	Beer	Sherry	Spirits	Beer	Sherry

Copy and complete the table to show this information.

Drink	Tally	Frequency
Beer		
Wine		
Spirits		
Sherry		
		Total 30

5 Here are the midday temperatures, in degrees Celsius, for 40 different towns.

18.6	19.3	21.2	17.8	18.3	18.4	22.8	19.6	18.8	17.2
16.3	17.0	21.4	18.0	16.2	19.1	22.2	18.4	17.9	15.4
15.8	22.5	20.8	21.7	18.9	18.5	17.6	18.3	20.1	20.0
17.6	22.0	21.4	19.3	18.0	16.6	20.1	19.2	20.2	18.3

(a) Design a data capture sheet on which these temperatures could be recorded. Use intervals of 1 degree, starting at 15 °C.

(b) Complete your data capture sheet for this data.

6 Billy's home is near a busy main road. He decides to carry out a survey of the different types of car that travel on the main road. Design a suitable data capture sheet for him to use.

7 Alex and June want to collect information on the type of music downloaded by students in their school.
Draw a suitable data collection sheet for this information.

1.4 Two-way tables

- You can use a **two-way table** to record or display data that is grouped in two categories.

Example 5

A travel company offers three types of holiday:
Beach Cities Lakes and mountains
Customers for these holidays are classified by gender as
Male or Female
Design a two-way table to collect and record the data about the choice of holiday for people of each gender.

A suitable table is:

	Beach	Cities	Lakes and mountains	Total
Male				
Female				
Total				

Example 6

This incomplete two-way table shows some information about the numbers of shirts sold on a market stall last week.

	Small	Medium	Large	Total
White		50		120
Red	79	35	27	
Blue	40	45		139
Total	135		135	400

Complete the table.

Looking at the first column, for **small** shirts:

The total number of **small** shirts sold was

white + red + blue = 135

i.e. white + 79 + 40 = 135

so white = 135 − 40 − 79

white = 16

Then looking across the first row, for **white** shirts:

small + medium + large = 120

i.e. 16 + 50 + large = 120

so large = 120 − 50 − 16

large = 54

Then looking across the second row, for **red** shirts:

small + medium + large = total

i.e. 79 + 35 + 27 = total

so total = 141

Then looking down the second column, for **medium** shirts:

total = white + red + blue

total = 50 + 35 + 45

total = 130

Then looking down the third column, for **large** shirts:

white + red + blue = total

54 + 27 + blue = 135

blue = 135 − 54 − 27

blue = 54

You can check that the fourth column of **totals** add to give 400.

120 + 141 + 139 = **400** so the values are correct.

The final table is:

	Small	Medium	Large	Total
White	**16**	50	**54**	120
Red	79	35	27	**141**
Blue	40	45	**54**	139
Total	135	**130**	135	400

Exercise 1D

1 The two-way table gives some information about the lunch arrangements of 85 students.

	School lunch	Packed lunch	Other	Total
Female	21		13	47
Male		5		
Total	40			85

Copy and complete the two-way table. [E]

2 Mary is conducting a survey into the ways students usually travel to school.
She has identified the four methods of travel as:

Walk Cycle Car Bus

She has also classified the students as:

KS3 KS4 Sixth form

Design a two-way table Mary could use to collect and record data.

3 Bob asked 100 adults which type of music they enjoyed the most. They could choose Jazz, Rock, Classical or Folk music.
The two-way table shows some information about their answers.

	Jazz	Rock	Classical	Folk	Total
Men	12		19	4	52
Women		23			
Total	21			11	100

Copy and complete the two-way table.

4 A reporter recorded the gender and age of the 35 people at a meeting of the European Parliament in Strasbourg.

Here are her results:

Male 33	Female 24	Female 58	Male 29
Male 48	Male 45	Female 57	Male 44
Male 46	Female 40	Female 49	Male 52
Female 33	Female 37	Female 52	Male 42
Male 54	Male 48	Male 56	Male 52
Male 49	Male 59	Male 56	Female 37
Male 34	Male 49	Male 39	Male 48
Male 49	Male 55	Female 32	Female 29
Male 37	Female 32	Male 50	

The European Parliament have monthly sessions in Strasbourg.

Record the data on a copy of the data capture sheet below.

Age (years)	Male	Female	Total
21–30			
31–40	|		
41–50			
51–60			
Total			35

Hint: Use tallies. This represents one male who is between 31 and 40 years old.

Mixed exercise 1

1 Gary is looking at the mileage of some second-hand cars. No car has completed more than 100 000 miles or less than 10 000 miles.

(a) Design a suitable data capture sheet for the data. Give reasons for your design.

In Gary's first sample of 40 cars, the mileages are:

12 850	23 402	16 011	76 852	57 113
45 206	93 444	15 347	25 143	17 642
56 442	33 449	18 730	42 665	85 472
22 225	43 571	88 432	19 002	52 000
17 036	83 202	66 661	57 349	14 027
95 671	75 420	34 006	23 975	62 510
44 921	48 632	34 285	37 848	26 936
44 502	11 032	63 021	51 128	24 137

(b) Record these values on your data capture sheet.

2 The maximum and minimum temperatures in degrees Celsius, were recorded one day for 15 different holiday resorts. The results are given in the table below.

Max.	37.1	42.0	16.2	24.1	22.1	17.4	26.7	27.3	29.0	27.4	22.4	18.6	31.7	30.0	33.5
Min.	26.8	27.2	12.1	26.2	14.2	12.3	22.0	19.8	22.1	19.3	13.8	10.5	23.7	22.0	24.7

(a) Design a data capture sheet for these temperatures. Give reasons for your design.

(b) Complete your data capture sheet for these temperatures.

3 Sumreen is doing a survey into how much time students in a school spend each week playing computer games. She is particularly interested to see whether there is any difference between the times for boys and for girls. Design, giving your reasons, a suitable data capture sheet she could use for her survey.

4 A student wanted to find out how many pizzas adults ate. He used this question on a questionnaire.

'How many pizzas have you eaten?'

☐ A few ☐ A lot

(a) Write down **two** things that are wrong with this question.

He gave his questionnaire to 10 of his teachers.

(b) Give **two** reasons why this is not a good way to find out how many pizzas adults ate. [E]

5 80 students each study one of three languages.

The two-way table shows some information about these students.

	French	German	Spanish	Total
Female				
Male		17		
Total	31	28		80

39 of the 80 students are female.
15 of the 39 female students study French.
Copy and complete the two-way table. [E]

Summary of key points

1. You can collect data:
   - by using a questionnaire
   - by making observations and recording the results
   - by carrying out an experiment
   - from records or a database
   - from the internet.
2. Data you collect yourself is called **primary data**. Data that has been collected by other people is called **secondary data**.
3. A **census** collects information from every member of a population.
4. A **sample** collects information from only part of a population. The larger the sample, the more reliable the results will be.
5. When you carry out a survey, select a **random sample** to avoid **bias**.
6. In a survey **bias** can result from:
   - leading questions, which invite a particular answer
   - unclear or ambiguous questions
   - people not answering every question.
7. When you are writing questions for a **questionnaire**:
   - be clear what you want to find out and what data you need
   - ask short, simple questions
   - provide tick boxes with possible answers
   - avoid questions which are vague, too personal or may influence the answer.
8. When you carry out a survey or an experiment you can use a **data capture sheet** to record your results.
9. Data that can be counted is called **discrete data**.
10. Date which is measured is called **continuous data**.
11. A **tally chart** is a way of recording and displaying data.
12. You can use a **two-way table** to record or display data that is grouped in two categories.

2 Representing and processing data

2.1 Bar charts and pictograms

- You can show discrete data, or data in words, in a **bar chart**. Remember to leave gaps between the bars.

Examples of data in words are 'red', 'small', 'blond'.

Example 1

Joanne surveys 30 swimmers in her swimming club. She records the colour of each person's swim suit.

Blue	Red	Red	Green	Black	Red	Yellow	Blue
Red	Pink	Red	Red	Blue	Black	White	Red
Yellow	Green	Red	White	Red	Blue	Yellow	White
Red	Blue	Green	Yellow	White	Red		

(a) Complete this tally chart for these results.

Colour	Tally	Frequency
Blue		
Red		
Green		
Black		
Yellow		
Pink		
White		

(b) Draw a bar chart to show this information.

(c) Which is the most common swimsuit colour for the swimming club?

(a)

Colour	Tally	Frequency
Blue	~~IIII~~	5
Red	~~IIII~~ ~~IIII~~ I	11
Green	III	3
Black	II	2
Yellow	IIII	4
Pink	I	1
White	IIII	4

A table that shows the number of times each data value occurs is called a **frequency distribution**.

(b)

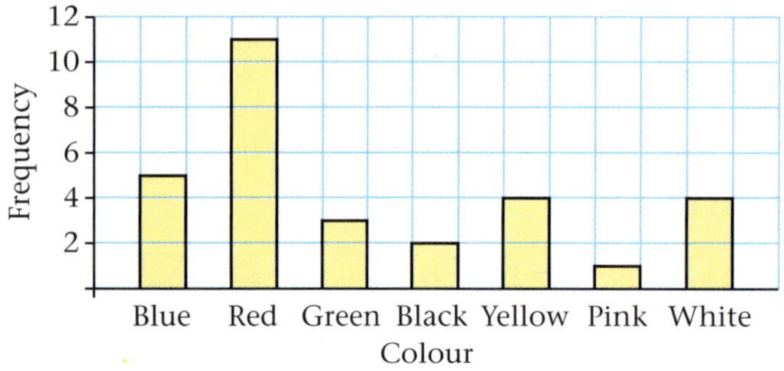

(c) The most common swimsuit colour is the one with the greatest frequency, so it is red.

A diagram that shows the number of times each data value occurs is called a **frequency diagram**.

Red has the tallest bar in the bar chart and the highest frequency in the tally chart.

Example 2

The bar chart shows some information about the number of megapixels each of four cameras use.

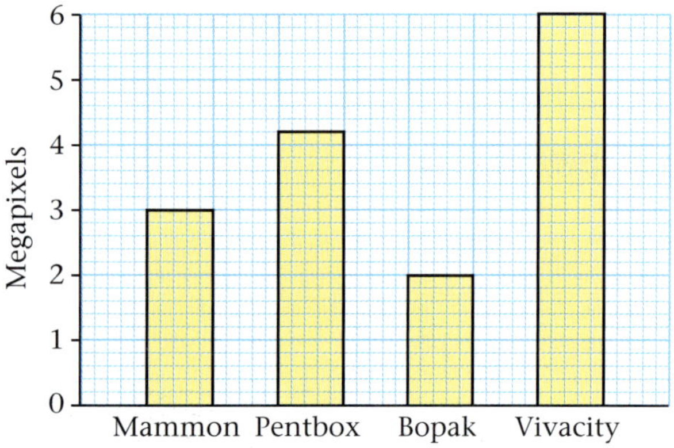

(a) Which camera uses the largest number of megapixels?

(b) Work out the difference in the number of megapixels used between the Mammon and the Pentbox cameras.

(c) An Optickler camera uses 4.8 megapixels. Show this on the bar chart.

(a) Vivacity

(b) $4.2 - 3 = 1.2$ megapixels

(c)

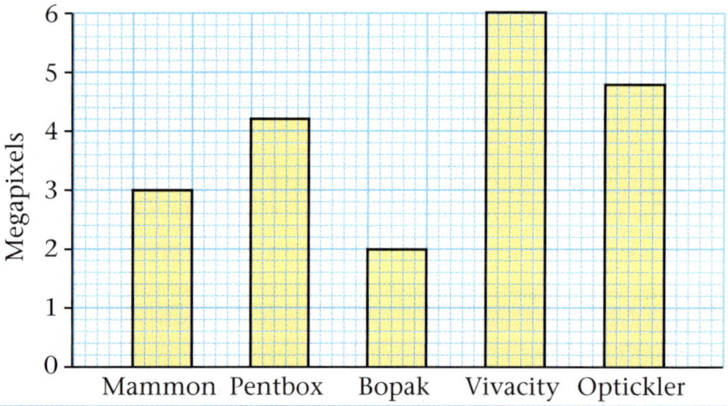

A pictogram uses symbols or pictures to represent a quantity.
It needs a **key** to show what one symbol represents.

Example 3

This pictogram shows the numbers of drivers caught by a speed camera in Askhorne last week.

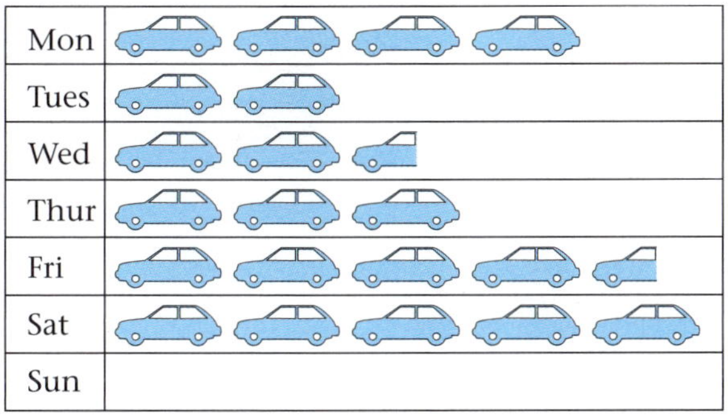

 = 20 drivers

(a) Write down the number of drivers caught by this speed camera
(i) last Monday (ii) last Wednesday (iii) last Friday.

Last Sunday 30 drivers were caught speeding.

(b) Draw symbols to show this.

(a) (i) 80
(ii) 50
(iii) 90

(b) 

4 car symbols = 4 × 20 drivers = 80 drivers

Half a symbol = 10 drivers

Exercise 2A

1 Forty people were asked the make of car they drive.
Their answers were:

Ford	Skoda	Ford	Vauxhall	Jaguar	BMW	Vauxhall	Ford
BMW	Rover	Vauxhall	Ford	Rover	Fiat	Ford	Fiat
Rover	Ford	Ford	Vauxhall	Ford	Jaguar	Vauxhall	Ford
Ford	Vauxhall	Rover	Ford	BMW	Fiat	Honda	Honda
Rover	Ford	Ford	Honda	Ford	Jaguar	Ford	Ford

(a) Draw and complete a tally chart for this information.

(b) Draw a bar chart for this information.

(c) For these 40 people, which is the most popular make of car?

2 The pictogram shows the number of swimmers who used the swimming pool on four days last week.

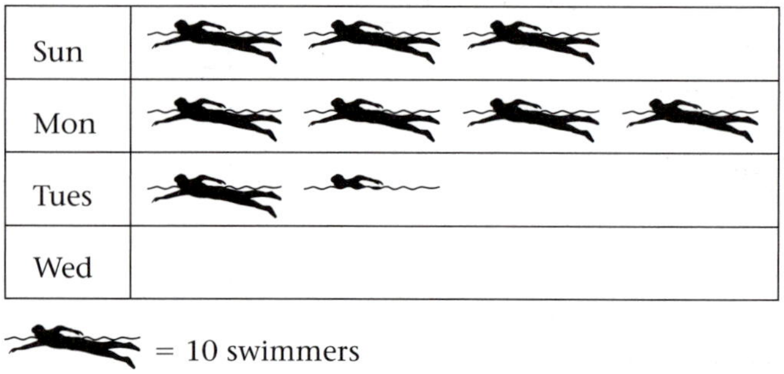

(a) How many swimmers used the swimming pool last Sunday?

(b) How many swimmers used the pool last Monday?

(c) On Wednesday 35 swimmers used the swimming pool. Draw symbols to show this.

3 The bar chart shows some information about the numbers of prescriptions a doctor gave in four days.

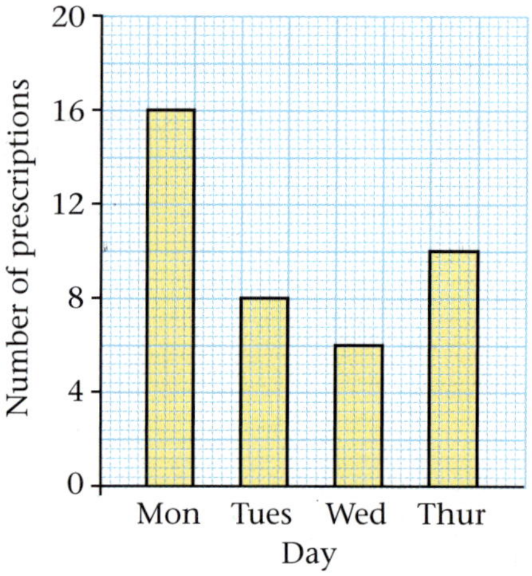

(a) On which day did the doctor give the smallest number of prescriptions?

(b) How many more prescriptions did the doctor give on Monday than on Thursday?

On Friday the doctor gave 14 prescriptions.

(c) Copy and complete the bar chart.

(d) Work out the total number of prescriptions the doctor gave in the week.

2.2 Pie charts and line graphs

20 Drawing pie charts
20 Interpreting pie charts

- A **pie chart** shows how something is shared or divided.
- The angles at the centre of a pie chart add up to 360°.

Example 4

The table shows the amount of oil used per day by five countries.

Country	Barrels of oil per day (millions)
United States	20
China	6
Japan	5
Russia	3
UK	2
Total	36

Draw a pie chart to show this information.

On the pie chart, the angle for the United States will be:

$\frac{20}{36} \times 360 = 200°$

Total number of barrels = 36
The US share is $\frac{20}{36}$

There are 360° in the whole pie chart.

The other angles are:

China: $\frac{6}{36} \times 360 = 60°$

Japan: $\frac{5}{36} \times 360 = 50°$

Russia: $\frac{3}{36} \times 360 = 30°$

UK: $\frac{20}{36} \times 360 = 20°$

So the pie chart is:

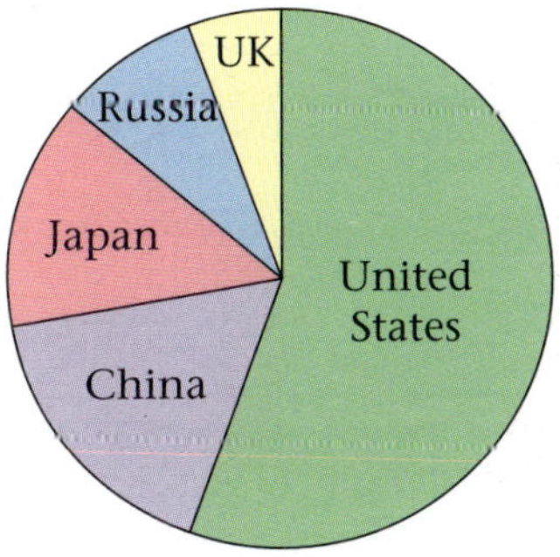

Example 5

The pie chart shows the proportions of people with blood groups A, O, B and AB. The data is for 500 people living in Weymouth.

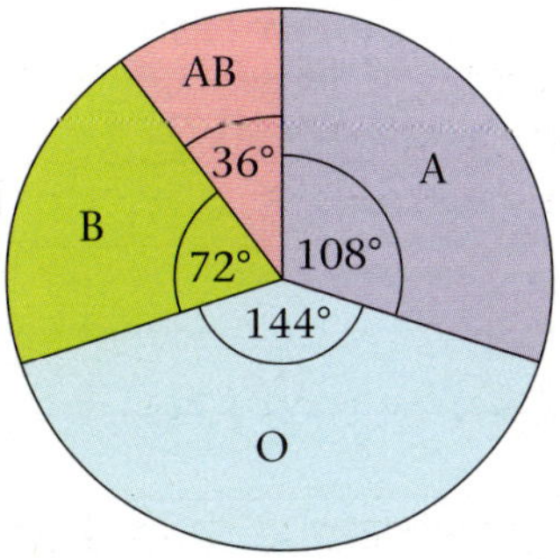

(a) Which blood group is most common?

(b) How many people were in each blood group?

(a) O is the most common blood group.
(b) The pie chart represents 500 people.
The angle for blood group O is 144°.
So the number of people with blood group O is
$\frac{144}{360} \times 500 = 200$ people

For the other blood groups:

Blood group A: $\frac{108}{360} \times 500 = 150$ people

Blood group AB: $\frac{36}{360} \times 500 = 50$ people

Blood group B: $\frac{72}{360} \times 500 = 100$ people

Check:
200 + 150 + 50 + 100 = 500 which is the correct total.

- You can show continuous data in a **line graph**.

A line graph that illustrates data collected at timed intervals (hourly, daily, weekly, etc.) is called a **time series**. There is more about time series graphs in Chapter 5.

Example 6

The table shows a baby's weight in kg over 6 weeks. Draw a line graph to show this information.

Week	1	2	3	4	5	6
Weight (kg)	2.4	2.2	2.4	2.7	2.9	3.2

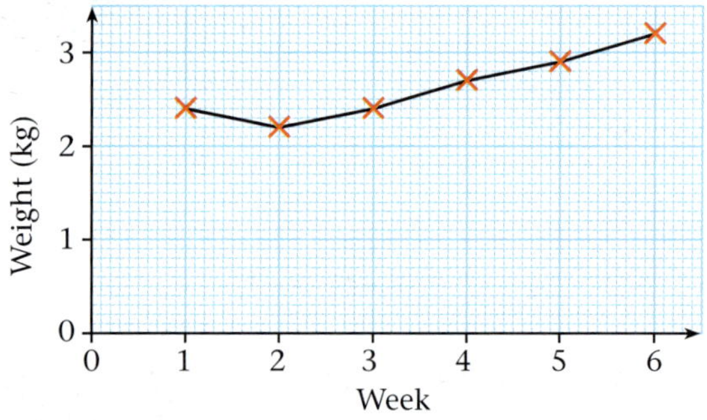

Exercise 2B

1 Harry collected data on the food some people bought in the restaurant today. Here are his results:

Food	Frequency
Pizza	5
Chicken tikka	12
Fish and chips	10
Baked potato	3

(a) Draw a bar chart to show this information.
(b) Show the information on a pie chart.

Use squared paper.

2 Sixty people used a sports centre one evening.
They each took part in only one of the following activities:

Aerobics Badminton Football Squash Tennis

The pie chart shows information about their activities.

(a) Which of the activities was most popular?

(b) How many of the 60 people took part in aerobics?

(c) What fraction of the 60 people took part in football?

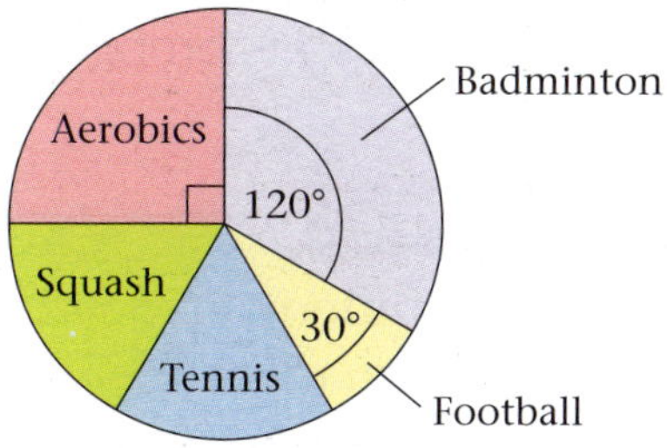

3 The table gives some information about which supermarket 90 people shopped in.

Supermarket	Frequency	Angle
Whiteways	36	
Baldy	18	
Miniver's		
Fine Fare		
Total	90	

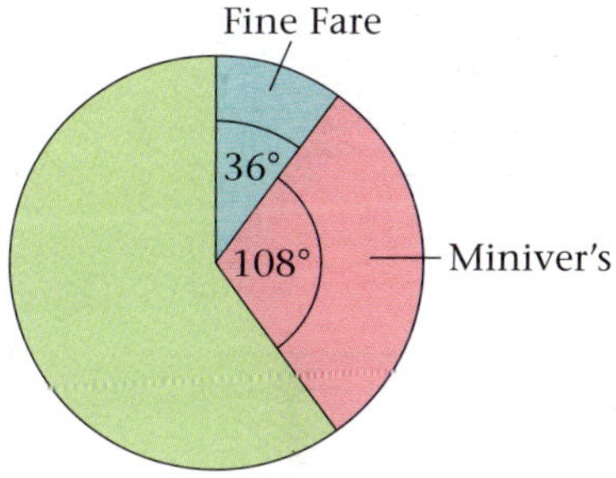

(a) Use the information in the table to copy and complete the pie chart.

(b) Use the information in the pie chart to copy and complete the table.

(c) Which of these four supermarkets is

(i) most popular (ii) least popular?

4 Draw a pie chart for the car data in Exercise 2A question **1**.

5 The table shows the depth of water in a pond over an eight-week period.
Copy the axes and draw a line graph to show this information.

Week	1	2	3	4	5	6	7	8
Depth (cm)	24	21	29	23	17	26	30	25

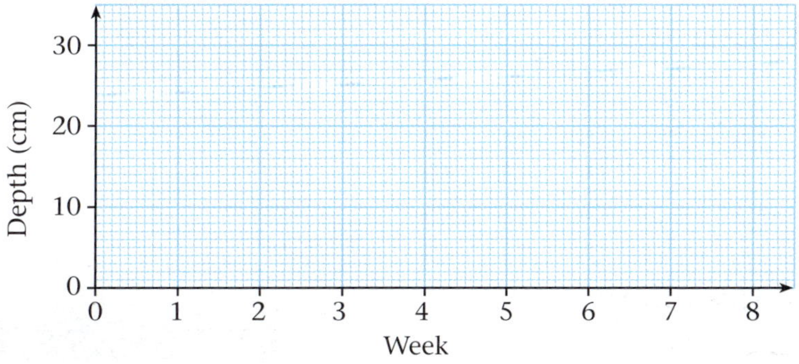

There are over 5000 known species of frog worldwide.

2.3 Stem and leaf diagrams

20 Drawing stem and leaf diagrams

- A **stem and leaf diagram** shows the shape of a distribution and keeps all the data values. It needs a **key** to show how the stem and leaf combine.

Example 7

The 30 students in Set 2 take a Science test marked out of 50. Their marks are given below.

32	41	17	24	43	36	47	12	26	32
45	16	9	22	35	27	28	20	37	34
19	7	18	26	33	29	48	37	25	23

Using the tens as the stem, represent this information as a stem and leaf diagram.

0	7 9
1	2 6 7 8 9
2	0 2 3 4 5 6 6 7 8 9
3	2 2 3 4 5 6 7 7
4	1 3 5 7 8

Key: 4 | 1 means 41

The stems are 0, 10, 20, 30 and 40.

Remember to give a key.

Exercise 2C

1 Here are Shinai's ten-pin bowling scores:

43	32	64	85	71	38	57	52	63	51
91	77	62	72	55	54	62	67	80	49
51	63	70	63	44	48	64	57	62	72
54	57	42	55	61	90	66	61	50	69

Represent this information as a stem and leaf diagram.

2 Carly did a survey into the ages of people using a library one day. Here are her results.

27	25	17	32	8	36	57	49	82	61
64	70	19	12	44	38	29	20	16	22
46	51	54	73	34	38	61	48	46	49
52	56	29	26	31	64	54	59	50	33
41	32	27	46	52	6	15	46	42	38
48	53	52	45	39	33	42	40	61	56

(a) Draw stem and leaf diagram to show these ages.

(b) Carly says 'There were more library users in their 60s than any other age group.' Is she correct?

3 The heights in cm of 30 athletes are recorded below:

170 167 172 185 159 176 186 179 168 201
164 191 182 183 169 177 173 186 183 192
149 181 171 169 173 184 188 173 179 168

Draw a stem and leaf diagram to show this data.

2.4 Frequency polygons

- You can show grouped continuous data in a **histogram**. A histogram has no gaps between the bars.
- A **frequency polygon** shows the general pattern of data in a histogram.

Example 8

The table shows the weekly rainfall, in millimetres, for one year.

Rainfall per week, r (mm)	Frequency
$0 \leq r < 5$	8
$5 \leq r < 10$	6
$10 \leq r < 15$	17
$15 \leq r < 20$	10
$20 \leq r < 25$	7
$25 \leq r < 30$	4

Draw a frequency polygon for this frequency distribution.

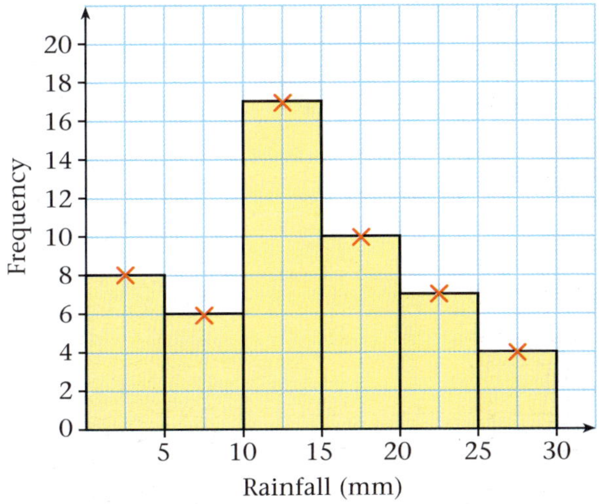

1. Draw the histogram.
2. Mark the mid-points of the bars.

3. Join the mid-points of the bars.

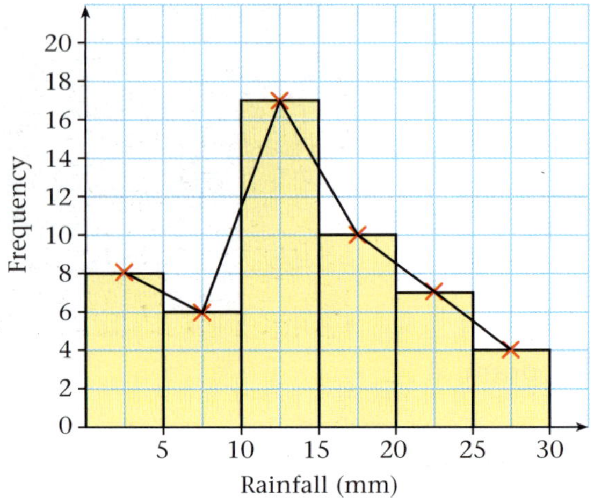

You could just plot the mid-points of each bar, like this.

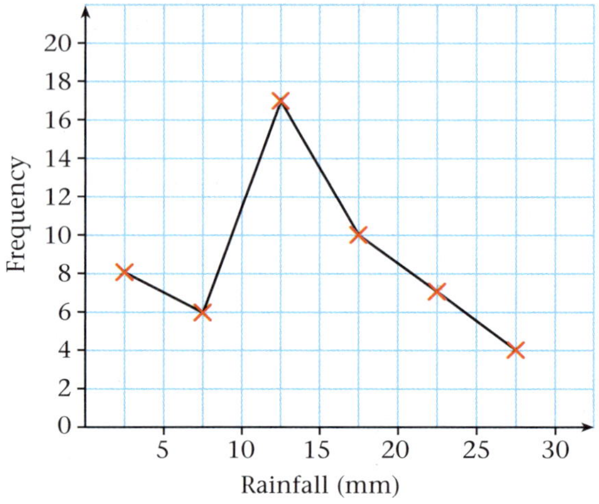

Exercise 2D

1 The police recorded the speeds of 100 vehicles on a dual carriageway. The results are shown in the table below.

Speed, s (mph)	Frequency
$20 < s \leqslant 30$	8
$30 < s \leqslant 40$	12
$40 < s \leqslant 50$	19
$50 < s \leqslant 60$	22
$60 < s \leqslant 70$	30
$70 < s \leqslant 80$	6
$80 < s \leqslant 90$	3

Represent this information as a frequency polygon.

2 The table shows the times, in minutes, for some people to complete a puzzle.

Time, t (minutes)	Frequency
$20 < t \leqslant 30$	8
$30 < t \leqslant 40$	12
$40 < t \leqslant 50$	16
$50 < t \leqslant 60$	14
$60 < t \leqslant 70$	10

Draw a frequency polygon to show this information.

3 The sizes of fish in a lake are recorded. The distribution of lengths of the fish is given in the table below.

Length, l (mm)	Frequency
$0 < l \leqslant 100$	2
$100 < l \leqslant 200$	8
$200 < l \leqslant 300$	15
$300 < l \leqslant 400$	10
$400 < l \leqslant 500$	5

Show this information as a frequency polygon.

Activity – Investigating height

- (Go to www.heinemann.co.uk/hotlinks, insert the express code 3827P and click on this activity.)
- Use the Mayfield database to select at random the heights of 50 students from Key Stage 4 (KS4).
- Record the data in a frequency table using the class intervals $1.3 \leqslant h < 1.4$, $1.4 \leqslant h < 1.5$, etc.
- Draw a frequency polygon for this information.
- Comment on the shape of your frequency polygon.

Mixed exercise 2

1 Forty people are asked their favourite type of music. Their answers are:

Pop	Classical	Jazz	Rock	Pop	Jazz
Pop	Rock	Pop	Pop	Jazz	Rock
Rock	Pop	Pop	Rock	Jazz	Pop
Pop	Rock	Rock	Classical	Pop	Pop
Jazz	Jazz	Rock	Pop	Rock	Pop
Pop	Classical	Pop	Rock	Rock	Pop
Pop	Pop	Jazz	Rock		

(a) Copy and complete the tally chart and frequency table.

Type of music	Tally	Frequency

(b) Draw a bar chart to show this information.

(c) Draw a pie chart for this information.

2 The pictogram shows the number of diamond rings sold by a shop in January, February and March.

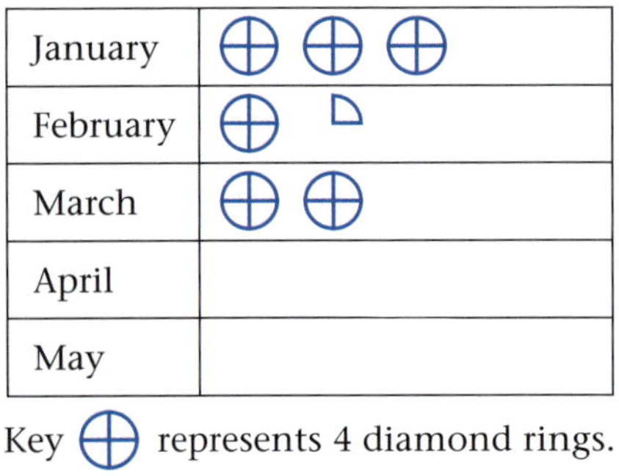

(a) Write down the number of diamond rings sold in January.

(b) Work out how many **more** diamond rings were sold in March than in February.

20 diamond rings were sold in April.
14 diamond rings were sold in May.

(c) Copy the pictogram. Use this information to complete it.

3 200 people were asked when and where they took their summer holiday: in the UK, Europe or elsewhere.
The incomplete table shows some of their responses.

	UK	Europe	Elsewhere	Total
July		20	8	40
August	36		16	
September		32		60
Total	56	100		

France is currently the world's most popular foreign holiday destination.

(a) Copy and complete the table.

(b) Draw a pie chart to represent the total numbers of people holidaying in each of the three months.

(c) Draw a second pie chart to represent the total numbers of people holidaying in the UK, Europe or elsewhere.

4 The table gives the share price of a company on the first ten days in one month.

Day	1	2	3	4	5	6	7	8	9	10
Share price (pence)	23	23	26	22	28	32	29	30	26	32

Copy and complete the line graph to show this information.

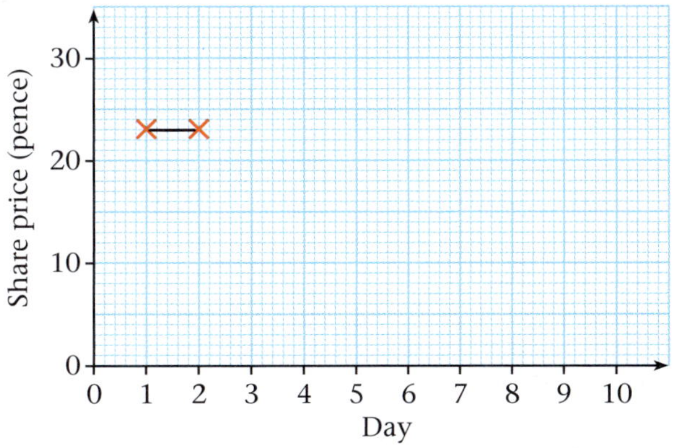

5 The monthly average midday temperatures are recorded in the table below.

Month	Temperature (°C)
October	−5
November	−17
December	−22
January	−24
February	−19
March	−11
April	−1
May	9

Represent this information as a line graph.

6 The pie chart provides some information about the colours of 120 cars in a car park.
Copy the frequency table.
Use the information from the pie chart to complete it.

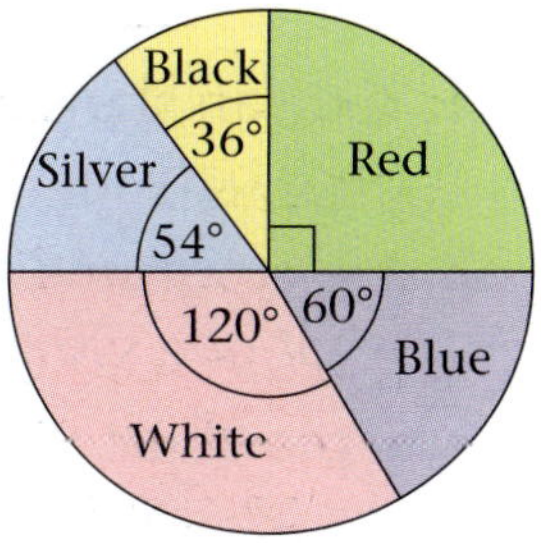

Colour	Frequency

7 The table shows information about the heights of Christmas trees in a garden centre.

Height, h (cm)	Frequency
$50 < h \leqslant 90$	7
$90 < h \leqslant 130$	15
$130 < h \leqslant 170$	12
$170 < h \leqslant 210$	5
$210 < h \leqslant 250$	3

Represent this information as a frequency polygon.

8 There are 27 boxes in a warehouse. The frequency polygon for their weights is shown opposite.

Represent this information as a frequency table.

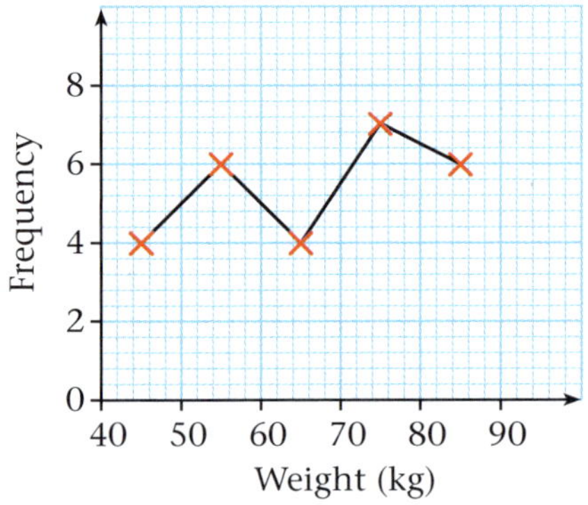

9 The costs per night, in £, for a double room in 24 hotels are:

110	118	125	110	134	132	169	125
127	141	110	111	120	149	99	159
120	125	127	180	163	170	109	115

Represent this information as a stem and leaf diagram.

Summary of key points

1. You can show discrete data, or data in words, in a **bar chart**. Remember to leave gaps between the bars.
2. A **pictogram** uses symbols or pictures to represent a quantity. It needs a **key** to show what one symbol represents.
3. A **pie chart** shows how something is shared or divided.
4. The angles at the centre of a pie chart add up to 360°.
5. A **stem and leaf diagram** shows the shape of a distribution and keeps all the data values. It needs a **key** to show how the stem and leaf combine.
6. You can show grouped continuous data in a **histogram**. A histogram has no gaps between the bars.
7. A **frequency polygon** shows the general pattern of data in a histogram.

3 Averages and spread

3.1 Ungrouped data

20 Introducing the median
20 Calculating the median

- The **mode** of a set of data is the value which occurs most often.
- The **median** is the middle value when the data is arranged in order of size.
- The **mean** of a set of data is the sum of the values divided by the number of values:

  $$\text{mean} = \frac{\text{sum of values}}{\text{number of values}}$$
- The **range** of a set of data is the difference between the highest value and the lowest value:
  range = highest value − lowest value
- The **modal class** is the group which has the highest frequency.

Example 1

Here are the numbers of nuclear reactors in each of ten non-European countries:

2 14 53 2 16 104 2 3 2 1

(a) Find the mode.
(b) Find the median.
(c) Work out the mean.
(d) Work out the range.

(a) The mode is 2.

The mode is the number that occurs most often.

(b) Putting the numbers in order of size gives

1 2 2 2 2 3 14 16 53 104

There are two middle values, 2 and 3,

so the median is $\frac{2+3}{2} = \frac{5}{2} = 2.5$ nuclear reactors.

The median is the mean of the two middle values.

(c) Mean $= \frac{2 + 14 + 53 + 2 + 16 + 104 + 2 + 3 + 2 + 1}{10}$

$= \frac{199}{10} = 19.9$ nuclear reactors

(d) Range = highest value − lowest value
= 104 − 1 = 103

Example 2

The stem and leaf diagram shows the number of complaints received by a television broadcasting company for each of 20 programmes.

0	2, 4, 5, 6, 8
1	0, 2, 2, 3, 5, 7, 7, 9
2	1, 1, 8, 8, 8, 8
3	0

11th value

10th value

Key: 3|0 means 30 complaints

(a) Find the mode.
(b) Find the median.
(c) Work out the range.

(a) The mode is 28.

(b) The median is the $\frac{20+1}{2}$ = 10.5th value = 16

(c) The range is 30 − 2 = 28

The average of the 10th and 11th values is $\frac{15+17}{2} = 16$

Example 3

The frequency diagram shows the distribution of ages for the population of Madwell village.
Write down the modal class for these ages.

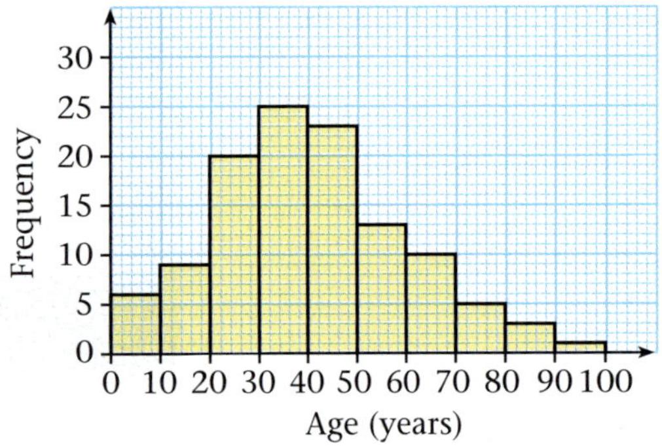

The modal class is the age group 30 to 40.

Exercise 3A

1 Here are the numbers of nuclear reactors in each of nineteen European countries:

27	13	5	11	9	1	6	30	1	1
2	4	19	59	4	6	6	7	1	

(a) Find the mode.
(b) Find the median.
(c) Work out the mean.
(d) Work out the range.

2 Last term Jenny did 14 homeworks in History.
Her marks were

$8\frac{1}{2}$ 7 6 8 4 5 5 9 8 8 4 $8\frac{1}{2}$ $7\frac{1}{2}$ $5\frac{1}{2}$

(a) Find the mode of these marks.
(b) Find the median of these marks.
(c) Work out the mean mark.
(d) Work out the range of these marks.

3 Here are the times, in minutes, of 10 films:

162 174 155 132 201 188 175 168 146 187

(a) Find the median time.
(b) Work out the range of the times.
(c) Work out the mean time.

4 The stem and leaf diagram shows the number of tree rings in each of 25 tree stumps.

2	5 5 5 5 6 8 9 9
3	0 0 2 2 6 7 7 8
4	3 3 5 7 7 8 8
5	1 3

Key: 5|1 means 51 tree rings

Find
(a) the mode
(b) the median
(c) the range.

5 Use the 'mean' function on your calculator to work out the mean of the numbers

3 7 8 5 9 10 7 8 6 2

Check your results without using a calculator.

The key may be labelled $\overline{X}$ or $\overline{x}$

6 The grouped frequency diagram shows the distribution of the weights of a group of people.
Write down the modal class interval.

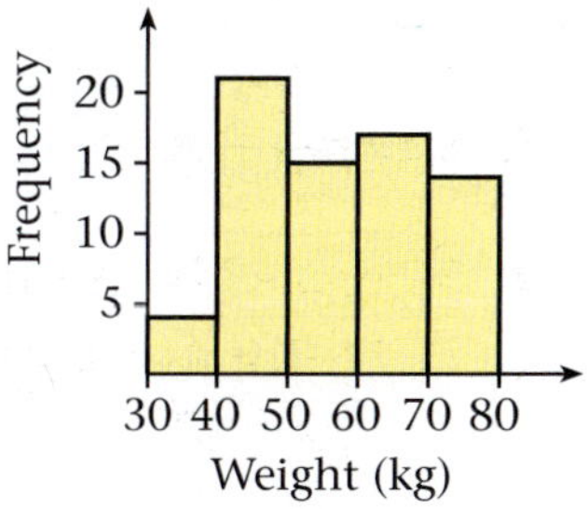

3.2 Frequency distributions

- When n values are written in ascending order:
  the median is the $\frac{n+1}{2}$th value.
- For a frequency distribution: mean $= \frac{\sum fx}{\sum f}$

Example 4

In a survey, Helen recorded the number of yogurts her friend ate on one particular weekend.
The results are shown in the table.

Number of yogurts, x	Frequency, f
0	4
1	11
2	6
3	4
Total	25

Work out

(a) the mode

(b) the median

(c) the mean

(d) the range.

(a) The mode is the value which occurs most often. In a frequency table this is the item of data with the highest frequency.
For this data the highest frequency is 11, for 1 yogurt.
The mode is 1 yogurt.

(b) The 25 data values in the table are written in ascending order. So the median value is

the $\frac{n+1}{2}$th $= \frac{25+1}{2} = 13$th value.

The 13th person in the table ate 1 yogurt.
The median is 1 yogurt.

Number of yogurts, x	Frequency, f
0	4
1	11

1st–4th people ate 0 yogurts

5th–15th ate 1 yogurt

(c)

Number of yogurts, x	Frequency, f	Frequency × number of yogurts, $f \times x$
0	4	0
1	11	11
2	6	12
3	4	12
Totals	$\sum f = 25$	$\sum fx = 35$

$\sum$ means 'the sum of'.
$\sum f$ = the sum of all the f values.
$f \times x$ is written fx.

$$\text{Mean} = \frac{\sum fx}{\sum x} = \frac{35}{25} = 1.4 \text{ yogurts}$$

(d) Range $= 3 - 0$
$= 3$ yogurts

Exercise 3B

1 The table shows the number of goals scored by Halifax Wanderers in 20 matches.

Work out

(a) the mode

(b) the median

(c) the mean.

Copy the table and add an $f \times x$ column.

Number of goals, x	Frequency, f
0	5
1	6
2	7
3	1
4	1
Total	20

2 The table shows the number of days lost through illness in April for 47 employees in a company.

Days	0	1	2	3	4
Frequency	27	9	6	3	2

Work out

(a) the range (b) the mean.

3 In a survey, Ross asks some people about the number of brothers and sisters that they each have. The table shows his results.

Brothers and sisters	0	1	2	3	4	5
Frequency	11	20	13	3	2	1

Work out

(a) the mode (b) the mean.

4 The table shows information about the number of people living in each of 100 houses.

Number of people, x	Frequency, f
1	5
2	13
3	20
4	25
5	19
6	11
7	7
Total	100

Work out

(a) the mode (b) the mean (c) the range.

3.3 Grouped frequency distributions

- For grouped data:
  - you can state the class interval that contains the median
  - the class interval with the highest frequency is called the **modal class**
  - you can calculate an estimate of the mean using the middle value of each class interval.

Example 5

The table provides information about the amount of rain that fell during the 52 weeks of one year.

Amount of rain, r (mm)	Number of weeks
$0 \leqslant r < 5$	8
$5 \leqslant r < 10$	6
$10 \leqslant r < 15$	17
$15 \leqslant r < 20$	10
$20 \leqslant r < 25$	7
$25 \leqslant r < 30$	4

Work out an estimate for the mean amount of rain that fell per week.

Add columns for the middle values (x) of the intervals and $f \times x$.

Rainfall	Middle value of interval (x)	Frequency (number of weeks, f)	$f \times x$
0 to <5	2.5	8	$8 \times 2.5 = 20$
5 to <10	7.5	6	$6 \times 7.5 = 45$
10 to <15	12.5	17	$17 \times 12.5 = 212.5$
15 to <20	17.5	10	$10 \times 17.5 = 175$
20 to <25	22.5	7	$7 \times 22.5 = 157.5$
25 to <30	27.5	4	$4 \times 27.5 = 110$
		$\sum f = 52$	$\sum fx = 720$

$$\text{Mean} = \frac{\sum fx}{\sum f}$$

$$= \frac{720}{52} = 13.846$$

The mean amount of rain per week is 13.85 mm (to 2 d.p.).

From the table, the maximum amount of rain is 30 mm and the minimum is 0 mm. So, as a rough guess, the mean is likely to be about halfway between 0 and 30, which is 15 mm.

Example 6

The frequency distribution shows the ages of 49 members of an aerobics class.

Age, a (years)	Frequency
$10 < a \leqslant 20$	4
$20 < a \leqslant 30$	18
$30 < a \leqslant 40$	10
$40 < a \leqslant 50$	14
$50 < a \leqslant 60$	3

(a) Write down the modal class interval for the ages.

(b) Work out which class interval contains the median age.

(c) Work out an estimate for the mean of the ages.

(d) Work out the maximum possible range for the ages.

(a) The modal class is $20 < a \leqslant 30$ years.

This is the group with the highest frequency.

(b) The data in the table is in order. There are 49 people altogether.

The median value is the $\frac{n+1}{2}$th $= \frac{49+1}{2} = 25$th value.

The interval $30 < a \leqslant 40$ contains the 25th value.

(c)

Age, a	Middle value of interval (x)	Frequency (f)	$f \times x$
$10 < a \leqslant 20$	15	4	60
$20 < a \leqslant 30$	25	18	450
$30 < a \leqslant 40$	35	10	350
$40 < a \leqslant 50$	45	14	630
$50 < a \leqslant 60$	55	3	165
		$\sum f = 49$	$\sum fx = 1655$

$$\text{Mean} = \frac{\sum fx}{\sum f}$$

$$= \frac{1655}{49} = 33.8 \text{ years correct to one decimal place.}$$

(d) The lowest possible age is 10 years. The highest possible age is 60 years.
So the maximum possible range is $60 - 10 = 50$ years.

Exercise 3C

1 The frequency table gives information about the number of text messages that Gina received each day in a month.

165 million text messages in the UK were sent on Jan 1st 2006.

Number of text messages	Frequency
0 to 2	8
3 to 5	13
6 to 8	6
9 to 11	3
12 to 14	1

(a) Write down the modal class interval.

(b) Work out the class interval which contains the median.

(c) Calculate an estimate for the mean number of text messages per day.

2 A farmer surveys the weight of some of the potatoes he grows. He weighs 40 potatoes. The distribution of weights is given in the table below.

Weight, w (g)	Frequency
$0 < w \leqslant 100$	2
$100 < w \leqslant 200$	16
$200 < w \leqslant 300$	10
$300 < w \leqslant 400$	9
$400 < w \leqslant 500$	3

(a) Work out an estimate for the mean weight of the potatoes.

(b) Write down the class interval which contains the median weight.

(c) Write down the modal class interval.

(d) Write down the maximum possible range for the weight of the potatoes.

3 A survey is conducted on the speeds of 80 vehicles on a main road at lunchtime. The results of the survey are:

Speed (s) in mph	Frequency
$0 < s \leqslant 10$	1
$10 < s \leqslant 20$	2
$20 < s \leqslant 30$	10
$30 < s \leqslant 40$	30
$40 < s \leqslant 50$	32
$50 < s \leqslant 60$	3
$60 < s \leqslant 70$	2

(a) Work out an estimate for the mean speed of these vehicles.

(b) Write down the modal class interval for the speed.

(c) Write down the class interval which contains the median.

The speed limit on the road is 45 mph.

(d) Estimate how many of the vehicles in the survey were exceeding the speed limit. Give your reasons.

Activity – Estimating the mean (an investigation)

Here are the times, in seconds for each of 50 people to complete a number puzzle:

80	65	57	30	61	91	67	61	86	51
38	44	81	40	63	45	86	33	67	88
65	81	94	41	55	94	52	53	75	58
86	57	35	65	64	31	53	97	61	85
47	85	49	56	46	93	60	68	47	68

1 Draw a grouped frequency table for this data. Use class intervals $30 \leqslant x < 40$, $40 \leqslant x < 50$, etc.

2 Use your grouped frequency table to calculate an estimate for the mean time to complete the number puzzle.

3 Repeat **1** and **2** using class intervals $30 \leqslant x < 45$, $45 \leqslant x < 60$, etc.

4 Repeat **1** and **2** using other equal, smaller class intervals, e.g. $30 \leqslant x < 40$, $40 \leqslant x < 50$, etc.

5 Calculate the actual mean of the times.

6 Comment on your findings.

Mixed exercise 3

1 Here are the number of cases of malaria that Dr Chang saw each month, for a year.

11 20 14 19 10 7 11 17 12 16 9 15

(a) Work out the median.

(b) Work out the range.

2 The stem and leaf diagram shows information about the areas of 32 photographs.

0	8 8 9
1	1 1 3 4 4 8 9
2	0 3 5 5 7 8 8 9
3	2 2 3 3 5 6 8 8
4	1 1 3 3 5 8

Key: 4|1 represents 41 cm^2

(a) Write down the number of photographs that have an area of 38 cm^2.

(b) Work out the median. [E]

3 Amanda collected 20 leaves and wrote down their lengths, in cm.

Here are her results.

5 6 5 2 4 5 8 7 5 4
7 6 4 3 5 7 6 4 8 5

(a) Copy and complete the frequency table to show Amanda's results.

Length in cm	Tally	Frequency
2		
3		
4		
5		
6		
7		
8		

(b) Write down the modal length.

(c) Work out the range. [E]

4 The midday temperatures, in °C, in 25 holiday resorts are shown below:

24 23 19 28 20 31 38 32 27 29 18 26 27
23 30 26 29 33 28 26 26 28 21 20 25

(a) Copy and complete the table for these temperatures.

Temperature, T (°C)	Tally	Frequency
$15 \leqslant T < 20$		
$20 \leqslant T < 25$		
$25 \leqslant T < 30$		
$30 \leqslant T < 35$		
$35 \leqslant T < 40$		

(b) Find the median temperature.
(c) Find the modal class interval.
(d) Work out the mean of the temperatures.

5 The mean of five numbers is 8.
Four of the numbers are 7, 9, 10, 3.
(a) Work out the fifth number.
(b) Find the median of the five numbers.

6 Rosie had 10 boxes of drawing pins.
She counted the number of drawings pins in each box.
The table gives information about her results.

Number of drawing pins	Frequency
29	2
30	5
31	2
32	1

(a) Write down the modal number of drawing pins in a box.
(b) Work out the range of the number of drawing pins in a box.
(c) Work out the mean number of drawing pins in a box. [E]

7 The speeds, in mph, of 30 motorbikes on a motorway are:

44 42 60 55 81 72 75 48 56 68
59 75 72 69 80 50 52 66 71 68
73 56 62 58 63 60 64 37 88 73

(a) Work out the mean speed of these motorbikes.
(b) Find the median speed.

(c) Work out the range of the speeds.

(d) Copy and complete the frequency table.

Speed (s) in mph	Tally	Frequency
$30 \leqslant s < 40$		
$40 \leqslant s < 50$		
$50 \leqslant s < 60$		
$60 \leqslant s < 70$		
$70 \leqslant s < 80$		
$80 \leqslant s < 90$		

(e) Write down the modal class interval for the speed.

8 There are 15 children in a choir.
Ten of the children are girls and five of the children are boys.
The mean age of the girls is 9.2 years.
The mean age of the boys is 7.4 years.
Work out the overall mean age of the 15 children.

9 The distribution of the ages, in years, of 60 women diagnosed with breast cancer is represented by the frequency diagram.

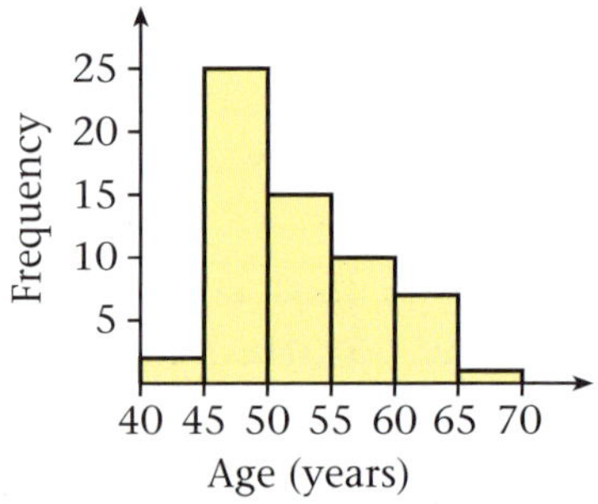

(a) In which class interval does the median age lie?

(b) Write down the modal class interval.

10 The number of people attending a Duke of Edinburgh's scheme was recorded over 28 weeks.
The highest number attending was 18 and the range was 8.
The group leader worked out that the mean number of people attending was 8.7.
Explain why the group leader's calculation for the mean number must be incorrect.

11 The grouped frequency table shows the lengths, in seconds, of some tracks on an MP3 player.

Samir works out an estimate for the mean time of the tracks.

He works out the answer to be 2840 seconds.

Without working out an estimate for the mean, explain why Samir's answer must be incorrect.

Time, t (seconds)	Frequency
$0 < t \leqslant 100$	4
$100 < t \leqslant 200$	16
$200 < t \leqslant 300$	25
$300 < t \leqslant 400$	14
$400 < t \leqslant 500$	1

12 Bill recorded the times, in minutes, taken to complete his last 40 homeworks.

The table shows information about the times.

Time, t (min)	Frequency	
$20 \leqslant t < 25$	8	
$25 \leqslant t < 30$	3	
$30 \leqslant t < 35$	7	
$35 \leqslant t < 40$	7	
$40 \leqslant t < 45$	15	

(a) Find the class interval in which the median lies.

(b) Calculate an estimate of the mean time it took Bill to complete each homework. [E]

Summary of key points

1 The **mode** of a set of data is the value which occurs most often.

2 The **median** is the middle value when the data is arranged in order of size.

3 The **mean** of a set of data is the sum of the values divided by the number of values:

$$\text{mean} = \frac{\text{sum of values}}{\text{number of values}}$$

4 The **range** of a set of data is the difference between the highest value and the lowest value:

range = highest value − lowest value

5 The **modal class** is the group which has the highest frequency.

6 When n data values are written in ascending order

the median is the $\frac{n+1}{2}$th value.

7 For a frequency distribution the mean $= \frac{\sum fx}{\sum f}$

8 For grouped data:

- you can state the class interval that contains the median
- the class interval with the highest frequency is called the **modal class**
- you can calculate an estimate of the mean using the middle value of each class interval.

You do not know the individual data values. So you can only calculate an **estimate** for the mean.

4 Interpreting data

4.1 Information from tables

- A **database** is an organised collection of information. It can be stored on paper or on a computer.

Example 1

Here is an extract from a computer database.

Country	Capital city	Highest mountain	Height (m)	Longest river	Length (km)	Currency
France	Paris	Mont Blanc	4807	Loire	1006	Euro
Germany	Berlin	Zugspitze	2963	Rhine	1320	Euro
Italy	Rome	Mont Blanc	4807	Po	652	Euro
Spain	Madrid	Pico del Teide	3478	Ebro	925	Euro
Sweden	Stockholm	Kebnekaise	2111	Klara-Göta	720	Krona
UK	London	Ben Nevis	1343	Severn	354	Pound

Use the database to answer the following questions.

(a) What is the capital city of Spain?

(b) Which countries do not have the euro?

(c) Which country has the longest river?

(d) Which countries have a mountain over 4000 m high? Comment on your answer.

(a) Madrid

(b) Sweden and the UK

(c) Germany

(d) France and Italy. It is the same mountain (Mont Blanc is on the border).

To answer questions like these using a computer database, you can use the program search tools.

Example 2

Here is a mileage chart.
Use the mileage chart to work out the distance between Cardiff and Salisbury.

Bristol				
44	Cardiff			
120	153	London		
73	107	56	Oxford	
52	98	85	70	Salisbury

Follow the arrows from Cardiff and Salisbury to find where they meet.
The distance between Cardiff and Salisbury is 98 miles.

Activity – Country facts database

Copy the database from Example 1 into a spreadsheet.

Find information about other countries to add to your database.

Remember: When you collect data from the internet make sure the data comes from a *reliable source* and that the data is *accurate* – check against other sources.

Exercise 4A

1 The table below is an extract from a travel company's advertisement for summer holidays.

Place	Month	Duration	Method of travel	Cost
Austria	August	14 days	Coach	£365
Majorca	August	7 days	Fly	£399
Tenerife	July	14 days	Fly	£650
Costa Brava	June	7 days	Coach	£199
Paris	June	3 days	Rail	£159
Barcelona	July	3 days	Fly	£269
Sorrento	July	14 days	Fly	£599
Minorca	June	14 days	Fly	£450
Capri	August	7 days	Fly	£859
Edinburgh	July	4 days	Rail	£249

When it was built in 1889 the Eiffel Tower was the tallest structure in the world at 300 m high.

(a) Write down the cost of a 14-day holiday to Sorrento in July.

(b) Peter can afford to spend a maximum of £300 on his holiday.
Write down the names of all the places from the above list he can afford to visit.

(c) Which two places could you go to by coach?

(d) Amy must take her holiday in August. She can only take a maximum of seven days and can afford no more than £500. Which is the only place she can visit?

2 The table shows the marks that six students received in some recent tests.

	English	Science	Mathematics
Gary	52	61	48
Fiona	73	34	69
Asif	55	73	67
Sumreen	57	68	83
Jane	81	66	72
Philip	56	39	47

(a) Who has the highest mark in Mathematics?
(b) Who has the lowest mark in Science?

The pass mark in English was 56.

(c) Who *did not* pass English?

3 Here is a mileage chart.

Athens				
1199	Baghdad			
693	796	Cairo		
3110	1960	2736	Delhi	
5310	4259	5048	2344	Hong Kong

The distances on the chart are all in miles.

(a) Work out the distance
  (i) between Athens and Delhi
  (ii) between Hong Kong and Baghdad.

(b) Which two cities are the closest together?
(c) Which two cities are the furthest apart?
(d) Simon travels from Athens to Cairo, then from Cairo to Delhi, and then from Delhi to Athens. How far does he travel in total?

4.2 Information from graphs and charts

- **Line graphs** can be used to show **continuous data**.

Example 3

Tony's pulse rate was taken every 6 hours over 3 days.
The graph shows his pulse rate in beats per minute.

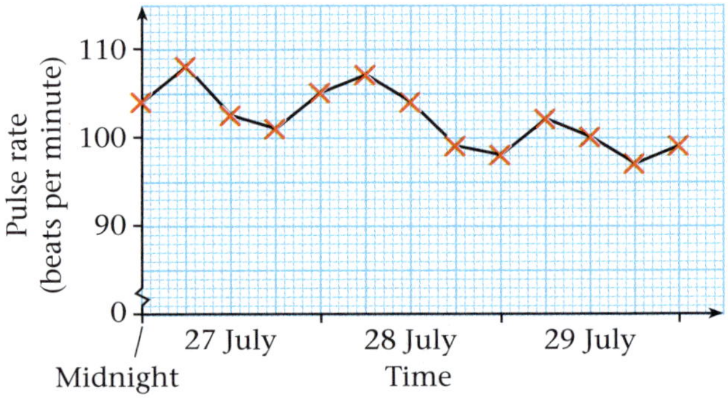

(a) Write down
  (i) Tony's lowest pulse rate during these three days
  (ii) when the pulse rate was recorded.

(b) Work out the difference between his highest and lowest pulse rates on 27th July.

(a) (i) The lowest pulse rate was 97 beats per minute.
  (ii) It was recorded at 6 pm on 29th July.

(b) On 27th July the highest and lowest recorded pulse rates were 108 and 101 beats per minute. The difference between these values is

$$108 - 101 = 7 \text{ beats per minute}$$

- You can compare sets of data represented in line graphs or bar charts.

Example 4

The line graphs show the average midday temperatures in England and Gibraltar for April to October.
Write three comments about these graphs.

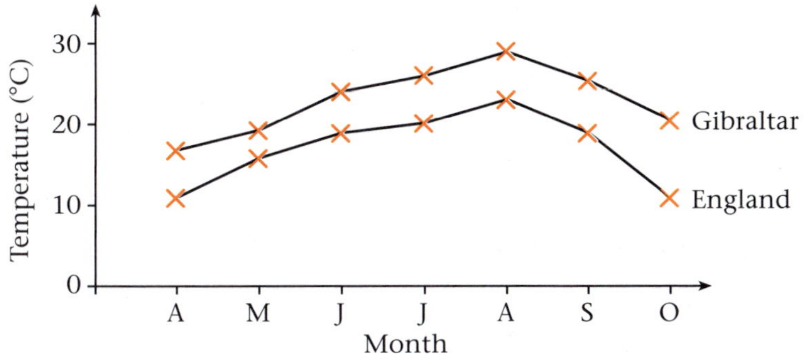

The Rock is Gibraltar's most famous feature. It is 426 metres high.

(i) The temperature in Gibraltar is consistently higher than the temperature in England.

(ii) The month when the temperature difference between Gibraltar and England is at its lowest is May.

(iii) The month when the temperature difference between Gibraltar and England is at its greatest is October.

Example 5

The diagram shows the maximum and minimum depths of a river over seven months.

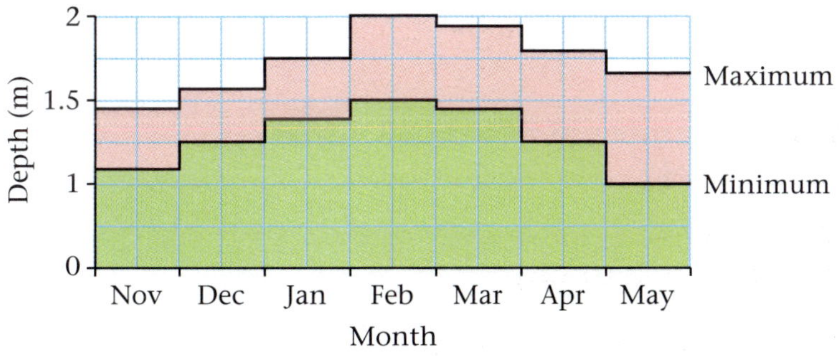

(a) During which month was the river's depth greatest?

(b) During which month was the difference between the maximum and minimum depths of the river the greatest?

(a) The greatest depth, of 2 metres, was in February.

(b) The greatest difference between the maximum and minimum depths of the river was in May.

Look for the tallest bar.

Look for the biggest difference between the two coloured sections.

Exercise 4B

1 The graphs below show information about the value of two cars over an eight-year period.
The engine sizes of the cars are 2000 cc and 1200 cc.

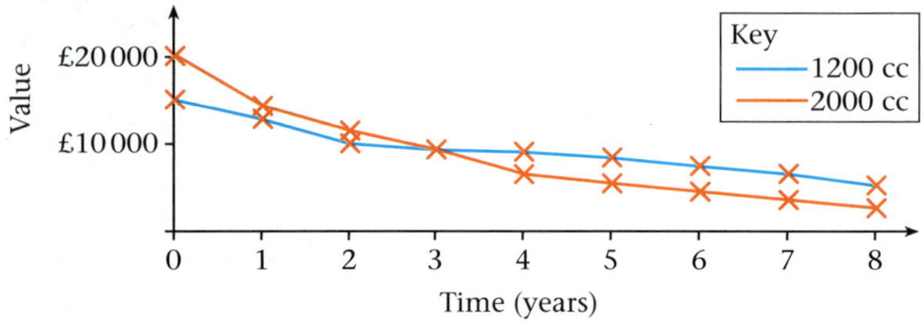

Write three comments about the relative prices of these two cars over the eight-year period.

2 The graphs below show information about the variation in average house prices in regions **A** and **B** over a ten-year period.

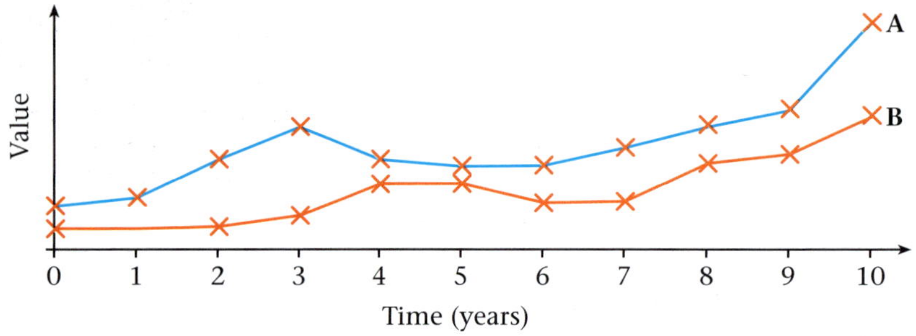

Comment as fully as possible on the information shown in the graphs.

3 Here is a bar chart showing the number of hours of TV that Helen and Robin watched last week.

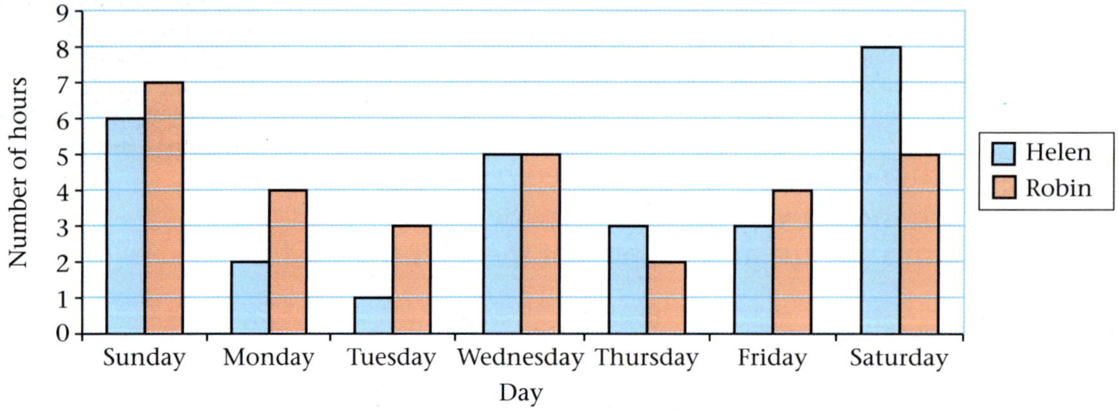

(a) Write down the number of hours of TV that Helen watched on Monday.

(b) On which day did Helen and Robin watch the same number of hours of TV?

(c) (i) Work out the total number of hours of TV that Robin watched on Friday and Saturday.

(ii) Who watched the greater number of hours of TV on Friday and Saturday? Show your working. [E]

4 The bar charts show the temperatures in London and Barcelona during the summer months.

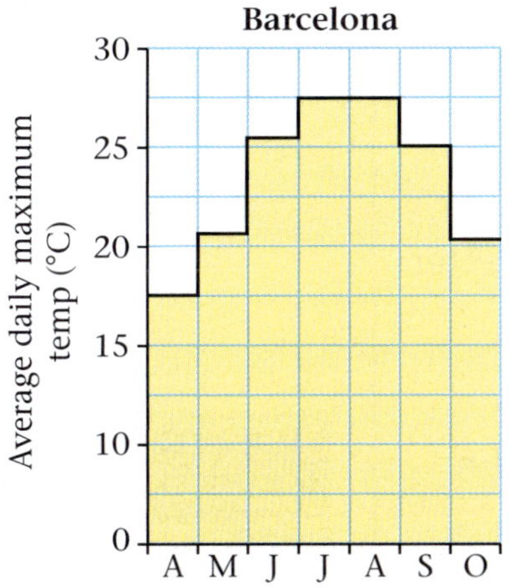

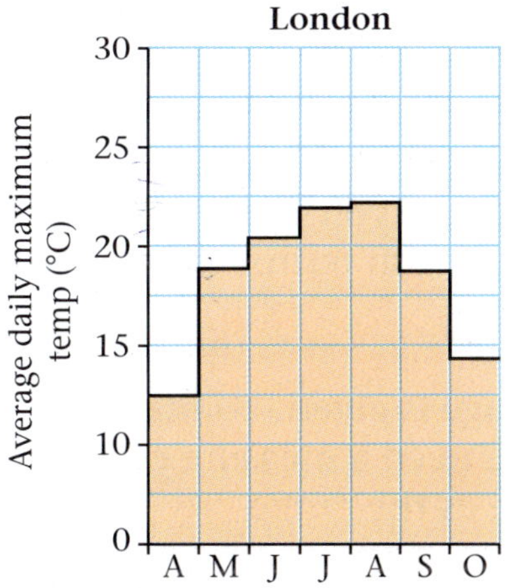

Las Ramblas in Barcelona is one of the most famous streets in the world.

(a) During which month is the temperature at its highest in London?

(b) Work out the difference between temperatures in London and Barcelona during May.

(c) Write a comment comparing the temperatures in Barcelona and London.

4.3 Comparing data sets

- You need a measure of average *and* a measure of spread to compare two sets of data.

The mean, mode and median are measures of average.

The range is a measure of spread.

Example 6

There are 15 girls and 15 boys in class 11T.
They took a spelling test with a maximum mark of 20.

The median mark for the girls was 16, with a range of 4.
The median mark for the boys was 12, with a range of 10.

By comparing the results explain whether the girls or the boys did better in the spelling test.

By just comparing the medians it looks as if the girls, on the whole, did better than the boys.
However, taking the ranges into account and given a maximum mark of 20 it could be possible that several boys scored higher than the maximum mark for the girls.
So the evidence is inconclusive about whether the girls or the boys did better.

Median for girls = 16
Median for boys = 12

Example 7

A group of men and a group of women took their driving theory test.
The average mark for the men was 50.
The average mark for the women was 60.

Explain, using an example if you wish, why it is not possible to say that, in general terms, the women did better in the test than the men.

Only a measure of average is given. To make a full and accurate comparison we need a measure of average and a measure of spread, such as the range.

Without both of these we cannot make a real comparison.

Suppose there were three men and three women.
The marks for the women were 55, 60 and 65.
The marks for the men were 70, 70 and 10.

The mean for the women is then $\frac{55 + 60 + 65}{3} = 60$

The mean for the men is then $\frac{70 + 70 + 10}{3} = 50$

So the average (mean) for the women is 60, which is greater than the average of 50 for the men.

But it is not possible to say that the women have, in general, done better than the men, because two-thirds of the men scored higher than all the women.

Exercise 4C

1 Mrs Rogers gave her class a mental arithmetic test.
The median mark for the boys was 7 and the range of the marks for the boys was 4.
The median mark for the girls was 6 and the range of the marks for the girls was 8.
Explain whether the boys or the girls did better in this mental arithmetic test.

2 A company researched a new product. It asked a group of girls and a similarly sized group of boys to rate the product. The average rating given by the girls was higher than the average rating given by the boys.
Explain whether or not it is possible to conclude that, in general, the girls rated the product higher than the boys.

3 In a game of golf the person with the lowest score wins. Nick and Tiger play five games of golf. Here are their scores.

Nick:	67	74	66	67	66
Tiger:	64	68	74	67	72

Who is the better player?
Give a reason for your answer.

Mixed exercise 4

1 The table shows the distances in kilometres between some cities in the USA.

Boston					
1589	Chicago				
4891	3366	Los Angeles			
2474	2184	4373	Miami		
342	1352	4539	2133	New York	
5067	3493	667	4990	4826	San Francisco

(a) Write down the distance between Los Angeles and New York.

One of the cities in the table is 2184 km from Miami.

(b) Write down the name of this city.

(c) Write down the name of the city which is furthest from San Francisco. [E]

2 The incomplete table and bar chart shows some information about the leisure activities of 100 people.

	Male	Female
Meal out	60	64
Cinema	52	47
Night club		
Spectator sports	31	13

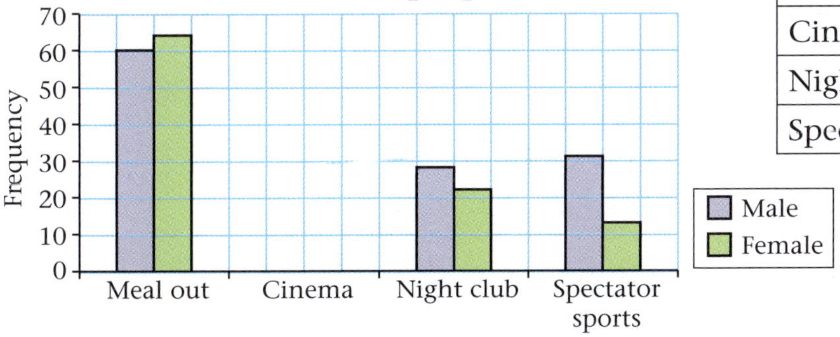

(a) Copy the table. Use the bar chart to complete it.

(b) Copy the bar chart. Use the table to complete it.

3 The mean weekly wage at Spencer and Sons is £210.
The mean weekly wage at Creswell Ltd is £250.
Is it fair to say that the people at Creswell Ltd are better paid than the people at Spencer and Sons? Explain your answer.

4 The graph shows the number of ice creams sold each day during one week.

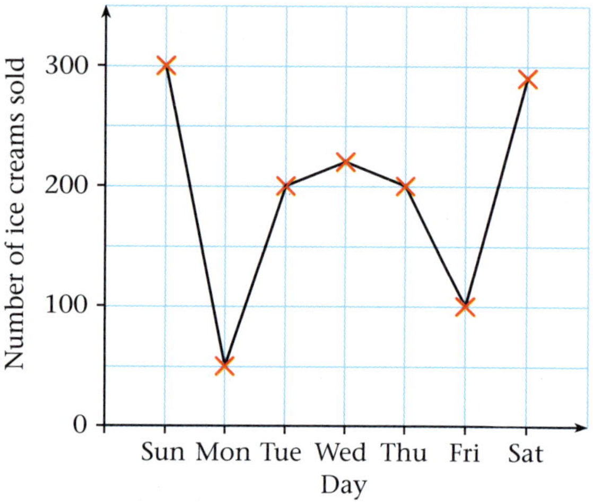

(a) How many more ice creams were sold on Tuesday than on Monday?

(b) Explain what might have happened on Monday. [E]

5 For a project on the prices of used cars, Gary collects information about the prices of two different makes of car.
He records the data in two frequency polygons:

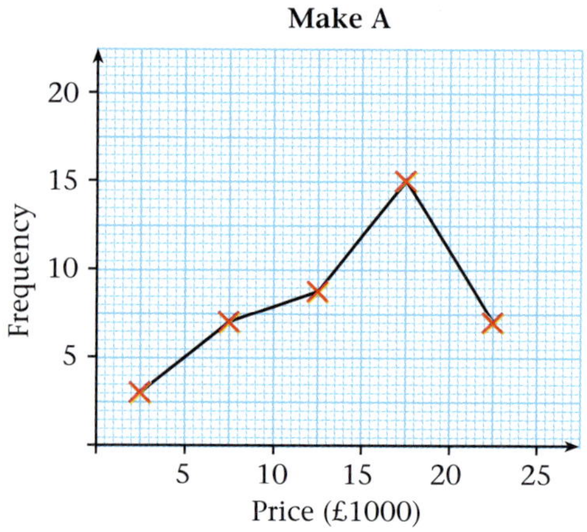

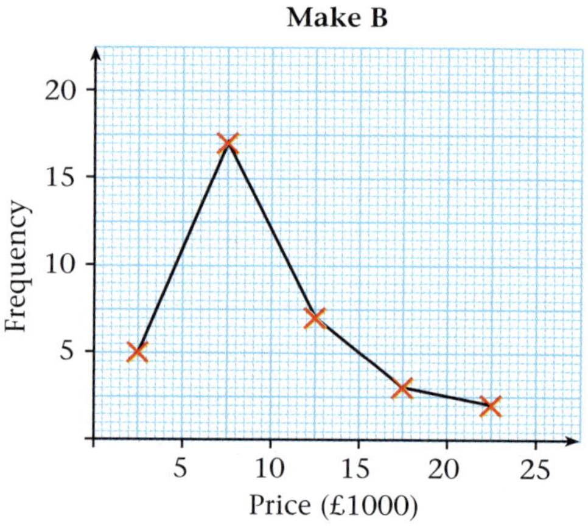

Compare, as fully as possible, the prices of the two makes of car.

6 The table below shows the pass rates (as percentages) for GCSE English in summer 2004 and summer 2005 at High School.

	A*	A	B	C	D	E	F	G	U
2004	3%	12%	21%	24%	18%	17%	3%	2%	0%
2005	2.8%	13.2%	23%	22%	17%	16%	3%	3%	0%

Make three valid comments about these pass rates.

7 Ali and Nick both sell second-hand cars.
Information about the values of the cars they have for sale is shown on the two frequency polygons.

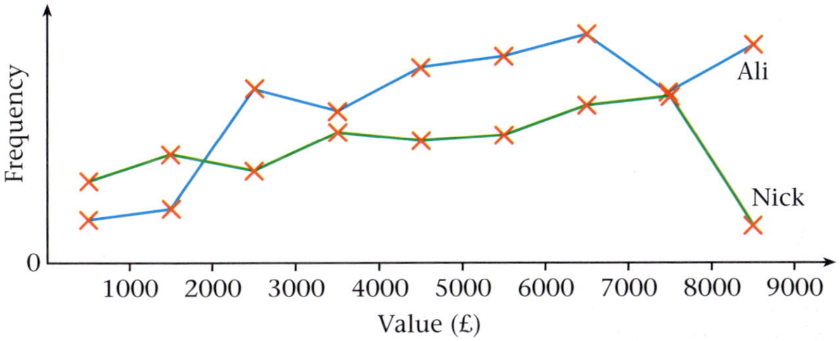

Make three valid comments comparing the values of the cars Ali has for sale with those that Nick has for sale.

8 Dominique asked 72 people at her school their shoe size. Here are her results.

7	4	5	6	7	4	3	5	5	7	8
5	3	6	6	6	4	5	4	5	8	9
5	6	6	5	6	7	6	5	4	4	5
6	6	6	5	3	9	11	6	7	8	6
6	8	4	9	10	8	6	10	7	7	7
4	4	10	9	7	8	6	5	4	3	11
10	9	6	5	6	5					

(a) Draw a tally chart and frequency table for this data.
(b) Represent the data on a bar chart.
(c) Represent the data on a pie chart.
(d) What is the mode of the shoe sizes?

Dominique's friend did a survey of shoe sizes in another school. She told Dominique that at the other school the mode of the shoe sizes was 7.

(e) Explain whether or not there is sufficient evidence to suggest that the students at the other school have, in general, larger feet than the students at Dominique's school.

9 During the summer of 2002, 32 countries took part in the finals of the football World Cup.
Correct to the nearest million and in millions, the populations of those countries at the time of the World Cup were:

38	10	176	16	1348	4	4	5
13	59	82	4	58	127	49	100
147	5	10	142	22	10	2	45
41	9	10	70	60	287	3	39

(a) Which of these population figures could be described as *exceptional*? Give your reasons.

(b) Explain whether the **mean**, **mode** or **median** would truly reflect the average population of a country taking part in the World Cup finals.

(c) Represent the population figures on a **stem and leaf** diagram.

The first World Cup final took place in 1930. The table below shows the countries that have subsequently won the World Cup, the number of times each country has won it and the population (in millions) of each country.

Country	Number of wins	Population
Brazil	5	176
Italy	4	58
Germany	3	82
Argentina	2	38
Uruguay	2	3
England	1	60
France	1	59

Uruguay's independence was recognised in 1828.

(d) Explain why this data gives the people of Uruguay every right to feel proud of their country's achievement in the World Cup.

Summary of key points

1 A **database** is an organised collection of information. It can be stored on paper or on a computer.

2 **Line graphs** can be used to show continuous data.

3 You can compare sets of data represented in line graphs or bar charts.

4 You need a measure of average *and* a measure of spread to compare two sets of data.

5 Scatter graphs, correlation and time series

5.1 Scatter graphs and correlation

24 Plotting scatter diagrams

- A linear relationship between two sets of data is called a **correlation**.

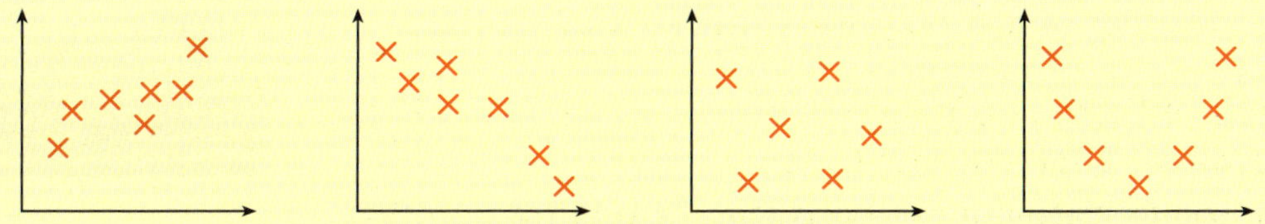

Positive correlation | Negative correlation | No correlation | No correlation (no linear relationship)

- The **line of best fit** is a straight line that passes through or is as close to as many of the plotted points as possible.
- A line of best fit gives a model for how two variables are related. The closer the plotted points are to the line the better the correlation.
- A line of best fit can be used to estimate other data values.

Example 1

The table shows the total hours of sunshine and the total rainfall in mm, in seven towns last summer.

Sunshine (hours)	660	465	550	430	615	400	630
Rainfall (mm)	12	20	16	20	13	28	15

These values are plotted as points on the scatter graph below.

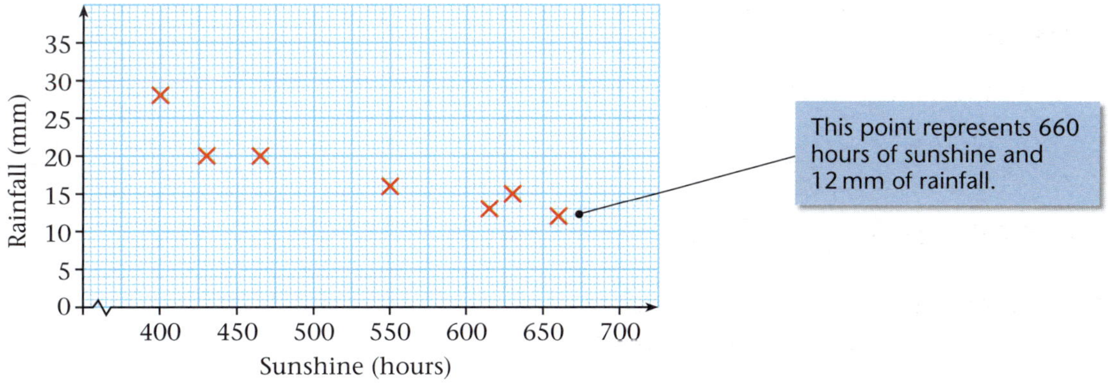

The hours of sunshine and rainfall in three other towns are shown in this table.

Sunshine (hours)	Rainfall (mm)
380	30
525	19
625	35

(a) Plot these extra pairs of values on the scatter graph.

(b) Describe the relationship between the hours of sunshine and the rainfall.

(c) Draw the line of best fit on the scatter graph.

(d) Use your line to find estimates of

(i) the rainfall in a town with 500 hours of sunshine

(ii) the number of hours of sunshine in a town that had 15 mm of rainfall.

(a) The complete scatter graph with the three extra points is

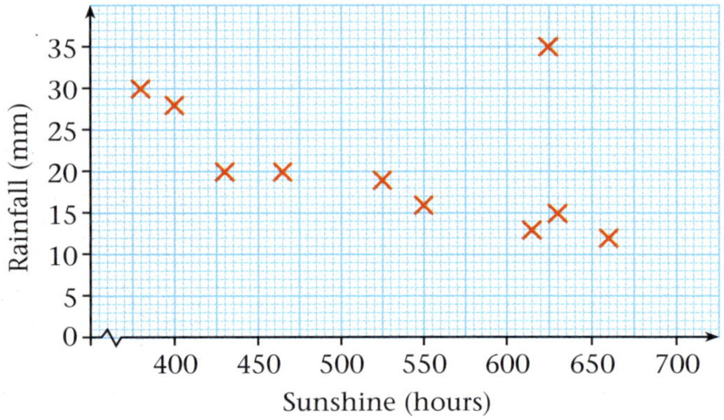

(b) The scatter graph shows that there is negative correlation. As hours of sunshine increase, rainfall decreases.

(c) The line of best fit is as shown.

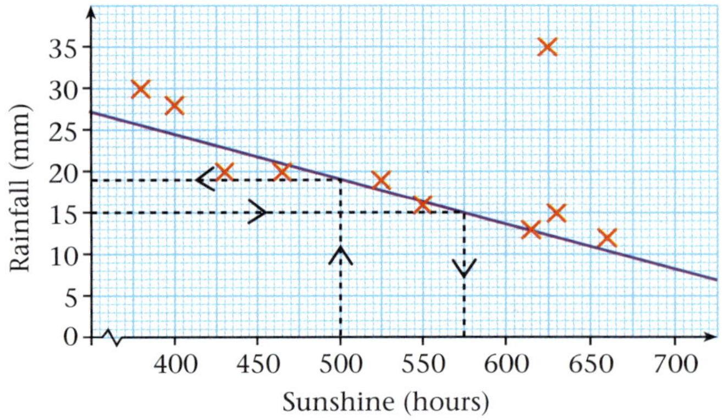

When drawing the line of best fit the point at (625, 35) was ignored. This point is so far from the other data points it is an **exception**. The pattern of weather in this town appears to be different to the other towns. It could perhaps be in a different country.

The points are close to the line of best fit. This shows strong correlation between the amount of sunshine and the amount of rainfall.

(d) The estimates from the line are

(i) 500 hours gives a rainfall figure of 19 mm

(ii) 15 mm of rain gives a sunshine figure of 575 hours.

Exercise 5A

1 Jade sells second-hand cars.
The table gives the value and mileage of eight cars on his forecourt.

Value (£)	6300	4200	8500	9500	2700	1850	3300	8200
Mileage	24 000	43 000	12 000	6500	94 000	101 000	51 000	14 000

(a) Plot these values as points on a scatter graph.
(b) Comment on the correlation between mileage and value.
(c) Draw a line of best fit on the scatter graph.
(d) Use your line of best fit to work out an estimate of
  (i) the likely mileage for a car valued at £5000
  (ii) the likely value of a car with a mileage of 72 000.

2 Kieran has conducted a survey examining the heights and weights of some of the people in his rowing club.
The results for six people are shown in the table below.

Height (cm)	Weight (kg)
178	80
157	57
182	81
155	53
148	42
175	74

These results are presented on the scatter graph below.

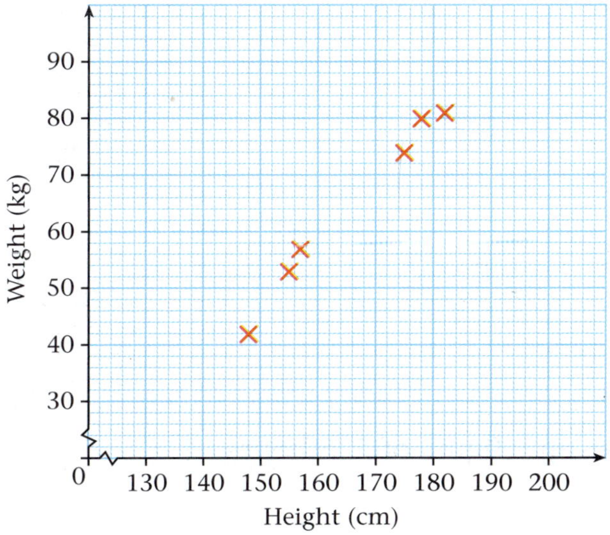

The results for a further four people are:

Height (cm)	192	138	163	180
Weight (kg)	88	36	60	79

(a) Plot these extra four values on a copy of the scatter graph.

(b) Describe the relationship between the heights and weights of these ten people.

(c) Draw a line of best fit on your scatter graph.

(d) Use your line of best fit to estimate
  (i) the likely weight of a person of height 150 cm
  (ii) the likely height of a person who weighs 72 kg.

5.2 Time series

- A **time series graph** is a line graph that shows data collected at timed intervals (e.g. hourly, daily, weekly, ...).

Example 2

The table below shows information about the average midday temperatures in Rhodes during the summer months.

Month	April	May	June	July	Aug	Sept	Oct
Temperature (°C)	18	21	26	29	31	27	23

(a) Draw a time series graph for this data.

During the same summer months, the average midday temperatures in the UK are:

Month	April	May	June	July	Aug	Sept	Oct
Temperature (°C)	13	18	20	22	22	19	14

(b) Draw a time series graph for this data on the same axes as for the Rhodes data.

(c) During which of these summer months is
  (i) the average midday temperature in Rhodes highest
  (ii) the average midday temperature in the UK lowest
  (iii) the smallest difference between the average midday temperatures in Rhodes and the UK
  (iv) the greatest difference between the average midday temperatures in Rhodes and the UK?

Mrs Jones wants to go on holiday to Rhodes when the average midday temperature is not above 30 °C. She wants to go when the difference between the average midday temperatures in Rhodes and the UK is as high as possible.

(d) During which month should Mrs Jones go to Rhodes?

(a) (b)

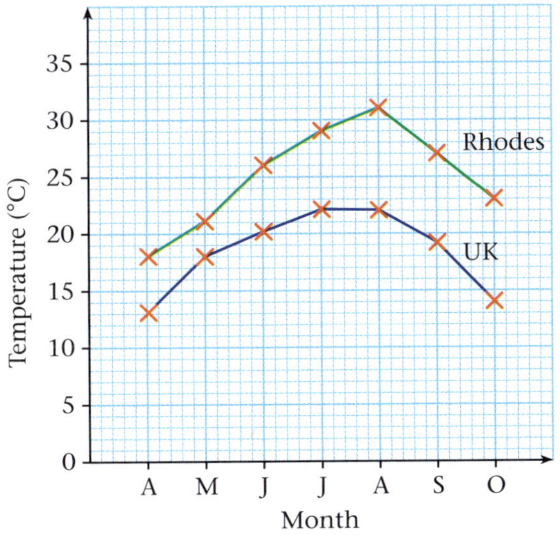

(c) (i) The average midday temperature in Rhodes is highest in August.

(ii) The average midday temperature in the UK is lowest in April.

(iii) The smallest difference between the midday temperatures in Rhodes and the UK is in May.

(iv) The greatest difference between the midday temperatures in Rhodes and the UK is in August and October.

(d) October

All these answers are read from the graph.

Months when temperature in Rhodes is not above 30 °C are April, May, June, July, September, October. Of these, the greatest difference between UK and Rhodes temperature is in October.

Example 3

As part of a project, Gemma has gathered information about the quarterly gas bill at her home over a period of four years.
The information is given in the table on page 56.

Date of bill	Amount
Feb 2002	£255
May 2002	£204
Aug 2002	£112
Nov 2002	£156

Date of bill	Amount
Feb 2003	£263
May 2003	£210
Aug 2003	£117
Nov 2003	£160

Date of bill	Amount
Feb 2004	£270
May 2004	£212
Aug 2004	£120
Nov 2004	£172

Date of bill	Amount
Feb 2005	£294
May 2005	£223
Aug 2005	£128
Nov 2005	£185

Represent this information as a time series.

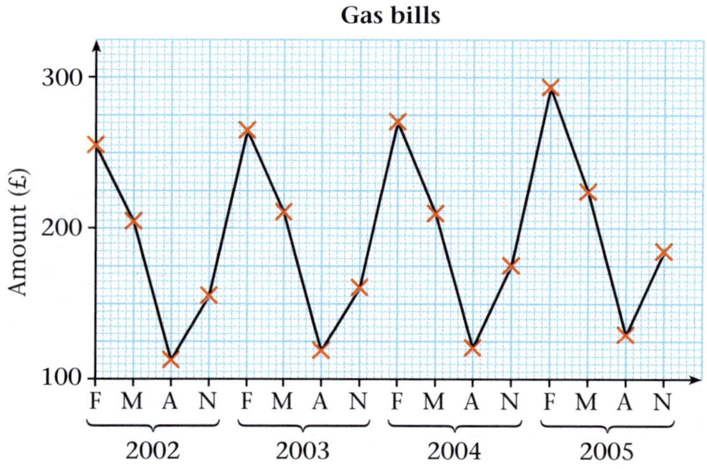

The time series graph shows seasonal variations. The bills are higher in the winter months, when more gas is used.

Activity – Fishing in the North Sea

This time series graph shows the effect of fishing on the numbers of cod in the North Sea.

Explain what the time series graph shows.

Investigate the effect of fishing on other types of fish.

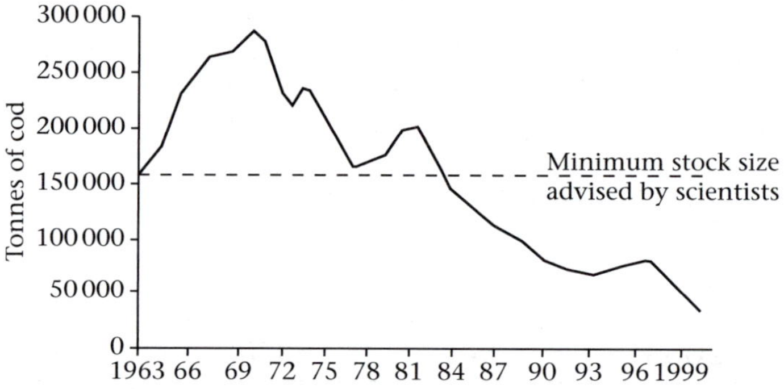

Source: http://dataservice.eea.eu.int

Exercise 5B

1 The table gives the average midday temperatures in the Costa del Sol and the UK during the winter months. All temperatures are in °C.

Month	Oct	Nov	Dec	Jan	Feb	Mar	Apr
Costa del Sol	24	19	17	16	17	18	21
UK	14	13	7	6	7	10	13

(a) On the same axes, draw a time series graph for each set of data.

(b) Which month has the smallest difference in average midday temperatures in the UK and the Costa del Sol?

(c) Work out the difference between the **means** of the average midday temperatures in the UK and the Costa del Sol during these months.

2 Wendy bought a beach hut in July 1992 for £34 000. The table shows its value in £1000s, for the next 13 years.

Year	92	93	94	95	96	97	98	99	00	01	02	03	04	05
Value	34	37	40	33	31	31	32	33	34	38	40	44	53	64

(a) Plot this data as points in a time series. Draw a time series graph for this data.

(b) Write *four* comments about how the value of Wendy's beach hut varied between 1992 and 2005.

3 The table shows information about Mrs Howe's gas bill, in £s, for the years from 2001 to 2005.

Year	1st quarter	2nd quarter	3rd quarter	4th quarter
2001	312	264	142	182
2002	325	271	150	190
2003	340	280	155	201
2004	346	288	172	218
2005	355	298	180	230

Represent this information graphically as a time series.

4 Joseph works as a salesman. His quarterly sales figures, in £1000, for the years from 2001 to 2005 are given below.

	2001	2002	2003	2004	2005
Jan	110	115	118	123	139
April	152	158	162	167	174
July	252	260	263	268	273
Oct	207	210	215	221	229

Represent this information as a time series.

5.3 Retail Prices Index

- The **Retail Prices Index** (RPI) measures the change in the prices of goods and services.

The government collects data on the cost of items each month, to update the RPI.

Example 4

Workwell is a small company. It keeps its wages in line with changes in the Retail Prices Index (RPI).

Sam joined Workwell on 1 January 1987.
His weekly wage then was exactly £200 and the RPI was 100.
For the next 19 years he stayed at Workwell doing the same job.
Work out what Sam's weekly wage would have been

(a) during January 1997, when the RPI was 154.4

(b) during January 2006, when the RPI was 193.4.

(a) In January 1987, the RPI was 100.
In January 1997, the RPI was 154.4.
So the proportional change (or factor) in the RPI

$$= \frac{154.4}{100} = 1.544.$$

So to keep in line with changes in the RPI, Sam's weekly wage in January 1997 was

wage in January 1987 × proportional change in RPI
= £200 × 1.544 = £308.80.

(b) In January 2006, the RPI was 193.4.
So the proportional change in RPI between January 1987 and January 2001 was $\frac{193.4}{100} = 1.934.$
So to keep in line with changes in the RPI, Sam's weekly wage in January 2006 was

£200 × 1.934 = £386.80.

Example 5

The table shows the Retail Prices Index in the UK and in Malta from January 1995 to January 2001.

Year	1995	1996	1997	1998	1999	2000	2001
(RPI) (UK)	146.0	150.2	154.4	159.5	163.4	166.6	171.1
(RPI) (Malta)	100	99.87	103.57	107.10	108.62	112.24	112.95

(a) Plot the RPI in Malta against the RPI in the UK as points on a scatter diagram.

(b) On your scatter diagram draw the line of best fit.

(c) Comment on the correlation between the RPI in Malta and the RPI in the UK.

The local newspaper in Malta claimed that price rises on the island between 1995 and 2001 had been lower than prices rises in the UK over the same period.

(d) Comment on the newspaper's claim.

(a) (b)

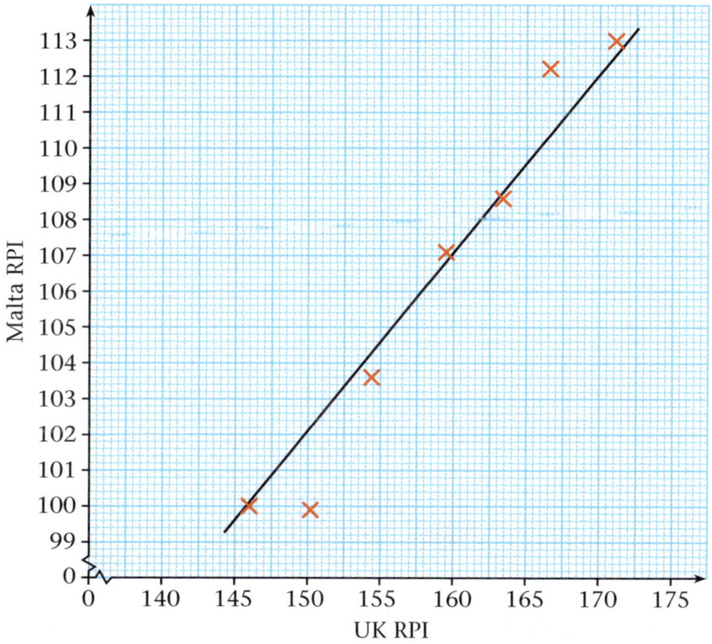

(c) The scatter diagram shows **positive correlation** between the RPI in the UK and the RPI in Malta.

As the RPI increased in the UK, it also increased in Malta.

(d) Between 1995 and 2001 the proportional changes in RPI were

For UK: $\frac{171.1}{140.0} = 1.1719$ For Malta: $\frac{112.95}{100} = 1.1295$

The change in RPI for the UK is greater than the change in RPI for Malta over the period from 1995 to 2001.

The newspaper's claim is correct.

Example 6

In January 2000 the RPI was 166.6.
A newspaper cost 65p in January 2000.
In January 2006 the RPI was 193.4.

(a) Use the RPI to work out the cost of a newspaper in January 2006.

(b) What assumptions did you make?

(a) January 2000 RPI = 166.6
January 2006 RPI = 193.4

Proportional change $= \frac{193.4}{166.6}$

Cost of newspaper in 2006 $= \frac{193.4}{166.6} \times 65\text{p}$
$= 75.45\ldots\text{p}$
$= 75\text{p}$

Round the answer to the nearest penny.

(b) The assumption was that the price of the newspaper increased in line with the RPI.

Exercise 5C

1 Asif joined Wellworkers Ltd in August 1996 at a salary of £12 500 per year.
The RPI in August 1996 was 153.1.
In August 2005 the RPI was 192.6.
Between August 1996 and August 2005, Asif's salary increased in line with the RPI.
Work out Asif's salary in August 2005.

2 In January 1975 the RPI was 30.39.
In January 2006 the RPI was 193.4.
In January 1975 the price of a loaf of bread was 12p.
Assuming that bread prices follow the changes in the RPI, work out the price of a similar loaf of bread in January 2006.

3 In December 2005 the RPI was 194.1.
In December 1960 the RPI was 12.62.
The price of a loaf of bread was 68p in December 2005.
Stating your assumptions, work out an estimate of the price of a similar loaf of bread in December 1960.

4 The table below provides information about the Retail Prices Index in the UK and on the island of Guernsey during the months of September from 1994 to 2001.

	1994	1995	1996	1997	1998	1999	2000	2001
UK	145.0	150.6	153.8	159.3	164.4	166.2	171.7	174.6
Guernsey	100.2	104.2	106.2	110.9	115.4	117.4	122.7	125.9

(a) Plot the two sets of data as points on a scatter graph.

(b) Draw the line of best fit on the scatter graph.

(c) Comment on the relationship between the RPI in the UK and the RPI on Guernsey.

A local radio station on Guernsey claims that during the years from 1994 to 2001 the price rises on the island have been lower than those on the mainland UK.

(d) Explain whether the table of RPIs provides evidence to support this claim or not.

Mixed exercise 5

1 Students' mark in a Mathematics examination and an English examination were as follows.

Mathematics	25	38	43	68	80	74	55	29	47	59	61
English	31	37	46	65	77	76	58	32	52	56	65

(a) Draw a scatter graph to represent this data.

(b) Comment on the relationship between the marks in the two subjects.

(c) Draw the line of best fit on your scatter graph.

A student took the Mathematics examination and scored a mark of 50.
The same student was ill on the day of the English examination and did not take it.

(d) Use the line of best fit to estimate a mark for this student in the English examination.

(e) Represent
(i) the Mathematics marks
(ii) the English marks
on a stem and leaf diagram.

2 The table shows the hours of sunshine and the snowfall, in mm, in ten towns during last winter.

Sunshine (hours)	450	255	360	230	420	200	440	175	320	420
Snowfall (mm)	20	40	30	58	48	56	28	60	50	40

The points for the first six results in the table have been plotted in a scatter graph:

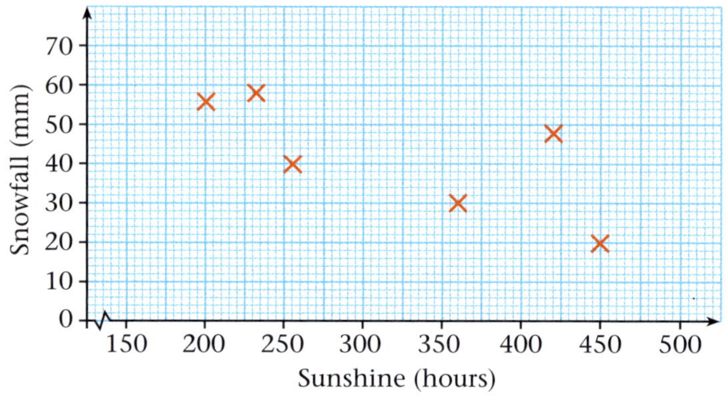

(a) Copy the scatter graph and plot the other four points.

(b) Describe the correlation between the hours of sunshine and the snowfall.

(c) Draw the line of best fit on your scatter graph.

(d) Represent the snowfall on a stem and leaf diagram.

3 The diagrams represent three scatter graphs:

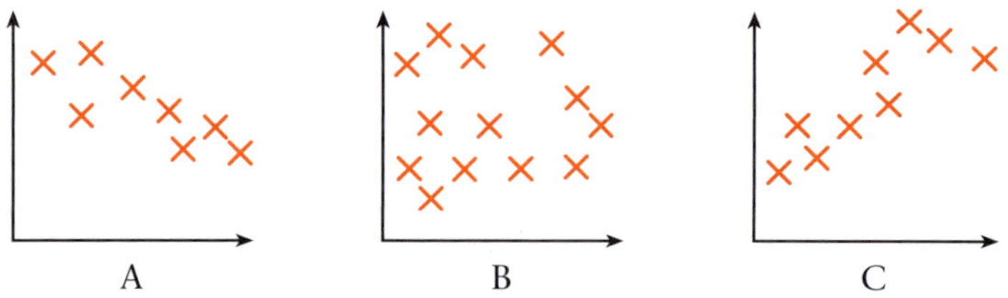

Use one of the following words to describe the correlation shown in each graph:

Positive Negative None

4 The scatter graph shows the Science mark and the Maths mark for 15 students.

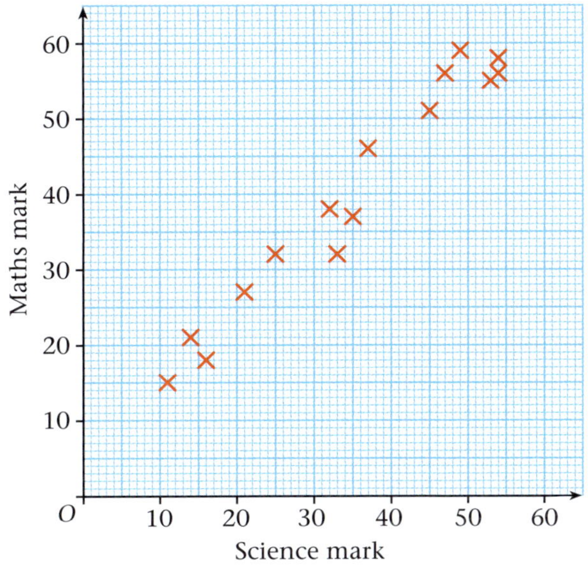

(a) What type of correlation does this scatter graph show?

(b) Copy the scatter graph. Draw the line of best fit.

Sophie's science mark was 42.

(c) Use your line of best fit to estimate Sophie's Maths mark. [E]

5 The scatter graph shows information about the value of a house and the area of floor space in the house.

Comment on this information.

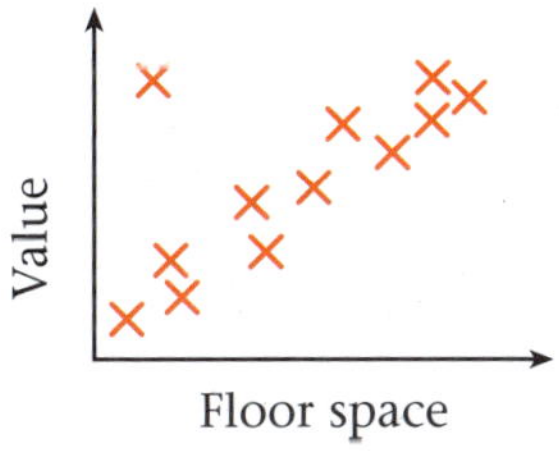

6 Mrs Sharma pays her gas bill in March, June, August and December each year.
The table below provides information about her gas bills for the years 2003 to 2005.

	March	June	August	December
2003	£268	£182	£121	£206
2004	£284	£191	£128	£217
2005	£301	£199	£140	£230

(a) Represent this information on a time series graph.

(b) Make three comments about how Mrs Sharma's gas bill varied from March 2003 to December 2005.

7 The government's estimate of the population of England in mid-2000 was 49 997 100.
It was estimated that the distribution of this population by region was:

English region	Population estimate
North East	2 577 300
North West	6 893 900
Yorkshire and Humber	5 057 900
East Midlands	4 207 900
West Midlands	5 335 400
East Anglia	5 459 600
London	7 375 100
South East	8 114 900
South West	4 975 100

(a) Represent this data on a bar chart.
(b) Represent this data on a pie chart.
(c) Which is the **modal** region?

The average price of a house in each of these English regions in the year 2000 is given in the table below.

(d) Write these average prices in order, starting with the smallest.
(e) Draw a scatter graph for the average price of a house against the population.
(f) Draw a line of best fit on your scatter graph.
(g) Comment on the relationship between house prices and population.

English region	Average house price
North East	£52 500
North West	£65 000
Yorkshire and Humber	£61 000
East Midlands	£68 850
West Midlands	£76 200
East Anglia	£82 500
London	£147 500
South East	£120 000
South West	£88 800

8 The quarterly figures (in 1000s) for the number of people visiting a theme park for the years 2002 to 2005 are given below.

Quarter	2002	2003	2004	2005
1st	112	113	102	124
2nd	206	204	185	223
3rd	517	510	470	540
4th	380	320	290	395

(a) Represent this information as a time series graph.
(b) Comment on any seasonal patterns in the data.

Summary of key points

1 A linear relationship between two sets of data is called a **correlation**.

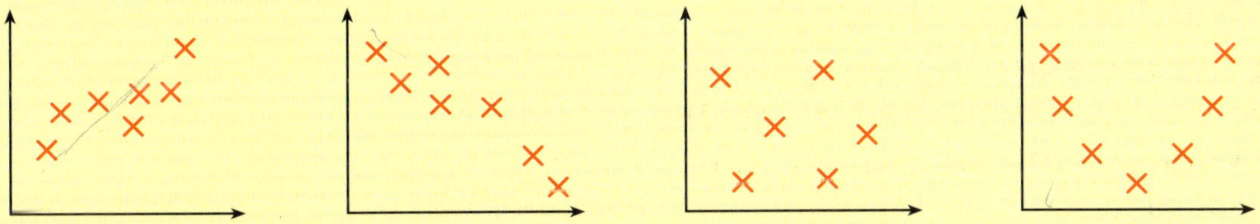

Positive correlation Negative correlation No correlation No correlation (no linear relationship)

2 The **line of best fit** is a straight line that passes through or is as close to as many of the plotted points as possible.

3 A line of best fit gives a model for how two variables are related. The closer the plotted points are to the line the better the correlation.

4 A line of best fit can be used to estimate other data values.

5 A **time series graph** is a line graph that shows data collected at timed intervals (e.g. hourly, daily, weekly, ...).

6 The **Retail Prices Index** (RPI) measures the change in the prices of goods and services.

6 Probability

6.1 Probability scales

- An event that is *certain* to happen has a **probability of 1**.
- An event that *cannot happen* has a **probability of 0**.
- The probability that an event will happen is always greater than or equal to 0 (impossible) and less than or equal to 1 (certain).
  This can be written:
  $0 \leqslant \text{probability} \leqslant 1$

Example 1

Here is a probability scale labelled in words.

impossible — unlikely — evens — likely — certain

On the scale mark the probability that
(a) it will snow in London on 1 August (use the letter A)
(b) the day before Christmas Day will be Christmas Eve (use the letter B)
(c) the bottom card of a well-shuffled pack of cards will be a black card (use the letter C)
(d) there will be at least one rainy day during March (use the letter D)
(e) ice cream will not melt if you put it in a hot oven for half an hour (use the letter E).

E	A	C	D	B
impossible	unlikely	evens	likely	certain

Example 2

Here is a probability scale.

0 — $\frac{1}{2}$ — 1

On the scale mark the probability that
(a) the next baby to be born will be female (use the letter F)
(b) the day immediately following Christmas Day will be Boxing Day (use the letter B)

(c) the next thing you see flying in the sky will be a pink elephant (use the letter E).

(a) We know that about half of newborn babies are boys and about half are girls. So the probability of the baby being a girl is about $\frac{1}{2}$.

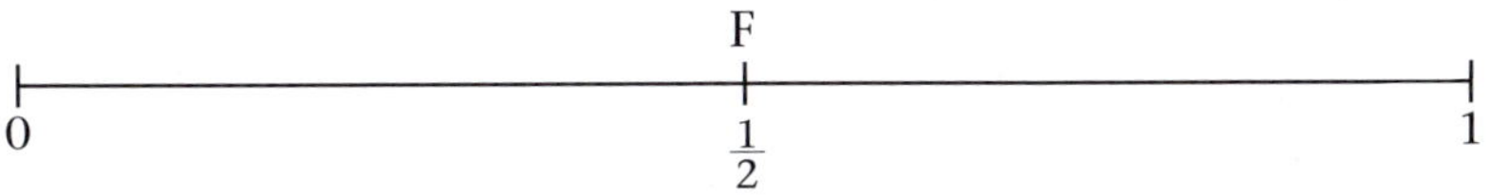

(b) It is a certainty that Christmas Day will be followed by Boxing Day, so the probability = 1.

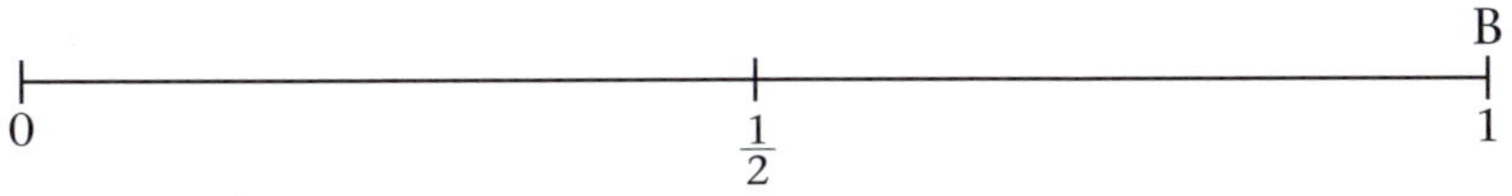

(c) We know that elephants cannot fly and neither are they pink. So it is impossible for you to see a flying pink elephant. So this probability = 0.

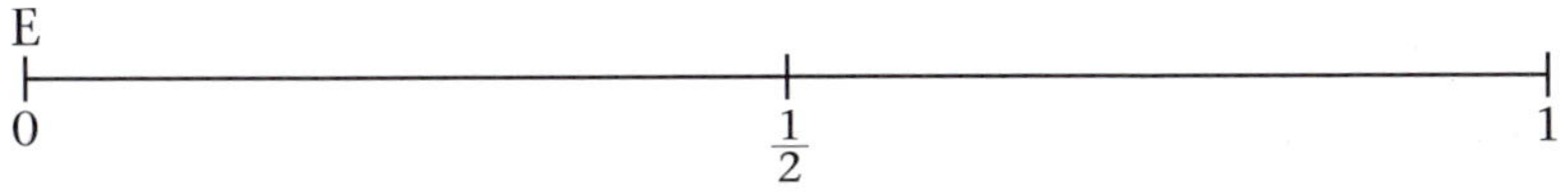

- If all the possible outcomes of an event are equally likely, the probability that the event will happen is

$$\text{probability} = \frac{\text{number of successful outcomes}}{\text{total number of possible outcomes}}$$

Example 3

On a probability scale, mark the probability that

(a) the top card on a well-shuffled pack of cards will be red

(b) the bottom card on a well-shuffled pack of cards will be a Heart

(c) when an ordinary dice is thrown it lands showing 5.

(a) Half of the cards in a pack are red.
So the probability that the top card is red is $\frac{1}{2}$.

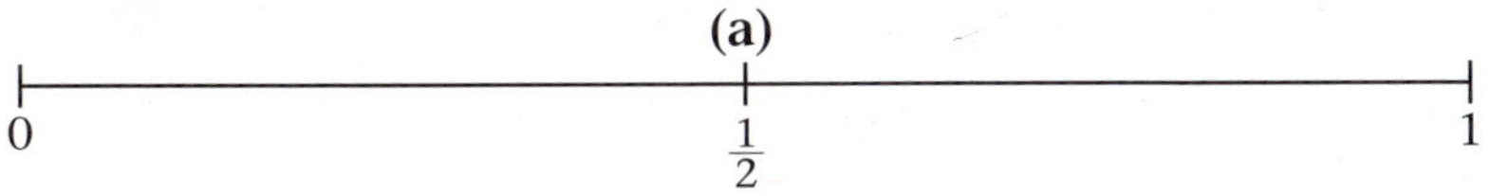

Each card is equally likely to end up on the top of the pack.

(b) There are 52 cards in a pack. 13 of them are Hearts.

Probability of a Heart $= \frac{13}{52}$

$= \frac{1}{4}$

> $\frac{\text{13 successful outcomes}}{\text{52 possible outcomes}}$

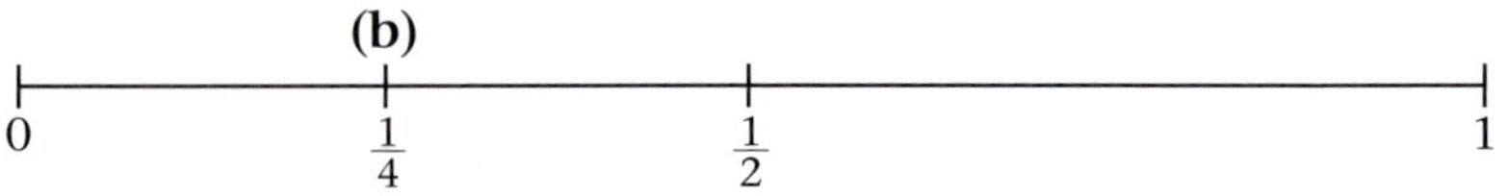

(c) Probability of a 5 $= \frac{1}{6}$

> $\frac{\text{1 successful outcome (the score 5)}}{\text{6 possible outcomes}}$

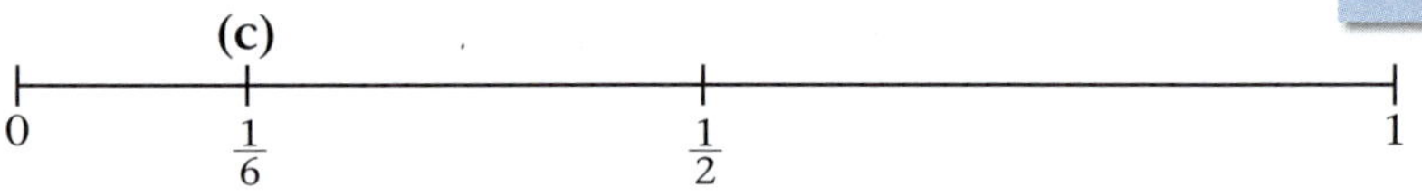

Exercise 6A

1 Copy this probability scale.

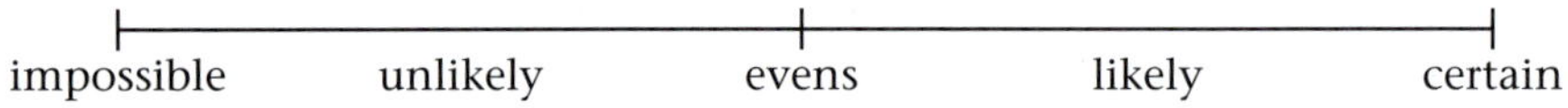

(a) Mark with T the likelihood of a fair coin landing tails when it is thrown once.

(b) Mark with C the likelihood of the day before Boxing Day being Christmas Day.

(c) Mark with S the likelihood of the sun shining in London on at least one day next July.

(d) Mark with D the likelihood that a dinosaur will walk down the main road tomorrow.

(e) Mark with J the likelihood that Mr Jones will cut his lawn at a time when it is pouring down with rain.

2 Copy this probability scale.

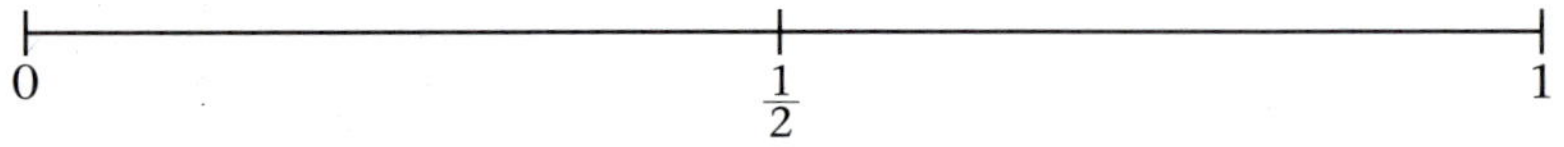

(a) Mark with T the probability of getting a tail when a fair coin is thrown.

(b) Mark with S the probability of getting a 9 when a fair six-sided dice is thrown.

(c) Mark with N the probability of getting a number less than 100 when a fair six-sided dice is thrown.

3 Three letters are marked on this probability scale.

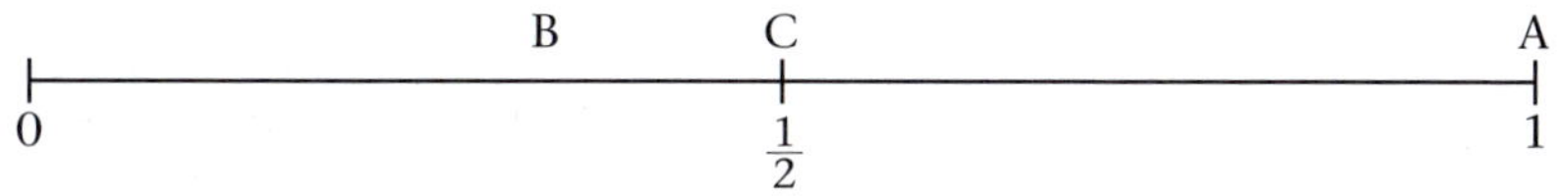

Match the letters to these probabilities:

(a) the probability that a fair six-sided dice will land with its top face showing a number less than 3

(b) the probability that the sun will set tomorrow

(c) the probability that when it is thrown once a fair coin will land heads.

4 Copy this probability scale.

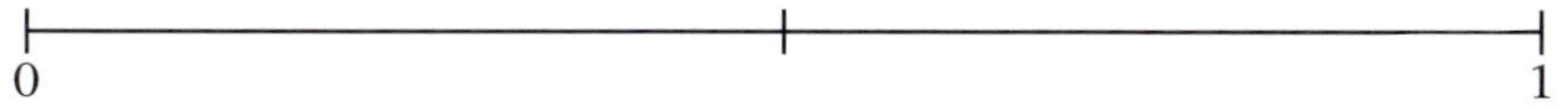

Mark

(a) with the letter S, the probability that it will snow in London in June.

(b) with the letter H, the probability that when a fair coin is thrown once it comes down heads.

(c) with the letter M, the probability that it will rain in Manchester next year. [E]

6.2 Mutually exclusive outcomes

- Outcomes are **mutually exclusive** when they cannot happen at the same time.

Example 4

This five-sided spinner is in the shape of a regular pentagon.
Each section of the spinner is labelled with a letter.
The spinner is spun once.
Write down the probability that it will land on

(a) the section labelled R

(b) a section labelled U

(c) a section labelled Z

(d) a section labelled with a letter of the alphabet

(e) a section labelled with a letter that is **not** a vowel

(f) a section labelled either U or R.

(a) The spinner could land on any one of five sections. But of these only one is labelled R. So the probability of it landing on this section is $\frac{1}{5}$.

(b) Of the five sections, two are labelled U, so P(U) $= \frac{2}{5}$.

(c) There are no sections labelled Z, so landing on one is impossible. Therefore P(Z) $= 0$.

(d) Each and every section is labelled with a letter. So it is a certainty that the spinner must land on a section labelled with a letter. So this probability $= 1$.

(e) The only vowel on the spinner is U. There are three sections with letters that are **not** vowels. So the probability of landing on a section with a letter that is not a vowel is $\frac{3}{5}$.

(f) There are two sections labelled U and one section labelled R. So there are three sections altogether labelled U or R. So the probability of landing on a section labelled either U or R is P(U or R) = P(U) + P(R) $= \frac{2}{5} + \frac{1}{5} = \frac{3}{5}$.

Instead of writing 'probability of R' you can write P(R).

Example 5

A four-sided dice labelled 1, 2, 3, 4 is thrown once.
What is the probability that the score is

(a) an even number (b) an odd number (c) a number less than 4?

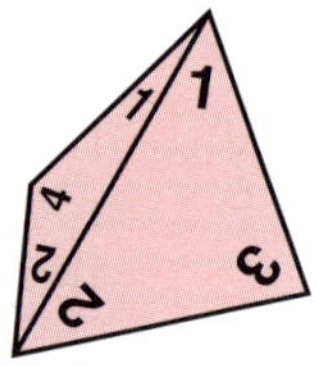

(a) P(even number) = P(2) + P(4)
$= \frac{1}{4} + \frac{1}{4} = \frac{1}{2}$

There are four equally likely outcomes: 1, 2, 3, 4.

(b) P(odd number) = P(1) + P(3)
$= \frac{1}{4} + \frac{1}{4} = \frac{1}{2}$

P(even number) = P(2 or 4) = P(2) + P(4).

(c) P(a number less than 4) = P(1) + P(2) + P(3)
$= \frac{1}{4} + \frac{1}{4} + \frac{1}{4}$
$= \frac{3}{4}$

The scores less than 4 are 1, 2 and 3.

Exercise 6B

1 Joan has three equal-sized coloured balls in a bag.
One ball is red, one ball is blue and the other ball is green.
She chooses a ball at random.
Write down the probability that

(a) the ball she chooses will be blue

(b) the ball she chooses will be yellow.

2 The faces of a six-sided dice are labelled 1 to 6.
The dice is rolled once.
Write down the probability that its upper face shows
(a) 4
(b) a number greater than 3
(c) an even number
(b) a number greater between 7 and 10.

3 Farouk has a box of 15 chocolates.
Eight are plain, six are milk and one is white.
He chooses a chocolate at random.
(a) Write down the probability that the chocolate chosen is white.
(b) Write down the probability of Farouk choosing a fruit gum.
(c) Write down the probability that the chocolate chosen is milk.
(d) Write down the probability that the chocolate chosen is either plain or white.

4 The diagram shows a six-sided fair spinner.
The spinner is in the shape of a regular hexagon.
The sections of the spinner are labelled with the letters A, B, C, D and E.
The spinner is to be spun once. Write down the probability
(a) that it will land on D
(b) that it will land on A
(c) that it will land on a vowel
(d) that it will land on P.

6.3 Listing outcomes

23 Combined events animation

Example 6

Each section of this square spinner is labelled with a number.
The coin has two faces – heads and tails.
The spinner is to be spun once.
The coin is to be thrown once.
One possible joint outcome of the two events is (1, heads)
(a) List all the possible joint outcomes of the two events.
(b) Explain why the probability of the spinner landing on 1 and the coin landing heads is $\frac{1}{8}$.

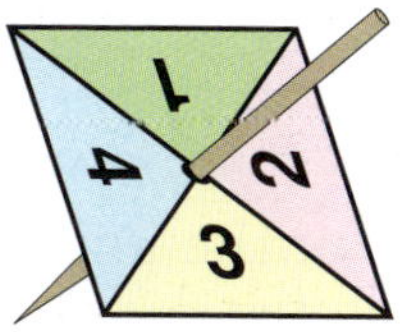

(a) (1, heads) (1, tails)
(2, heads) (2, tails)
(3, heads) (3, tails)
(4, heads) (4, tails)

List all the outcomes systematically.

(b) There are 8 possible outcomes.
Each of these outcomes is equally likely.
The outcome (1, heads) is one of these outcomes.
So the probability of this outcome is $\frac{1}{8}$.

The 8 possible outcomes are listed in part **(a)**.

- A **sample space diagram** shows all possible outcomes of one or more events.

Example 7

The diagram represents a fair coin and a fair spinner.
The spinner is in the shape of an equilateral triangle.
Asif throws the coin once and spins the spinner once.

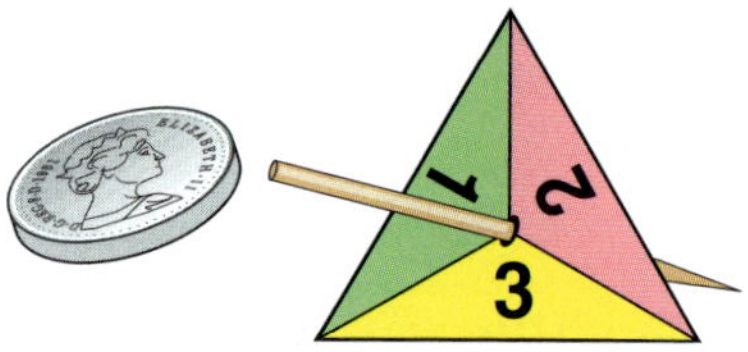

(a) Construct a sample space diagram to show all the possible outcomes.

(b) Work out the probability of the joint outcome heads and a number less than 3.

(a) The sample space diagram is:

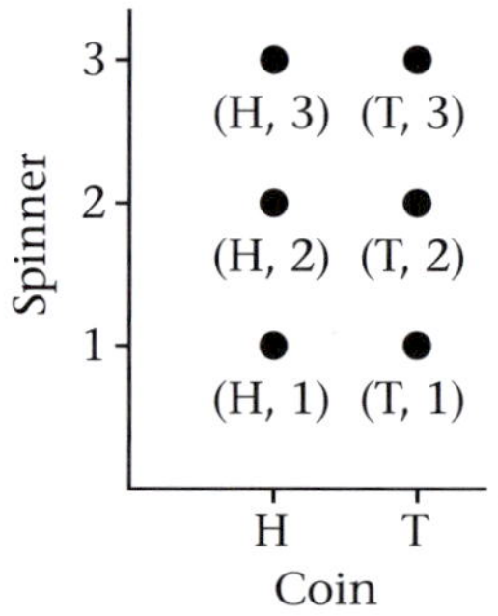

(b) For the joint outcome of heads and a number less than 3, the 'successful' outcomes are

(H, 1) (H, 2)

Two successful outcomes.

From the sample space diagram, there are six joint outcomes in total.
So probability (H and number < 3) $= \frac{2}{6} = \frac{1}{3}$

Exercise 6C

1 Tamsin has four places to visit:

London, Manchester, Bristol and Edinburgh.

In each case she has three possible methods of travel:

car, bus or train.

One possible journey she could make is

London by train.

List all the possible journeys Tamsin could make.

2 This fair spinner is to be spun once and the dice rolled once.

One possible outcome could be (A, 1).

A on the spinner
1 on the dice

(a) Draw a sample space diagram to show the possible joint outcomes.

(b) Write down the probability of the joint outcome (A, 1).

(c) Write down the probability of the joint outcome (D, 3).

3 A game is played with two fair spinners. The spinners are spun at the same time.

The diagram below shows the result (red, 3).

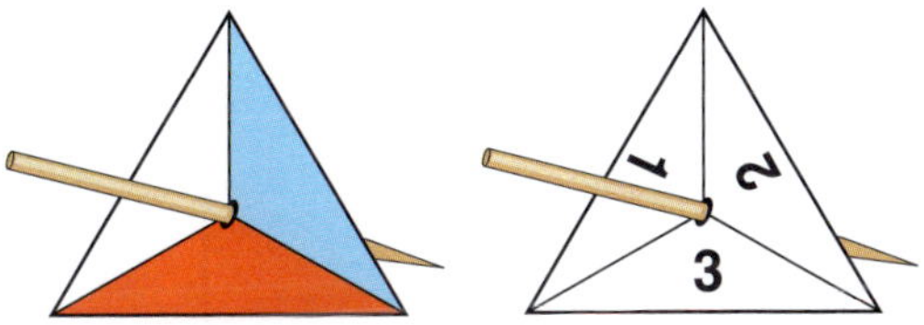

(a) Draw a sample space diagram to show all the possible results when the spinners are spun once.

(b) Use your list to work out the probability of (blue, 1) when the spinners are spun once.

4 Kylie has a fair coin and a fair six-sided dice.

She throws the coin once.

She rolls the dice once.

The diagram shows the outcomes (head, 3).

(a) Draw a sample space diagram to show all the possible outcomes when the coin is thrown once and the dice is rolled once.

(b) Work out the probability of (tail, 6).

5 The diagram shows two fair spinners.
Each spinner is spun once and the joint outcomes recorded.

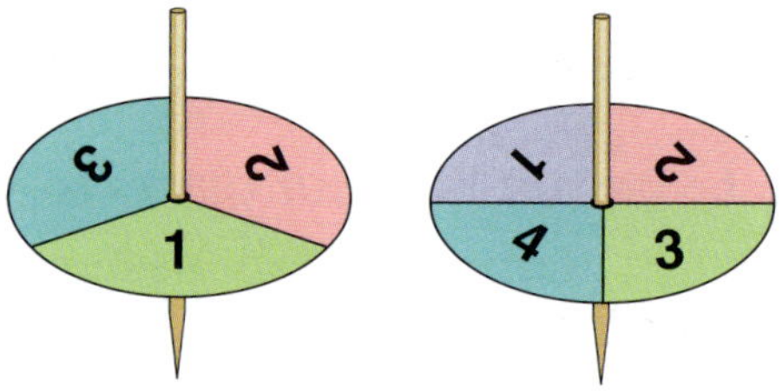

(a) Draw a sample space diagram for the joint outcomes.

(b) Find the probability of the joint outcome
first spinner stops on 3 and second spinner stops on 4.

The numbers on the two sections that the spinners land on are added to give a total score.

(c) Work out the probability of obtaining a total score
  (i) of 4
  (ii) which is an even number
  (iii) which is an odd number.

6.4 Probability of an event not happening

- The probabilities of all the mutually exclusive outcomes of an event add to 1.
- The probabilities of an event **not** happening
  = 1 − probability of the event happening.
  P(not A) = 1 − P(A)

'Event happens' and 'event does not happen' are mutually exclusive. So P(happens) + P(does not happen) = 1

Example 8

Jack has a box of chocolates.
Twelve are plain, five are milk and three are white.
Jack takes a chocolate at random.
What is the probability that the chocolate is

(a) milk

(b) not plain

(c) a caramel?

'At random' means every chocolate is equally likely to be chosen.

(a) There are 20 chocolates. 5 are milk.
P(milk) $= \frac{5}{20} = \frac{1}{4}$

You can simplify the fraction but you don't **need** to unless the question asks you to.

(b) P(not plain) $= 1 - \text{P(plain)}$
$= 1 - \frac{12}{20}$
$= \frac{20}{20} - \frac{12}{20}$
$= \frac{8}{20} = \frac{2}{5}$

20 chocolates; 12 plain
P(plain) $= \frac{12}{20}$

(c) There are no caramels in the box, so
P(caramel) = 0

- You can write probabilities as fractions, decimals or percentages.

Example 9

The probability of a new light bulb being faulty is 0.002. Work out the probability of a new light bulb *not* being faulty.

Probability of not being faulty = 1 − probability of being faulty
= 1 − 0.002
= 0.998

Example 10

The diagram represents a spinner in the shape of a pentagon. The spinner is biased.

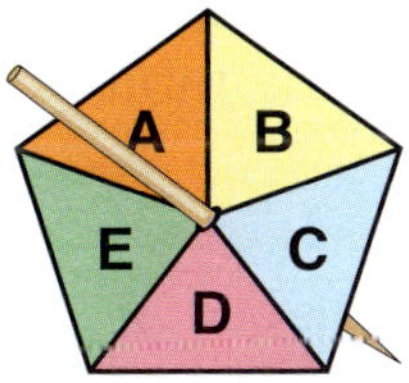

When it is spun once, the probability of it stopping on each of the sections A, B, C and D is shown in the table below.

Section	A	B	C	D	E
Probability	0.23	0.18	0.16	0.22	

The spinner is spun once.

(a) Work out the probability that it stops on section E.

(b) Work out the probability of it *not* stopping on section A.

(a) The sum of the probabilities = 1

So 0.23 + 0.18 + 0.16 + 0.22 + P(E) = 1

0.79 + P(E) = 1

P(E) = 1 − 0.79 = 0.21

So probability of stopping on E = 0.21

(b) Probability of not A = 1 − probability of A
= 1 − 0.23
= 0.77

It is certain that the spinner will land on A or B or C or D or E, so the sum of the probabilities = 1.

Exercise 6D

1 The probability of a newly laid egg being cracked is 0.03.
Work out the probability of a newly laid egg *not* being cracked.

2 The probability of a train being late is 23%.
Work out the probability of the train *not* being late.

3 Debbie has a bag which contains ten equal-sized coloured counters.
Six of the counters are red, three are blue and one is white.
She selects a counter at random from the bag.
Work out the probability that the selected counter is
(a) blue (b) not white
(c) either red or white (d) green.

4 A dice has faces numbered, 1, 2, 3, 4, 5 and 6.
The dice is biased.
Some of the probabilities of it landing with each face uppermost when it is rolled once are shown in the table below.

Face	1	2	3	4	5	6
Probability	0.20	0.11	0.17	0.19	0.21	

The dice is to be rolled once.
Work out the probability of it landing with 6 on the uppermost face.

5 A train can be either **early**, **late** or **on time**.
The probability of the train being early is 0.07.
The probability of the train being late is 0.24.
Work out the probability of the train being on time.

6 Imran has a box of 25 felt-tip pens.
Twelve of the pens are red.
Eight of the pens are blue.
The rest of the pens are black.
Imran chooses one pen at random from the box.
What is the probability that Imran will choose
(a) a red pen
(b) a black pen
(c) a pen that is not blue?

6.5 Estimating likely outcomes

Example 11

On Sarita's MP3 player, 30% of the tracks are indie, 50% are hip hop and 20% are pop.
Sarita sets the player to 'shuffle', so it selects and plays tracks at random.

(a) What type of track is it most likely to play?
(b) What type of track is it least likely to play?

Write down the probability that the first track played is

(c) not pop
(d) folk.

(a) It is most likely to play hip hop, as this has the highest percentage of tracks.
(b) It is least likely to play pop, as this has the lowest percentage of tracks.
(c) P(pop) = 20%

$$\text{So P(not pop)} = 100\% - \text{P(pop)} = 100\% - 20\% = 80\%$$

P(not pop) = 1 − P(pop)
100% = 1

(d) There is no folk on the MP3 player, so
P(folk) = 0

Example 12

The probability of a new computer being faulty is 0.002.

(a) Work out the probability of a new computer *not* being faulty.

A computer superstore has 12 000 new computers in stock.

(b) Work out an estimate of the number of these new computers likely to be faulty.

(a) Probability (not faulty) = 1 − probability (faulty)
= 1 − 0.002
= 0.998

(b) Probability of being faulty is 0.002 (i.e. 2 out of every 1000 will be faulty).
So the likely number of faulty computers out of a batch of 12 000 is

$$0.002 \times 12\,000 = 24$$

$0.002 = 2$ thousandths $= \frac{2}{1000}$

Exercise 6E

1 A bag contains 20 coloured snooker balls.
Nine of the balls are red, six are blue, three are white and two are black.
A ball is to be selected at random from the bag.

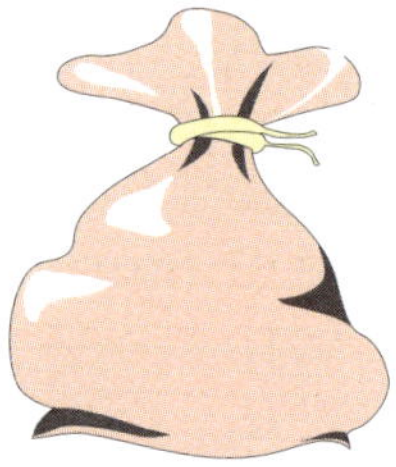

(a) Which colour is the ball selected least likely to be? Give your reasoning.

(b) Write down the probability of the selected ball being blue.

(c) Work out the probability of the selected ball being

(i) blue or black **(ii)** red, white or black
(iii) not red **(iv)** green.

2 The probability of a newly laid egg being cracked is 0.004.

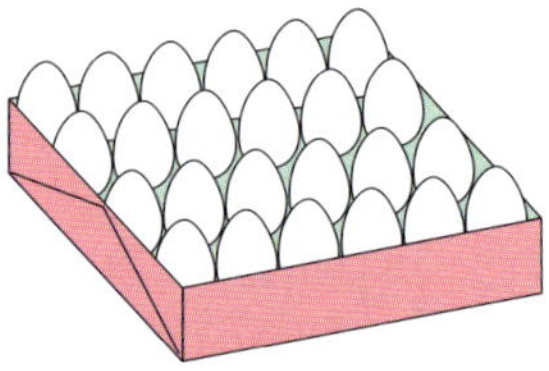

(a) Work out the probability of a newly laid egg *not* being cracked.

A supermarket took delivery of 140 000 newly laid eggs.

(b) Work out, showing all of your reasoning, the most likely number of eggs out of the 140 000 to be cracked.

3 The probability of a train being late is $\frac{1}{15}$.
Work out the probability of the train *not* being late.

4 The probability of the school bus being late is estimated to be 15%. During the year the school bus makes 195 journeys to the school.
Work out an estimate for the most likely number of times the school bus will be late during the year.

5 James write books. The probability of him spelling a word incorrectly is 0.003.
James's last book contained 120 000 words. Work out an estimate of the most likely number of words in this book to be spelled incorrectly.

6.6 Estimating probability

- The **relative frequency** of an outcome in an experiment is

$$\text{relative frequency} = \frac{\text{number of successful trials}}{\text{total number of trials}}$$

- For a trial or experiment the **estimated probability** is given by the relative frequency.

Example 13

The four candidates standing at the local electon are

Anderson, Barnes, Clarke and **Deyhna**.

Shortly before the election, a market research company ask a random sample of 1000 voters the question.

Which candidate do you intend to vote for?

The responses are:

Name	Anderson	Barnes	Clarke	Deyhna
Number of voters	125	462	285	128

A voter is selected at random.
Using the information in the table, work out the best estimate for

(a) the probability of this voter voting for Clarke

(b) the probability of this voter *not* voting for Barnes.

(a) The best estimate for

$$\text{P(Clarke)} = \frac{\text{number saying they will vote for Clarke}}{\text{total number of people asked}}$$

$$= \frac{285}{1000}$$

$$= 0.285$$

(b) The best estimate for

$$\text{P(not Barnes)} = 1 - \text{P(Barnes)}$$

$$= 1 - \frac{462}{1000}$$

$$= 1 - 0.462$$

$$= 0.538$$

Example 14

The diagram represents a spinner.
It is thought that the spinner is biased.
Chantal spins the spinner 100 times and records the letter it stops on.
Her results are:

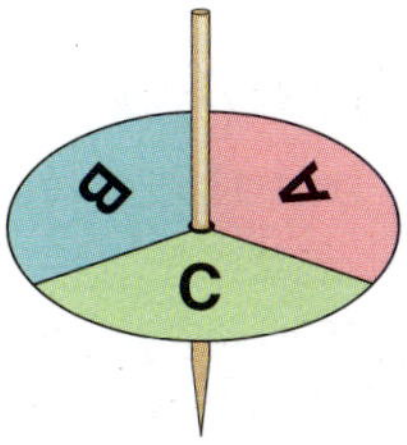

Letter	A	B	C
Frequency	28	30	42

Zoë then spins the spinner 100 times and records the letter it stops on.

Her results are:

Letter	A	B	C
Frequency	26	36	38

(a) Explain why there is a difference between the two sets of results.

(b) Use the information to work out the *best* estimates for the probability of the spinner stopping on each of the three letters.

(c) Explain whether or not the spinner appears to be biased.

(a) The results of spinning the spinner are random, so it is very unlikely that two sets of spins will give exactly the same results.

(b) Combining Chantal's and Zoë's results gives:

Letter	A	B	C
Frequency	$28 + 26 = 54$	$30 + 36 = 66$	$42 + 38 = 80$

The best estimates are

$$P(A) = \frac{54}{200} = 0.27$$

$$P(B) = \frac{66}{200} = 0.33$$

$$P(C) = \frac{80}{200} = 0.40$$

(c) For an unbiased spinner the probabilities of stopping on A, B and C would be

A	B	C
$\frac{1}{3} = 0.3\dot{3}$	$\frac{1}{3} = 0.3\dot{3}$	$\frac{1}{3} = 0.3\dot{3}$

We cannot be certain, but the estimated probabilities of

A	B	C
0.27	0.33	0.40

based on 200 trials, suggest that the spinner is biased.

Increasing the number of trials gives a more accurate result. For the *best* estimate, combine the results.

This is the **theoretical probability** – what should happen 'in theory'.

To see if a spinner is fair, you compare its experimental results with the theoretical probability.

Activity – Drawing pin

Throw a drawing pin 10 times and count the number of times it lands point up.

Repeat for more sets of 10 throws, up to 100 throws in total.

Copy and complete the table.

Number of throws	Number of times drawing pin lands point up	Relative frequency
10		
20		
…		
…		
100		

Draw a graph to show estimated probability for different numbers of throws.

Comment on your results.

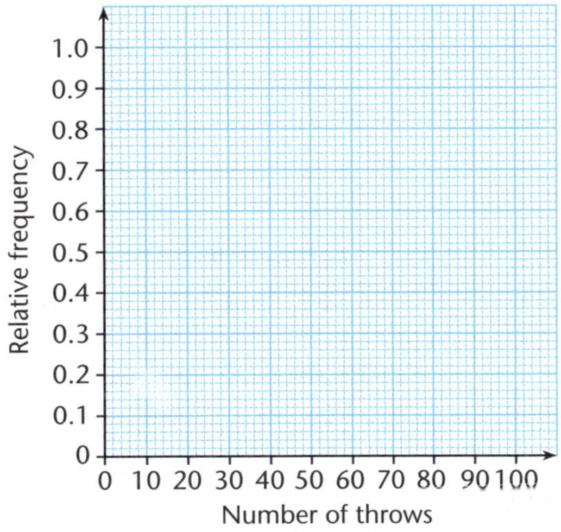

Exercise 6F

1 A market research company conducts a survey into students' travel to school. They choose a random sample of 2000 students from all types of school across the country.
The results of the survey are:

Method of travel	Walk	Car	Train	Cycle	Bus
Frequency	758	352	206	103	581

(a) Work out the best estimates for the probability that a student chosen at random will normally
  (i) travel to school by bus
  (ii) travel to school by car
  (iii) *not* walk to school.

(b) Explain what the market research company will need to do to improve on these estimates.

2 The diagram represents a spinner.
The spinner is thought to be biased.
John spins the spinner 100 times and records the letter it stops on each time.
His results are:

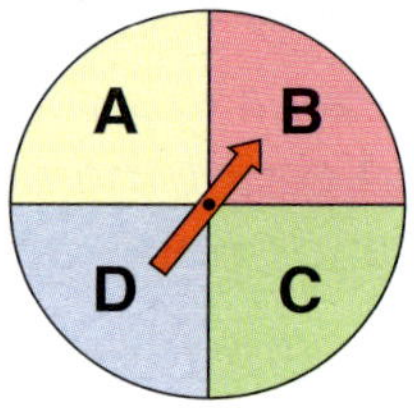

Section	A	B	C	D
Frequency	12	42	17	29

Mandy spins the spinner 300 times.
Her results are:

Section	A	B	C	D
Frequency	41	129	58	72

Mandy spins the spinner three times as many as John.

(a) Explain why the frequencies in Mandy's table are not three times those in John's table.

(b) Use the results to work out the best estimate for the probability of the spinner

(i) stopping on section C when it is spun once

(ii) not stopping on section B when it is spun once.

(c) Explain whether or not there is evidence to suggest that the spinner might be biased.

3 In a batch of 1000 mugs produced in a pottery, seven are found to be cracked.
Work out an estimate of the probability of a mug not being cracked.

4 An airline checks the departure times of 200 flights. Of the 200 flights

12 are early, 142 are on time and the remainder are late.

Use this evidence to work out the best estimate of the probability that a randomly selected flight departs late.

5 George throws a coin 100 times.
It lands heads 57 times.
Jane throws the same coin 100 times.
It lands heads 45 times.

(a) Explain why George and Jane's results are not the same.

(b) Explain whether or not there is sufficient evidence to suggest that the coin is biased.

Mixed exercise 6

1 Tristan has ten marbles in a bag.
Six of the marbles are red, three are blue, and one is white.
He picks a marble at random.
Write down the probability that the marble he picks is

(a) white (b) blue
(c) either blue or white (d) yellow.

2 The diagram represents a fair spinner in the shape of a regular hexagon.
The sections of the spinner are labelled with letters.
The spinner is spun once.
Write down the probability that it lands on a section marked

(a) A (b) B
(c) C (d) D.

3 This spinner is spun once.

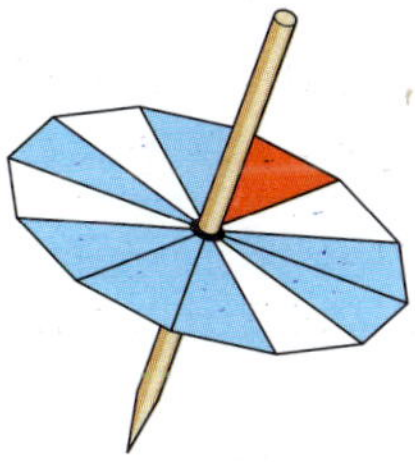

(a) On which colour is it most likely to land?
Give a reason for your answer.

(b) Copy the probability scale.
Mark with an X the probability that the spinner lands on red.

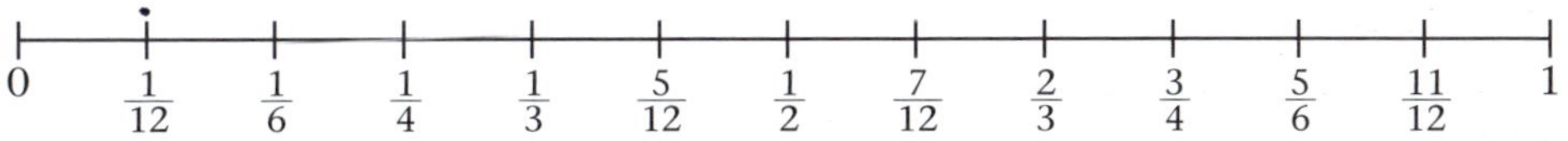

(c) Write down the probability that it lands on white.

4 This four-sided dice is biased. Its vertices are labelled 1 to 4.
Here are Jim's estimates for the probability of getting each score.

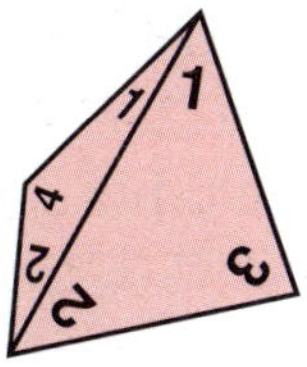

Score	1	2	3	4
Estimated probability	0.28	0.31	0.26	0.23

Explain why these estimates cannot all be correct.

5 Ben's bus to work can be **late**, **on time** or **early**.
The probability of it being late is 0.26.
The probability of it being on time is 0.65.
Work out the probability of Ben's bus being early.

6 A bag contains 12 equal-sized coloured balls. Five of the balls are red, four are blue and three are white.
Work out the probability of the selected ball being

(a) blue (b) either red or blue
(c) green (d) not red.

7 The probability of Jenny winning the raffle is $\frac{3}{1000}$.
Work out the probability of Jenny not winning the raffle.

8 The probability of a new DVD being faulty is 0.002.
(a) Work out the probability of a new DVD not being faulty.
(b) A batch of 30 000 DVDs is released.
Estimate the number of faulty DVDs in this batch.

9 The probability of Lola getting an A* in Mathematics is 96%.
Work out the probability of Lola not getting an A* in Mathematics.

10 A biased dice is rolled once. The probabilities for some scores are:

Score	1	2	3	4	5	6
Probability	0.13	0.17	0.18	0.12		0.20

(a) Work out the probability of a score of 5.
(b) Work out the probability of a score less than 4.
(c) Work out the probability of a score that is a prime number.

11 Joshua rolls an ordinary dice once.
It has faces marked 1, 2, 3, 4, 5 and 6.
(a) Write down the probability that he gets
(i) a 6 (ii) an odd number
(iii) a number less than 3 (iv) an 8.

Ken rolls a different dice 60 times.
This dice also has six faces.
The table gives information about Ken's scores.

Score on dice	Frequency
1	9
2	11
3	20
4	2
5	8
6	10

(b) Explain what you think is different about Ken's dice.[E]

12 On the school sports day Patrick enters the 100 metres and the long jump.

It is estimated that

the probability of Patrick winning the 100 metres = 0.7
the probability of Patrick winning the long jump = 0.5.

Explain fully what is wrong with the following statement:

'The probability of Patrick winning the 100 metres or the long jump = 0.7 + 0.5 = 1.2'

13 A football team can win, lose or draw a match.
The team plays two matches.
List all the possible joint outcomes of the two matches.

14 A game is played with these two fair spinners.

(a) Draw a sample space diagram to show all the possible joint outcomes when the spinners are each spun once.

(b) Work out the probability of the joint outcome (red, 3).

15 A sandwich bar offers all fillings in one of three options:

wrap   baguette   sliced bread.

The five fillings are:

chicken, tuna, cheese, ham, hummus.

One possible sandwich is hummus in a wrap.
Draw a sample space diagram to show all the possible sandwich options.

16 Jim spins the spinner shown in the diagram twice.
He records the sum of the two scores.

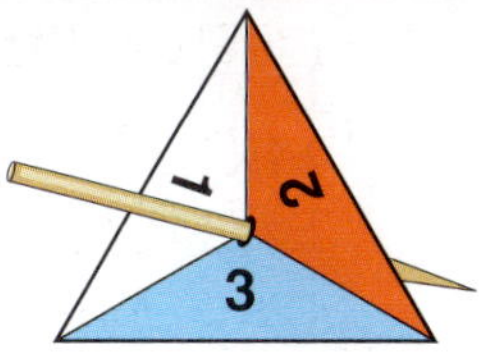

(a) Copy and complete this table to show all the possible results.

2nd spin

1st spin		1	2	3
	1			
	2			5
	3			

(b) Work out the probability of a score of

(i) 6   **(ii)** 3   **(iii)** 8.

17 A market research team conducts a survey into the main method of travel people used to travel to their holiday destination.
They choose a random sample of 1200 people taken from across the country. The results of the survey are shown in the table below.

Method of travel	Plane	Coach	Train	Car	Did not go on holiday
Frequency	451	106	124	474	45

(a) Work out the best estimate for the probability that someone, chosen at random
- **(i)** did not go on holiday
- **(ii)** did **not** travel to their holiday destination by train.

There are approximately 700 000 people in Maidford.

(b) Work out the estimate of the most likely number of people who went on holiday by car.

18 The diagram shows a biased spinner.
Michael spins the spinner 100 times.
His results are:

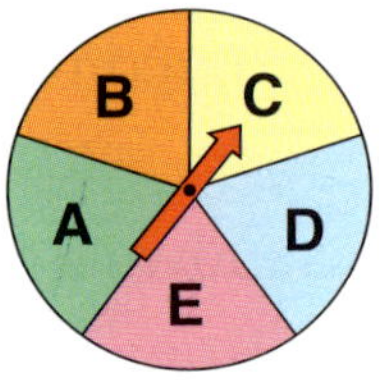

Letter	A	B	C	D	E
Frequency	17	26	31	9	17

Jenny spins the spinner 200 times.
Her results are:

Letter	A	B	C	D	E
Frequency	39	48	69	21	23

(a) Jenny spins the spinner twice as many times as Michael.
Explain why the frequencies in Jenny's table are not twice those in Michael's table.

(b) Work out the best estimate of the probability of the spinner stopping on the sections marked
(i) B **(ii)** D **(iii)** with a vowel
when it is spun once.

(c) The spinner is spun 1000 times.
Work out an estimate for the likely number of times it will land on D.

Use your estimate for P(D) from part **(b)**.

19 The diagram represents a spinner.
The spinner was spun 10 000 times and the faces it stopped on were recorded. The results were:

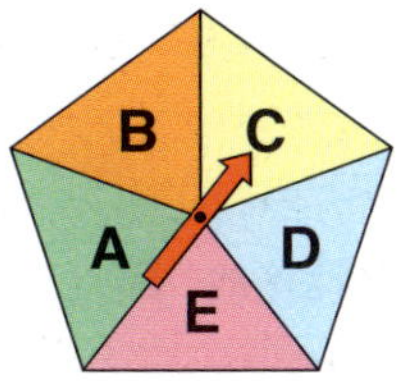

Face	A	B	C	D	E
No. of times	593	4009	1427	2003	1968

Explain clearly whether or not this information suggests that the spinner is biased.

Summary of key points

1 An event that is *certain* to happen has a **probability of 1**.

2 An event that *cannot happen* has a **probability of 0**.

3 The probability that an event will happen is always greater than or equal to 0 (impossible) and less than or equal to 1 (certain).

This can be written:

$0 \leqslant \text{probability} \leqslant 1$

4 If all the possible outcomes of an event are equally likely, the probability that the event will happen is

$$\text{probability} = \frac{\text{number of successful outcomes}}{\text{total number of possible outcomes}}$$

5 Outcomes are **mutually exclusive** when they cannot happen at the same time.

6 A **sample space diagram** shows all possible outcomes of one or more events.

7 The probabilities of all the mutually exclusive outcomes of an event add to 1.

8 The probability of an event **not** happening = 1 − probability of the event happening.

$P(\text{not } A) = 1 - P(A)$

9 The **relative frequency** of an outcome in an experiment is

$$\text{relative frequency} = \frac{\text{number of successful trials}}{\text{total number of trials}}$$

10 For a trial or experiment, the **estimated probability** is given by the relative frequency.

Examination practice paper

Section A (calculator)

1 Ann bought a bag of sweets.

She counted the number of red, yellow, orange and green sweets.

Here are her results.

Colour	Number of sweets
Red	7
Yellow	4
Orange	8
Green	2

On a copy of the grid, draw a bar chart to show to this information.

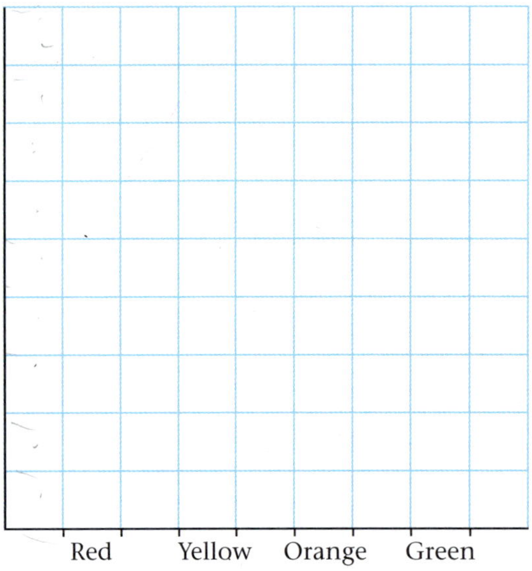

(2 marks)

2 Haleem made a list of his homework marks.

9 8 3 5 7 8 6 8 8 8

(a) Write down the range of his homework marks. **(1 mark)**

(b) Write down the mode of his homework marks. **(1 mark)**

(c) Work out his mean homework mark. **(3 marks)**

3 The table gives information about the types of central heating used by households in a village.

Type of central heating	Frequency	
Electricity	6	
Gas	42	
Oil	24	

Copy and complete this diagram.
Draw an accurate pie chart to show this information.

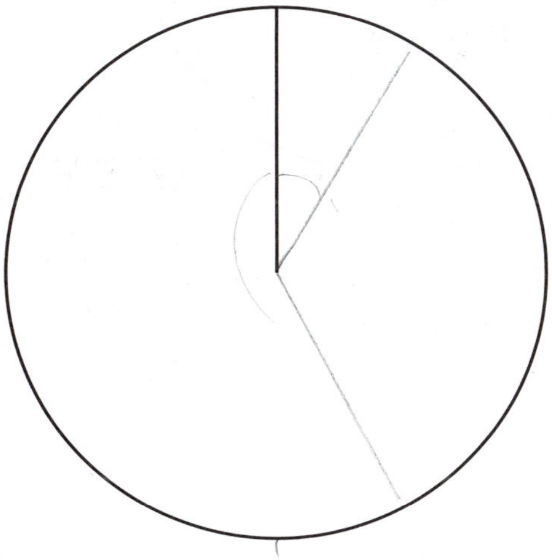

(4 marks)

4 A bag contains yellow, red and blue balls.

Carl takes one ball at random from the bag.

The table shows the probabilities that Carl takes a yellow ball or a red ball.

Colour	Yellow	Red	Blue
Probability	0.25	0.3	

(a) Work out the probability that Carl takes a yellow ball or a red ball. **(2 marks)**

(b) Work out the probability that Carl takes a blue ball. **(2 marks)**

Total for Section A: 15 marks

Section B (non-calculator)

1 Josh carried out a survey of his friends' favourite flavour of crisps.

Here are his results.

Salt and vinegar	Cheese and onion	Plain
Bacon	Plain	Bacon
Plain	Cheese and onion	Salt and vinegar
Cheese and onion	Cheese and onion	Salt and vinegar
Salt and vinegar	Bacon	Cheese and onion
Cheese and onion	Plain	Salt and vinegar
Cheese and onion	Cheese and onion	Plain
Bacon	Bacon	Plain
Bacon		

(a) Copy and complete the table to show Josh's results.

Flavour of crisps	Tally	Frequency
Salt and vinegar		
Cheese and onion		
Plain		
Bacon		

(2 marks)

(b) Write down the number of Josh's friends whose favourite flavour was bacon. **(1 mark)**

(c) Which flavour is the most popular among Josh's friends? **(1 mark)**

2 The diagram shows a fair spinner in the shape of a regular hexagon.

The spinner can land on A or B or C.

Lindsey spins the spinner.

(a) On which letter is the spinner most likely to land? Explain your answer. **(2 marks)**

(b) Write down the probability that the spinner will land on A. **(1 mark)**

3 Fiona says

'The median of a set of data is the value which occurs most often.'

She is **wrong**. Explain why. **(1 mark)**

4 150 people each win a prize.

They win one of a badge, a flag or sticker.

The two-way table shows some information about the prizes they win.

Copy and complete the two-way table.

	Badge	Flag	Sticker	Total
Male	27			81
Female	15		17	
Total		68		150

(3 marks)

5 The scatter graph shows information about the height and arm span for nine students.

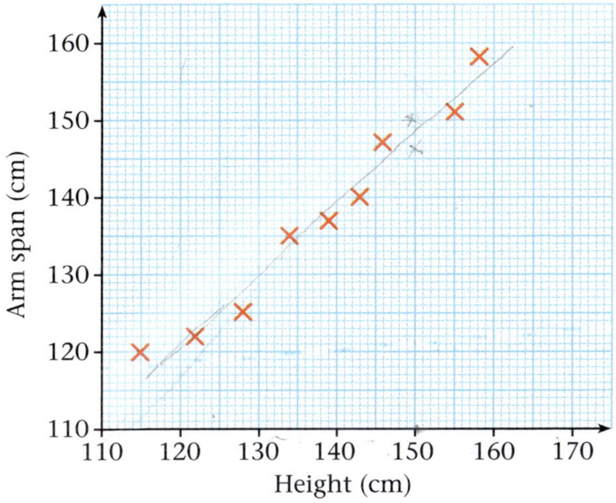

Another student has a height of 130 cm and an arm span of 134 cm.

(a) Plot this information on a copy of the scatter graph. **(1 mark)**

(b) What type of correlation does this scatter graph show? **(1 mark)**

(c) Draw a line of best fit on your copy of the scatter graph. **(1 mark)**

The height of another student is 150 cm.

(d) Use your line of best fit to find an estimate for the arm span of this student. **(1 mark)**

Total for Section B: 15 marks

Answers

Exercise 1A

1 A
2 B
3 C
4 A
5 **(a)** Everyone in the school.
(b) The results are accurate.
(c) There is a lot of data to process.
6 **(a)** **(c)** and **(f)** secondary; **(b)**, **(d)** and **(e)** primary

Exercise 1B

1 List the types of sweet available. Give numberical options regarding how many of each type are consumed per week on average.
2 **(a)** D He can then calculate how far people have travelled (people might not know the actual distances they've travelled). This way will also show if there is one particular area for which the cafe is very popular.
(b) More people than on average for other days might use the internet cafe on a Friday and therefore his results might be a little exaggerated.
3 **(a)** The questions omits many possible methods of communication and cannot be answered by the Yes/No tick boxes.
(b) The number of e-mail addresses is not relevant to how teenagers communicate with each other.
4 The question should specify a time period, e.g. each week. The options are too specific. They should give a range, for example: less than £1, £1 to £1.99, £2 to £2.99, £3 to £3.99, £4 or more.

Exercise 1C

1 **(a)** Continuous **(b)** Discrete
(c) Discrete **(d)** Continuous
(e) Continuous

2

Number of bids	Tally	Frequency
1–5	𝍸 |	6
6–10	𝍸 𝍸 |	11
11–15	||||	4
16–20	|||	3

3

Height, h (m)	Tally	Frequency
$0 \leqslant w < 5$	||||	4
$5 \leqslant w < 10$	𝍸 ||||	9
$10 \leqslant w < 15$	𝍸 𝍸 |	11
$15 \leqslant w < 20$	||||	4
$20 \leqslant w < 25$	||	2

4

Drink	Tally	Frequency
Beer	𝍸 𝍸 ||	12
Wine	𝍸 |||	3
Spirits	𝍸 |	6
Sherry	𝍸 ||||	9

5

Temperature	Tally	Frequency
$15 \leqslant t < 16$	||	2
$16 \leqslant t < 17$	|||	3
$17 \leqslant t < 18$	𝍸 |	6
$18 \leqslant t < 19$	𝍸 𝍸 |	11
$19 \leqslant t < 20$	𝍸	5
$20 \leqslant t < 21$	𝍸	5
$21 \leqslant t < 22$	||||	4
$22 \leqslant t < 23$	||||	4

6

Type of car	Tally	Frequency
Vauxhall		
Rover		
BMW		
…		
…		
(etc.)		

7

Type of music	Tally	Frequency
Classical		
Pop		
Jazz		
Rock		
…		
…		
(etc.)		

Exercise 1D

1

	School lunch	Packed lunch	Other	Total
Female	21	**13**	13	47
Male	**19**	5	**14**	**38**
Total	40	**18**	**27**	85

2

	Walks	Cycle	Car	Bus	Total
KS3					
KS4					
Sixth form					
Total					

3

	Jazz	Rock	Classical	Folk	Total
Men	12	**17**	19	4	52
Women	**9**	23	**9**	**7**	**48**
Total	21	**40**	**28**	11	100

4

Age (years)	Male	Female	Total
21–30	1	2	3
31–40	4	6	10
41–50	11	1	12
51–60	7	3	10
Total	23	12	35

Mixed exercise 1

1 **(a)** Mileage is continuous so we should group the data. We will use a class interval of 5000 miles. We know there are no cars with mileage less than 10000 or greater than 100000, so our sheet will only be between these mileages. We use tallies and frequencies.

(b)

Mileage in thousands (m)	Tally	Frequency
$10 \leqslant m < 15$	|||	3
$15 \leqslant m < 20$	~~||||~~ |	6
$20 \leqslant m < 25$	||||	4
$25 \leqslant m < 30$	||	2
$30 \leqslant m < 35$	|||	3
$35 \leqslant m < 40$	|	1
$40 \leqslant m < 45$	||||	4
$45 \leqslant m < 50$	||	2
$50 \leqslant m < 55$	||	2
$55 \leqslant m < 60$	|||	3
$60 \leqslant m < 65$	||	2
$65 \leqslant m < 70$	|	1
$70 \leqslant m < 75$		0
$75 \leqslant m < 80$	||	2
$80 \leqslant m < 85$	|	1
$85 \leqslant m < 90$	||	2
$90 \leqslant m < 95$	|	1
$95 \leqslant m < 100$	|	1

2 **(a)** We will record the min. and max. temperatures in separate tables. Since the data is continuous we will group the data. We will use a class interval of 5 °C. The max. temperature is not lower than 15 °C or higher than 45 °C, and the min. temperature is not lower than 10 °C or higher than 30 °C, so these are the ranges we will use. We use tallies and frequencies.

(b)

Max. temperature (T) in °C	Tally	Frequency
$15 \leqslant T < 20$	|||	3
$20 \leqslant T < 25$	|||	3
$25 \leqslant T < 30$	||||	4
$30 \leqslant T < 35$	|||	3
$35 \leqslant T < 40$	|	1
$40 \leqslant T < 45$	|	1

Min. temperature (T) in °C	Tally	Frequency
$10 \leqslant t < 15$	~~||||~~	5
$15 \leqslant t < 20$	||	2
$20 \leqslant t < 25$	~~||||~~	5
$25 \leqslant t < 30$	|||	3

3 She should have two separate tables for boys and girls. She will need to group the data, since times are continuous. A class interval of 1 hour would be OK. She will need to allow for times from 0 to 28 hours or more.

4 He needs to specify a time period, e.g. each week or each month. People will not all mean the same by 'a few' and 'a lot' so he needs to give numbers, e.g. 0–2, 3–5, …

5

	French	German	Spanish	Total
Female	**15**	**11**	**13**	**39**
Male	**16**	17	**8**	**41**
Total	31	28	**21**	80

Exercise 2A

1 **(a)**

Car	Tally	Frequency
Ford	~~||||~~ ~~||||~~ ~~||||~~ |	16
Skoda	|	1
Vauxhall	~~||||~~ |	6
Jaguar	|||	3
BMW	|||	3
Fiat	|||	3
Rover	~~||||~~	5
Honda	|||	3

(b)

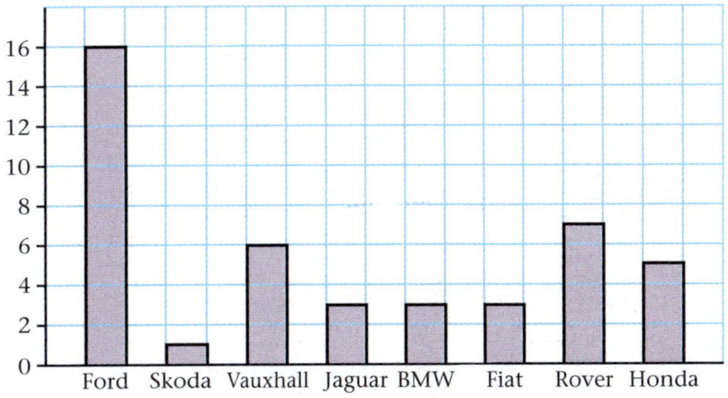

(c) Ford

2 **(a)** 30 **(b)** 40

(c)

Wed	

3 (a) Wednesday (b) 6

(c)

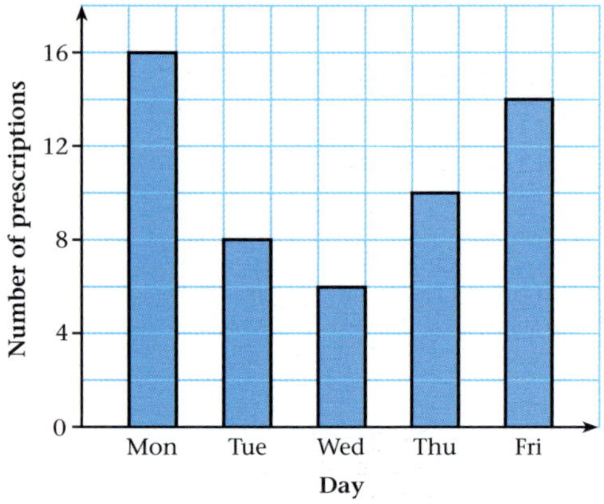

(d) 54

(b)

Subject	Frequency	Angle
Whiteways	36	**144°**
Baldy	18	**72°**
Miniver's	**27**	**108°**
Fine Fare	**9**	**36°**
Total	90	**360°**

(c) (i) Whiteways (ii) Fine Fare

4

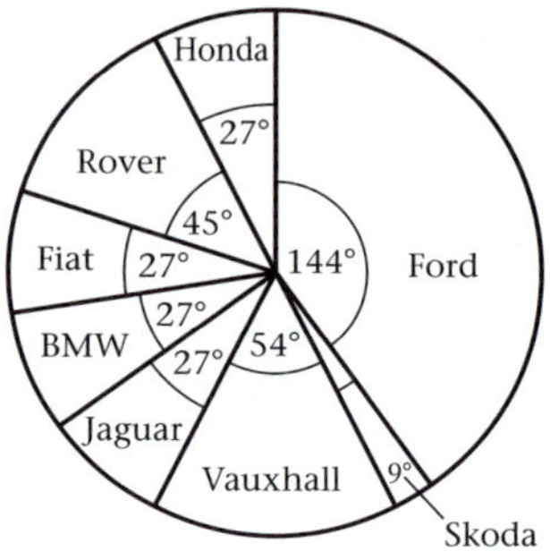

5

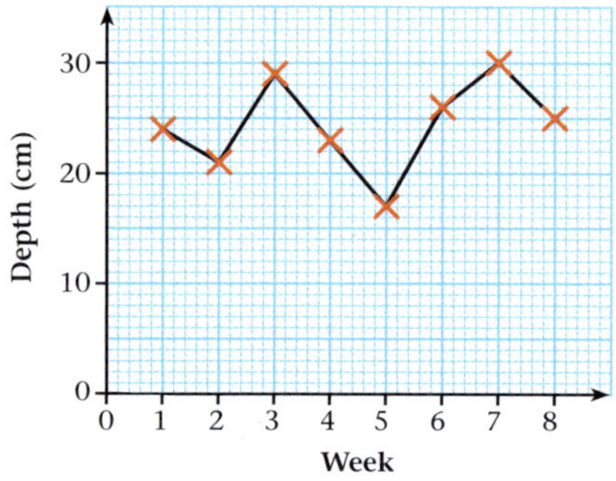

Exercise 2B

1 (a)

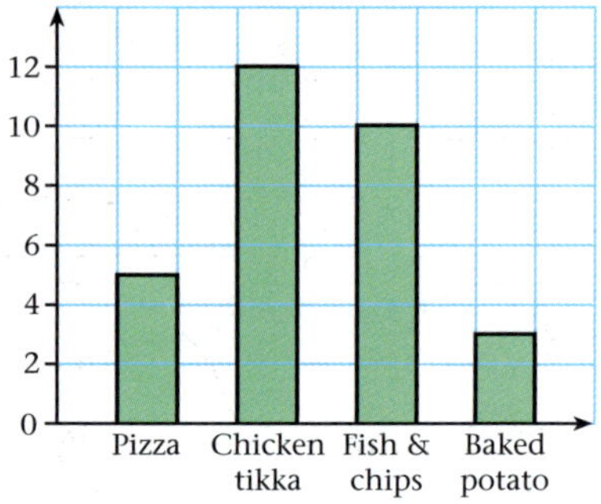

(b)

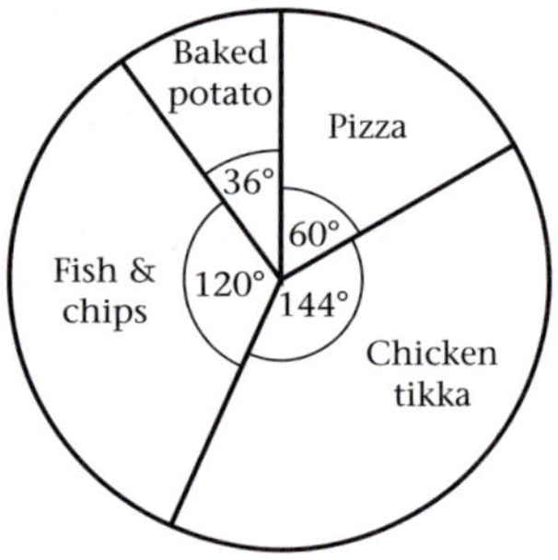

2 (a) Badminton

(b) 15 people

(c) $\frac{1}{12}$

3 (a)

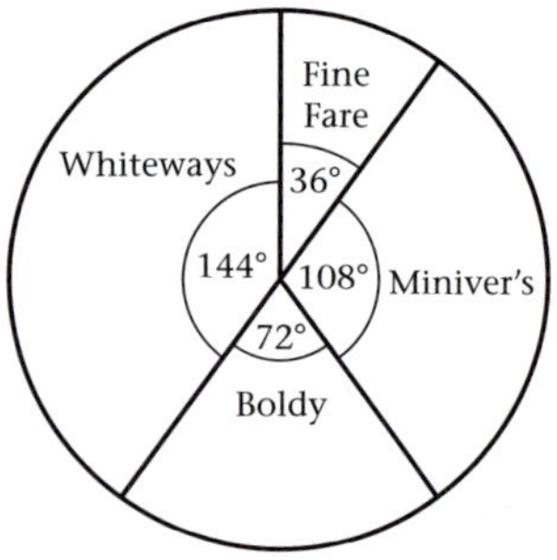

Exercise 2C

1

3	2, 8
4	2, 3, 4, 8, 9
5	0, 1, 1, 2, 4, 4, 5, 5, 7, 7, 7
6	1, 1, 2, 2, 2, 3, 3, 3, 4, 4, 6, 7, 9
7	0, 1, 2, 2, 7
8	0, 5
9	0, 1

Key: 3|2 means 32

2 (a)

0	6, 8
1	2, 5, 6, 7, 9
2	0, 2, 5, 6, 7, 7, 9, 9
3	1, 2, 2, 3, 3, 4, 6, 8, 8, 8, 9
4	0, 1, 2, 2, 4, 5, 6, 6, 6, 6, 8, 8, 9, 9
5	0, 1, 2, 2, 2, 3, 4, 4, 6, 6, 7, 9
6	1, 1, 1, 4, 4
7	0, 3
8	2

Key: 3|1 means 31

(b) No, there are more in their 40s than any other age group.

3

14	9
15	9
16	4, 7, 8, 8, 9, 9
17	0, 1, 2, 3, 3, 3, 6, 7, 9, 9
18	1, 2, 3, 3, 4, 5, 6, 6, 8
19	1, 2
20	1

Key: 14|9 means 149

Exercise 2D

1

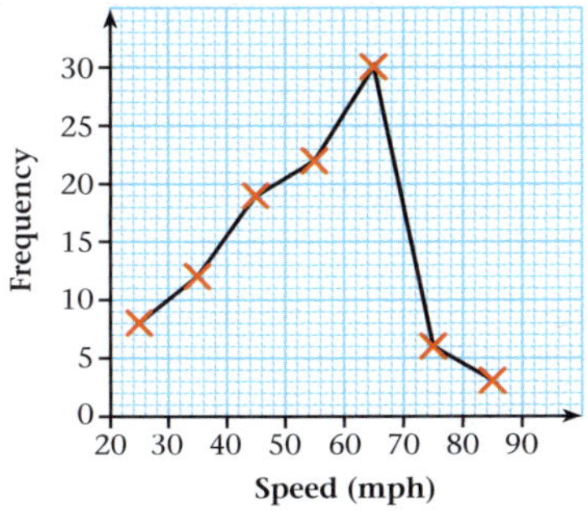

2

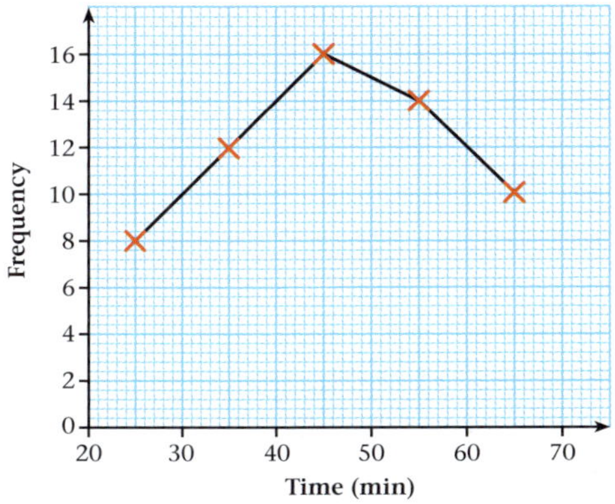

3

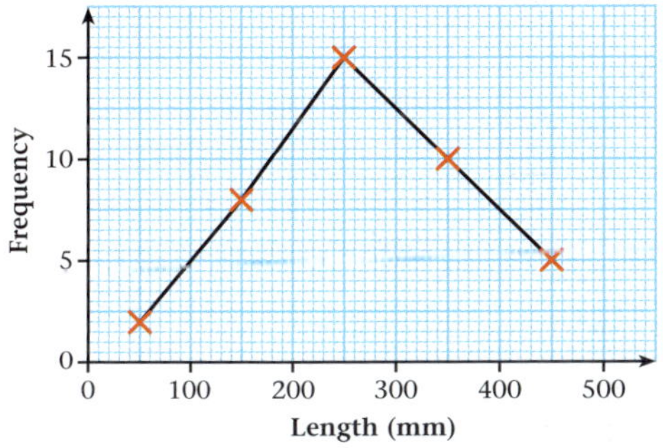

Mixed exercise 2

1 (a)

Type of music	Tally	Frequency
Pop	卌 卌 卌 |||	18
Classical	|||	3
Jazz	卌 ||	7
Rock	卌 卌 ||	12

(b)

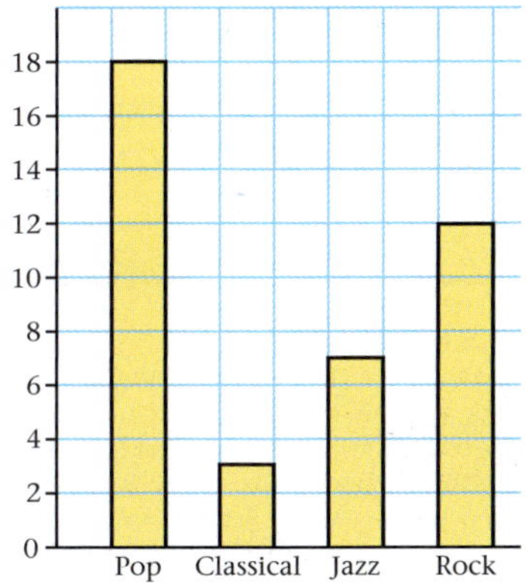

(c)

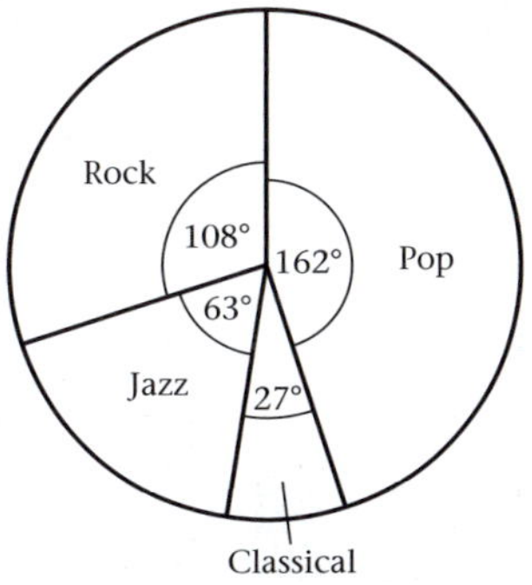

2 (a) 12 (b) 3

(c)

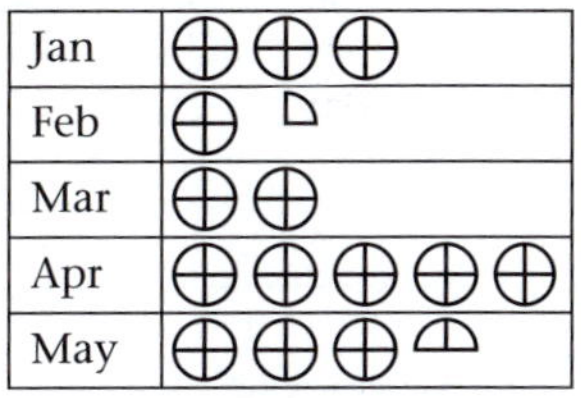

3 (a)

	UK	Europe	Elsewhere	Total
July	**12**	20	8	40
Aug	36	**48**	16	**100**
Sept	**8**	32	**20**	60
Total	56	100	44	**200**

(b)

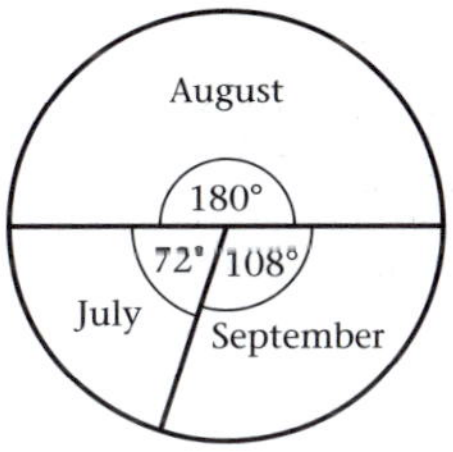

(c)

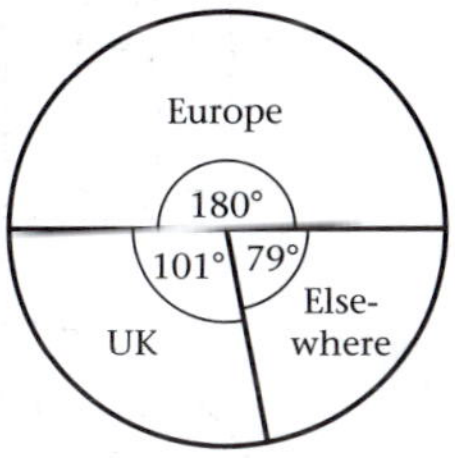

4

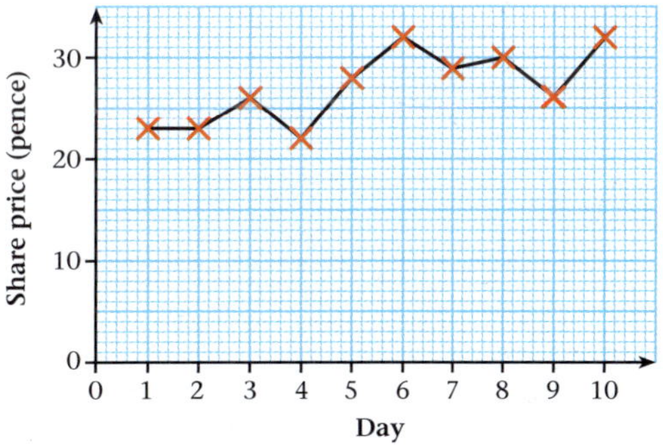

5

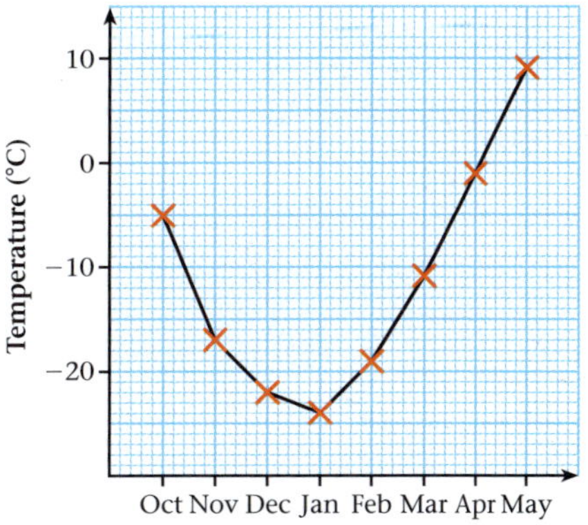

6

Colour	Frequency
Silver	18
Black	12
Red	30
Blue	20
White	40

7

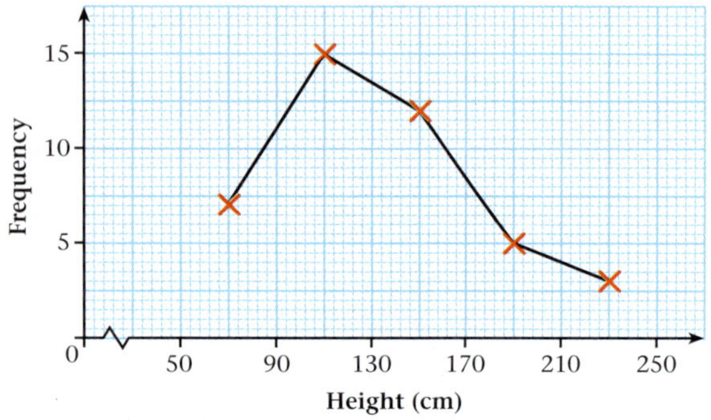

8

Weight, w (kg)	Frequency
$40 < w \leqslant 50$	4
$50 < w \leqslant 60$	6
$60 < w \leqslant 70$	4
$70 < w \leqslant 80$	7
$80 < w \leqslant 90$	6

9

9	9
10	9
11	0, 0, 0, 1, 5, 8
12	0, 0, 5, 5, 5, 7, 7
13	2, 4
14	1, 9
15	9
16	3, 9
17	0
18	0

Key: 10|9 means 109

Exercise 3A

1 (a) 1 (b) 6 (c) 11.16 (d) 58
2 (a) 8 (b) 7.25 (c) 6.71 (d) 5
3 (a) 171 min (b) 69 min (c) 168.8 min
4 (a) 25 (b) 36 (c) 28
5 6.5
6 40 kg to 50 kg

Exercise 3B

1 (a) 2 goals (b) 1 goal (c) 1.35 goals
2 (a) 4 days (b) 0.81 days
3 (a) 1 (b) 1.36
4 (a) 4 people (b) 4.01 people (c) 6 people

Exercise 3C

1 (a) 3 to 5 messages (b) 3 to 5 messages
(c) 4.68 messages
2 (a) 237.5 g (b) $200 < w \leqslant 300$ g
(c) $100 < w \leqslant 200$ g (d) 500 g

3 (a) Estimate mean speed is 38.4 mph (3 s.f.)
(b) $40 < s \leqslant 50$ mph (c) $30 < s \leqslant 40$ mph
(d) 21 vehicles

Activity – Estimating the mean

1 Frequencies: 5, 8, 9, 13, 1, 9, 5
2 Estimated mean: 63.8 seconds
3 Frequencies: 8, 14, 13, 10, 5
Estimated mean: 64.5 seconds
5 Mean: 63.1 seconds
6 Estimating the mean makes the assumption that the values are uniformly distributed within the class intervals. As values are not uniformly distributed, the estimated mean will depend on the class intervals chosen.

Mixed exercise 3

1 (a) 13 (b) 13
2 (a) 2 (b) 28 cm^2
3 (a)

Length in cm	Tally	Frequency
2	|	1
3	|	1
4	||||	4
5	𝍸 |	6
6	|||	3
7	|||	3
8	||	2

(b) 5 cm (c) 6 cm

4 (a)

Temperature, T (°C)	Tally	Frequency
$15 \leqslant T < 20$	||	2
$20 \leqslant T < 25$	𝍸 |	6
$25 \leqslant T < 30$	𝍸 𝍸 ||	12
$30 \leqslant T < 35$	||||	4
$35 \leqslant T < 40$	|	1

(b) Median temperature = 26°C
(c) Modal class interval is $25 \leqslant T < 30$
(d) Mean temperature = 26.28°C

5 (a) Fifth number = 11 (b) Median = 9
6 (a) 30 (b) 3 (c) 30.2
7 (a) Mean speed = 63.2 mph (1 d.p.)
(b) Mean speed = 63.5 mph
(c) Range = 51 mph
(d)

Speed, s (mph)	Tally	Frequency
$30 \leqslant s < 40$	|	1
$40 \leqslant s < 50$	|||	3
$50 \leqslant s < 60$	𝍸 ||	7
$60 \leqslant s < 70$	𝍸 ||||	9
$70 \leqslant s < 80$	𝍸 ||	7
$80 \leqslant s < 90$	|||	3

(e) Modal class interval is $60 \leqslant s < 70$ mph

8 Overall mean = 8.6 years
9 (a) 50 to 55 years (b) 45 to 50 years
10 The highest mark was 18 so the lowest mark was 10. The mean lies between the highest and lowest marks.
11 The greatest possible time of any track is 500 seconds so the mean must be less than 500 seconds.
12 (a) $35 \leqslant t < 40$ (b) 34.75 min or 34 min 45 sec

Exercise 4A

1 (a) £599
(b) Costa Brava, Paris, Barcelona, Edinburgh
(c) Austria, Costa Brava
(d) Majorca

2 (a) Sumreen (b) Fiona (c) Gary, Asif

3 (a) (i) 3110 miles (ii) 4259 miles
(b) Athens and Cairo
(c) Athens and Hong Kong
(d) 6539 miles

Exercise 4B

1 During the first 3 years the value of the 2000 cc car was greater than that of the 1200 cc car.
At 3 years old the value of the cars was the same.
The greatest difference in value was at the start.
During the final 5 years the 1200 cc car was the more valuable.

2 The difference in average house prices between the two regions was least in year 5 and greatest in year 10.
Average house prices were consistently higher in region A.
Average house prices in both regions had increased at the end of the 10-year period.

3 (a) 2 hours (b) Wednesday
(c) (i) 9 hours (ii) Helen (11 hours)

4 (a) August (b) 1.5 °C
(c) Throughout the period April to October temperatures in Barcelona were higher than in London.

Exercise 4C

1 The median mark for the boys was higher than for the girls. However, the spread was greater for the girls than for the boys, so some girls may have received higher marks than any of the boys.

2 To reach any conclusion we need to know which measure of average was used, and we need a measure of spread. For example consider the girls' marks of 1, 2, 4, 5 and 5 with the boys' marks of 3, 3, 3, 6 and 8.
The mode and median for the girls are higher than for the boys, but the boys' marks are better than the girls'.
Or consider girls' marks of 8, 9 and 10, with mean of 9, and boys' marks of 0, 12, and 12 with mean of 8.
The girls' mean is higher, but two of the three boys had higher marks than all three girls, so it is not possible to conclude that the girls rated the product higher than the boys.

3 Nick was the better player. They each won 2 matches but Nick had the lower average score and a smaller range than Tiger, so he is a more consistent player.

Mixed exercise 4

1 (a) 4539 km (b) Chicago (c) Boston

3 You cannot know whether the people at Creswell Ltd are better paid. There may be one highly paid manager whose salary raises the mean wage, while most of the staff have lower wages than at Spencer and Sons.

4 (a) 150
(b) If the ice cream seller was outside, bad weather may have kept people indoors. If the ice cream seller was at an indoor venue, beautiful weather may have persuaded people to stay outside.

5 The modal price range for Make A cars is £15 000–£20 000, compared to £5000–£10 000 for Make B. There were more Make B than Make A in the under £5000 and £5000–£10 000 price ranges and more Make A than Make B cars in all the higher price ranges.

6 For example
The mode grade in 2004 was C.
The mode grade in 2005 was B.
The percentage of students getting grades A*–B has gone up from 36% in 2004 to 39% in 2005.

7 For example
Ali generally has more cars at a particular range than Nick; an exception to this is for cars of value £0–£2000.
The price range where the difference in the number of cars they have is greatest, is £8000–£9000.
The price range where the difference in the number of cars they have is smallest, is £7000–£8000.

8 (a)

Shoe size	Tally	Frequency
3	IIII	4
4	𝍸 𝍸	10
5	𝍸 𝍸 IIII	14
6	𝍸 𝍸 𝍸 III	18
7	𝍸 IIII	9
8	𝍸 I	6
9	𝍸	5
10	IIII	4
11	II	2
	Total	72

(b)

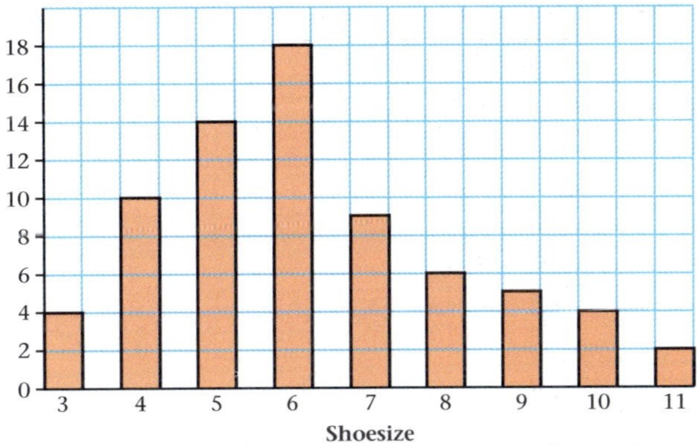

(c)

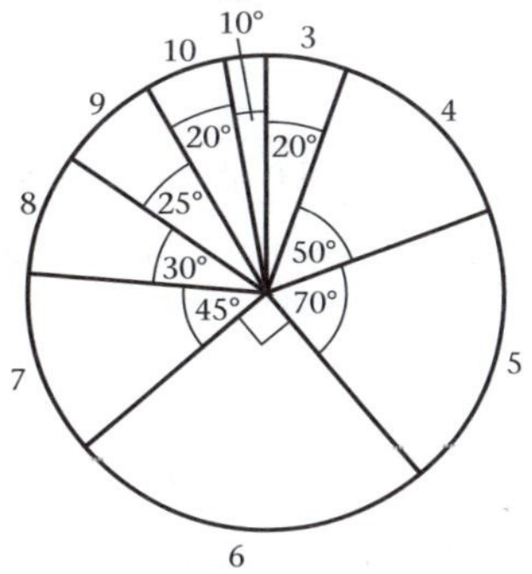

(d) size 6

(e) There is not sufficient evidence, as there might be more students with shoe size between 3 and 6 at the other school than at Dominique's school. Also sample size must be known, as well as range, etc.

9 (a) 1 348 000 000, is much larger than the other populations.
(b) The median would truly reflect the average population. The mean will not since the exceptional value will affect it. It does not make sence to use the mode since the data is not grouped.

(c)

Stem	Leaf
0	2, 3, 4, 4, 4, 5, 5, 9
1	0, 0, 0, 0, 3, 6
2	2
3	8, 9
4	1, 5, 9
5	8, 9
6	0
7	0
8	2
9	
10	0
11	
12	7
13	
14	2, 7
15	
16	
17	6
⋮	
28	7
⋮	
134	8

Key: 8|2 means 82

(d) Out of the seven countries Uruguay has the largest number of wins per million people; we expect that the higher this is, the better the country is at football. Despite having a small population, Uruguay have found footballers good enough to win the World Cup two times.

Exercise 5A

1 (a) and (c)

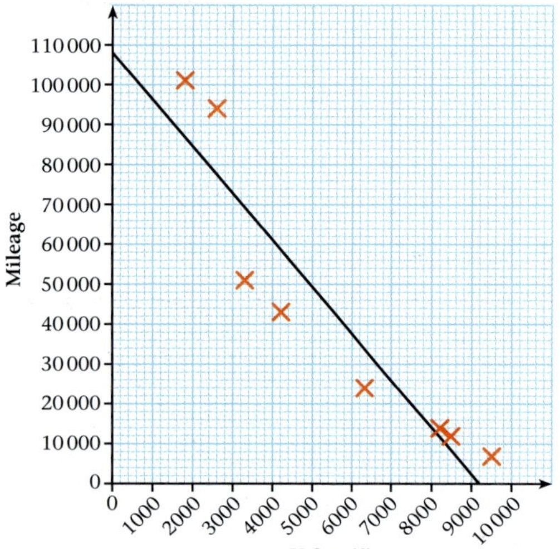

(b) Correlation between mileage and value is negative.

(d) (i) 50 000 miles (ii) £3100

2 (a) and (c)

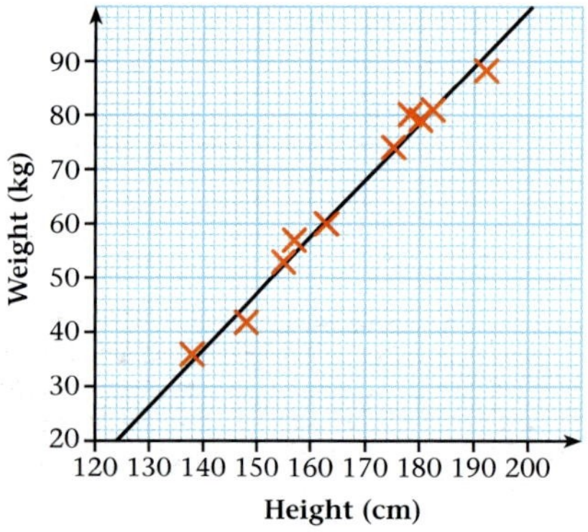

(b) Positive correlation between height and weight of these people.

(d) (i) 47 kg (ii) 174 cm

Exercise 5B

1 (a)

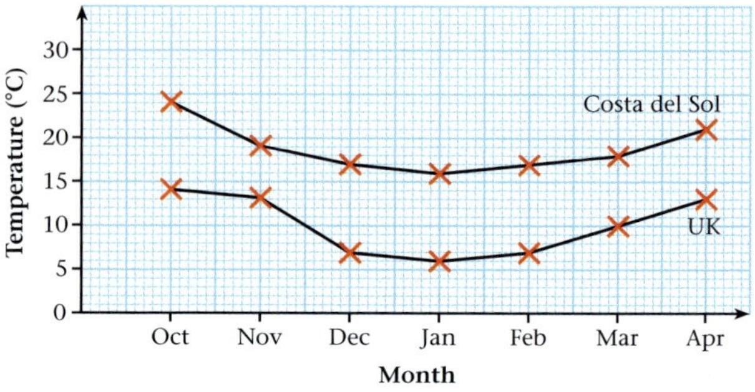

(b) November (c) 8.86 °C (2 d.p.)

2 (a)

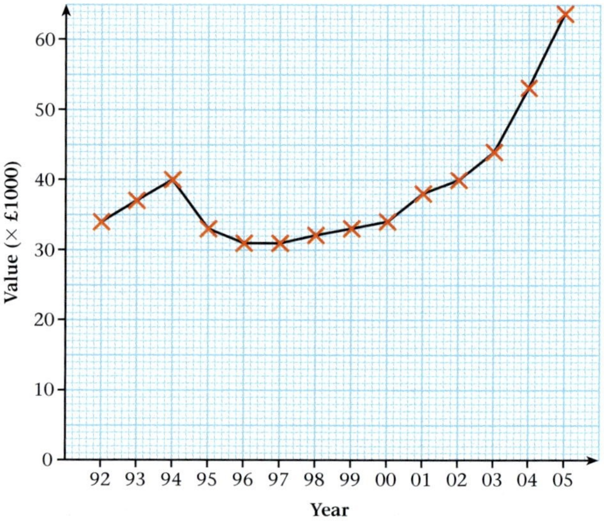

(b) Between 1992 and 1994 the value increased steadily.
Between 1994 and 1995 the value sharply decreased, to lower than the value when Wendy bought the house.
The value of the house was lowest in 1996 and 1997, but between 1997 and 2000 the value slowly increased.
Between 2000 and 2005 the value increased very sharply, and from 2001 it increased by more each year, to its highest point in 2005.

3

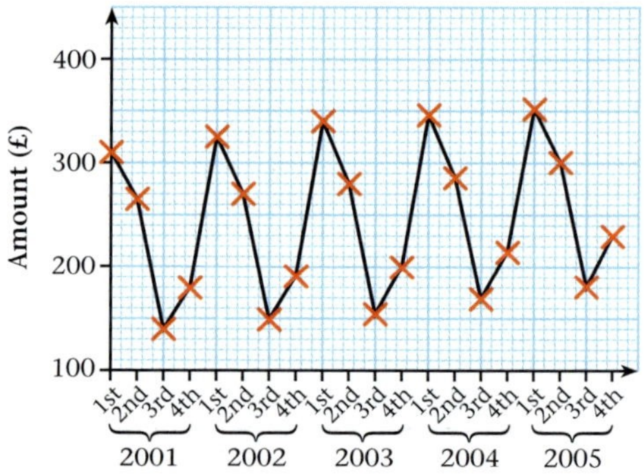

4

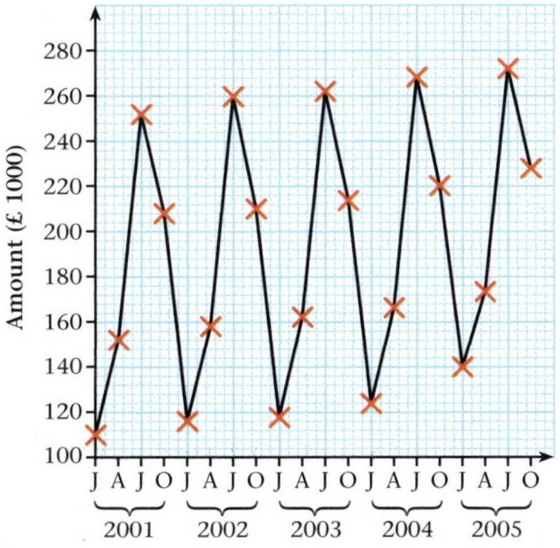

Exercise 5C

1 £15 725.02   2 76p

3 Assuming bread prices follow the changes in the RPI, a similar loaf would cost 4p.

4 (a) (b)

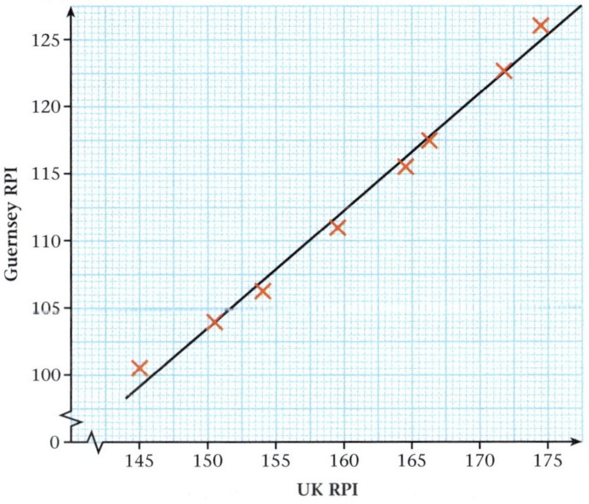

(c) Scatter graph shows positive correlation between the UK and Guernsey RPIs.

(d) Proportional changes to RPI have been:

For UK: $\frac{174.6}{145.0} = 1.204$ For Guernsey: $\frac{125.9}{100.2} = 1.256$

Change in RPI is less for UK than for Guernsey. So, no evidence to support claim.

Mixed exercise 5

1 (a), (c)

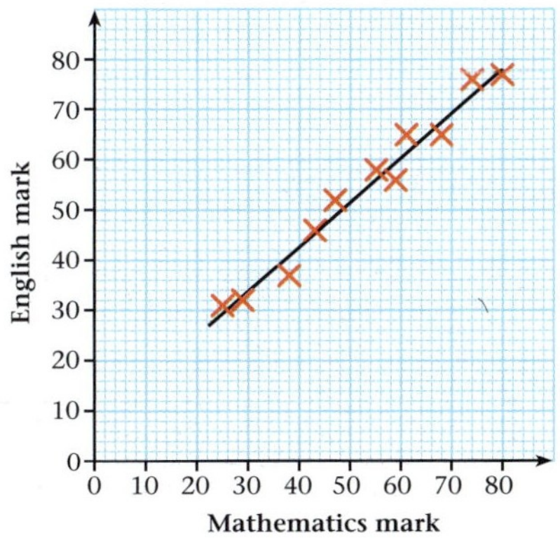

(b) There is a positive correlation between the marks scored in Mathematics and in English.

(d) 52 marks in English exam.

(e) Using 10s as the stem in both case, we have

(i) Mathematics

2	5, 9
3	8
4	3, 7
5	5, 9
6	1, 8
7	4
8	0

(ii) English

3	1, 2, 7
4	6
5	2, 6, 8
6	5, 5,
7	6, 7

Key: 2|5 means 25

2 (a), (c)

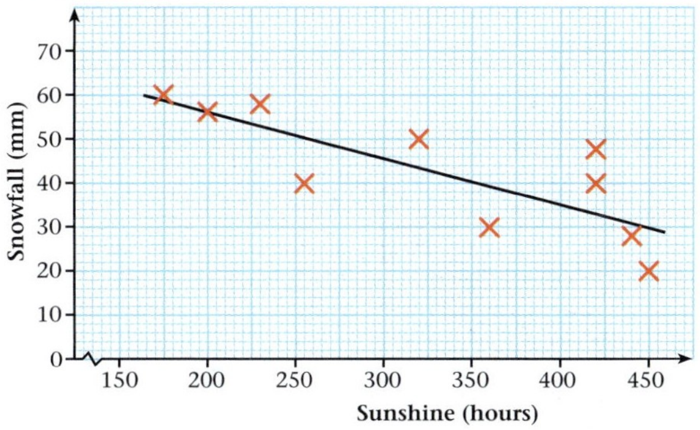

(b) There is a negative correlation between the hours of sunshine and the snowfall.

(d)

2	0, 8
3	0
4	0, 0, 8
5	0, 6, 8
6	0

Key: 2|0 means 20

3 A – Negative, B – None, C– Positive

4 (a) The scatter diagram shows positive correlation

(b)

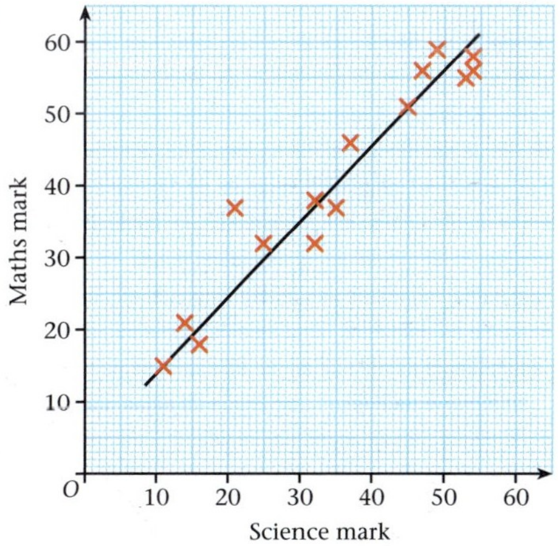

(b) 48 marks

5 The scatter diagram shows there is a positive correlation between value and area of floor space. There is one point on the scatter diagram which does not fit the correlation and is an exception (possibly due to the house being in a more expensive area than the others).

6 (a)

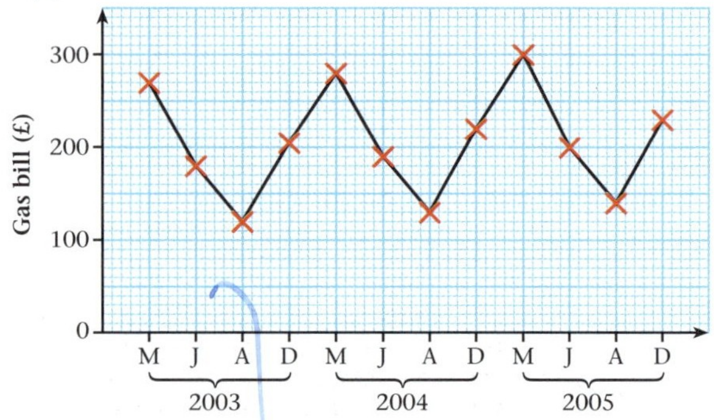

(b) In each year the gas bill decreased from March to August.
In each year the gas bill increased from August to March of the next year.
Comparing the same months in different years we see that the overall trend is an increase in the gas bill over the three years.

7 (a)

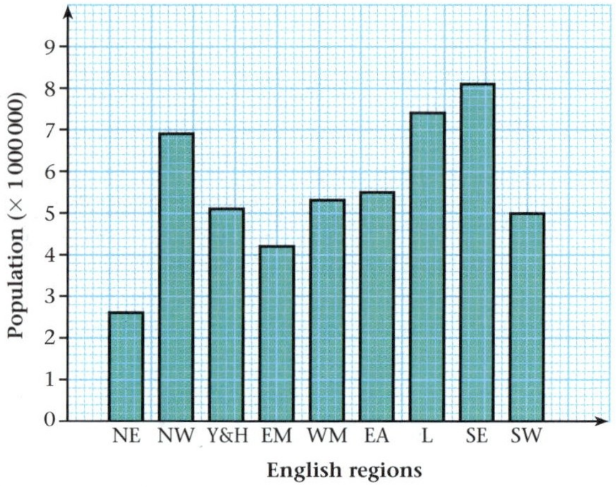

(b)

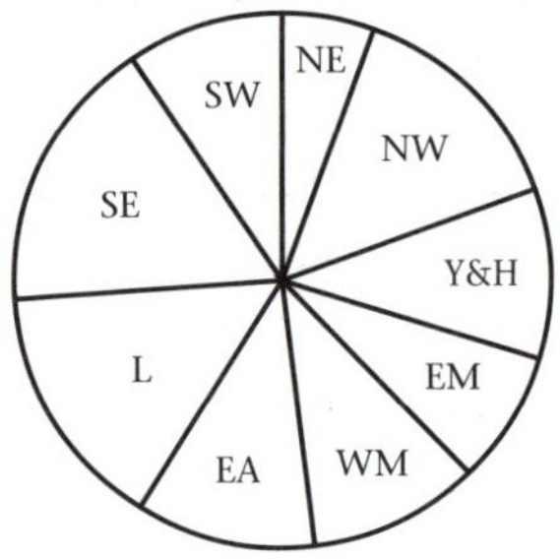

(c) South East

(d) £52 500, £61 000, £65 000, £68 850, £76 200, £82 500, £88 800, £120 000, £147 500

(e) (f)

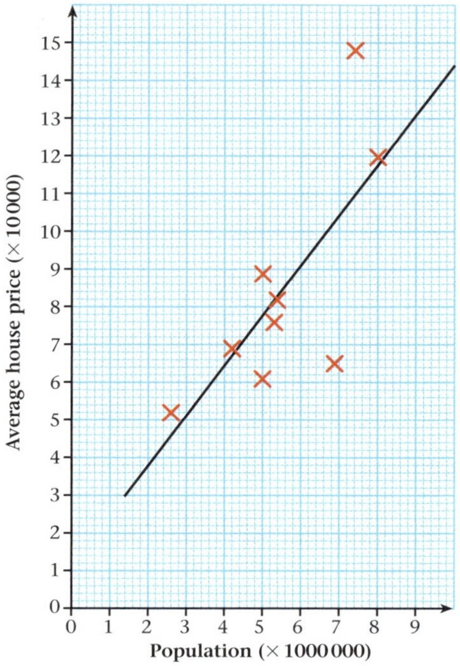

(g) There is a positive correlation between house prices and population.

8 (a)

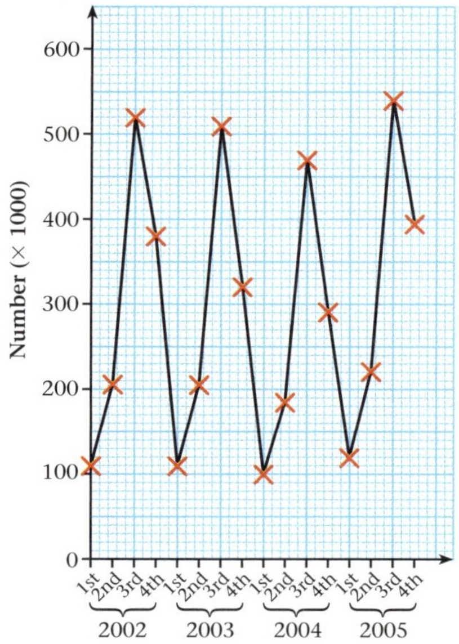

(b) In each year the bill is lowest in the first quarter. It increases in the second quarter, increases greatly in the third quarter then falls to the fourth quarter, and falls greatly to the first quarter of the next year.

Exercise 6A

1

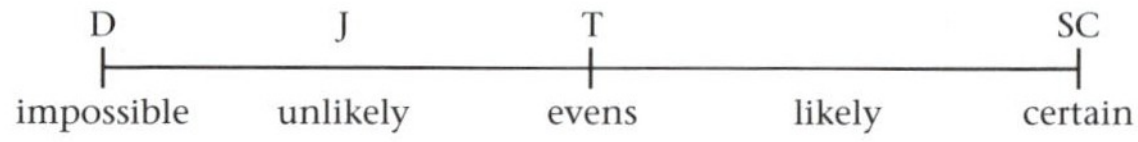

2

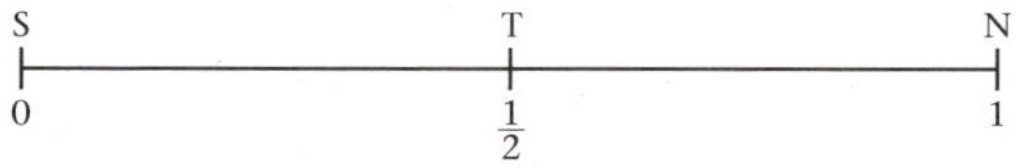

3 **(a)** B **(b)** A **(c)** C

4 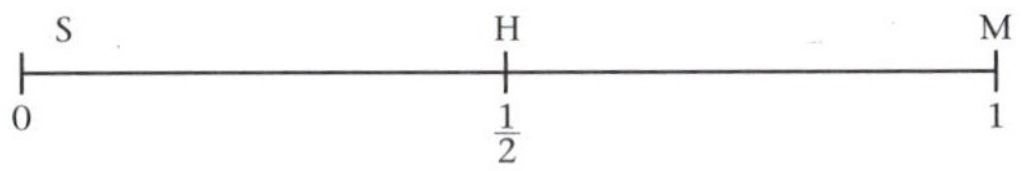

Exercise 6B

1 (a) $\frac{1}{3}$ (b) 0

2 (a) $\frac{1}{6}$ (b) $\frac{3}{6} = \frac{1}{2}$ (c) $\frac{3}{6} = \frac{1}{2}$ (d) 0

3 (a) $\frac{1}{15}$ (b) 0 (c) $\frac{6}{15}$ (d) $\frac{8}{15} + \frac{1}{15} = \frac{9}{15} = \frac{3}{5}$

4 (a) $\frac{1}{6}$ (b) $\frac{2}{6} = \frac{1}{3}$ (c) $\frac{3}{6} = \frac{1}{2}$ (d) 0

Exercise 6C

1 London by car, London by bus, London by train
Manchester by car, Manchester by bus, Manchester by train
Bristol by car, Bristol by bus, Bristol by train
Edinburgh by car, Edinburgh by bus, Edinburgh by train

2 (a) (A, 1); (A, 2); (A, 3); (A, 4); (A, 5); (A, 6)
(B, 1); (B, 2); (B, 3); (B, 4); (B, 5); (B, 6)
(C, 1); (C, 2); (C, 3); (C, 4); (C, 5); (C, 6)
(b) $\frac{1}{18}$ (c) $\frac{1}{18}$

3 (a) (R, 1); (R, 2); (R, 3)
(B, 1); (B, 2); (B, 3)
(W, 1); (W, 2); (W, 3)
(b) $\frac{1}{9}$

4 (a) (H, 1) (H, 2) (H, 3) (H, 4) (H, 5) (H, 6)
(T, 1) (T, 2) (T, 3) (T, 4) (T, 5) (T, 6)
(b) $\frac{1}{12}$

5 (a)

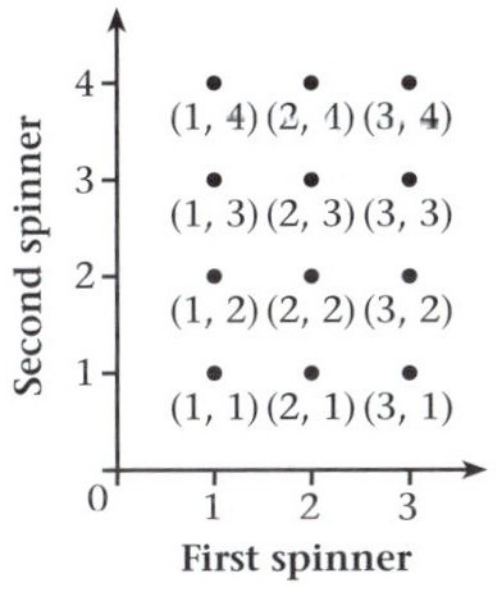

(b) $\frac{1}{12}$
(c) (i) $\frac{1}{4}$ (ii) $\frac{1}{2}$ (iii) $\frac{1}{2}$

Exercise 6D

1 0.97

2 77%

3 (a) $\frac{3}{10}$ (b) $\frac{9}{10}$ (c) $\frac{7}{10}$ (d) 0

4 0.12

5 0.69

6 (a) $\frac{12}{25}$ (b) $\frac{1}{5}$ (c) $\frac{17}{25}$

Exercise 6E

1 (a) Black, since there is the least number of these.
(b) $\frac{3}{10}$
(c) (i) $\frac{2}{5}$ (ii) $\frac{7}{10}$ (iii) $\frac{11}{20}$ (iv) 0

2 (a) 0.996
(b) Probability of being cracked = 0.004
So the most likely number of eggs to be cracked
= 140 000 × 0.004
= 560 eggs

3 $\frac{14}{15}$

4 29 times

5 360 words

Exercise 6F

1 (a) (i) 0.2905 (ii) 0.176 (iii) 0.621
(b) The company will need to ask more students, i.e. take a larger sample; this will make the estimates better.

2 (a) The outcome of the spinner is governed by the laws of chance, so it is likely that each time we spin the spinner 100 times we will get a different set of outcomes. So it is unlikely that Mandy will have 3 times the frequencies that John got.
(b) (i) 0.1875 (ii) 0.5725
(c) Our best estimates are P(A) = 0.1325
P(B) = 0.4275
P(C) = 0.1875
P(D) = 0.2525
If the spinner was unbiased the probabilities would each be 0.25, so the spinner appears to be biased.

3 0.993

4 0.23

5 (a) The outcome of a coin toss is governed by the laws of chance, so it is likely that each time we toss a coin 100 times we will get a different number of heads.
(b) 57 + 45 = 102
Best estimate is P(H) = $\frac{102}{200}$ = 0.51
If the coin is unbiased this probability should be about 0.5, so our estimate does not give sufficient evidence to suggest the coin is biased.

Mixed exercise 6

1 (a) $\frac{1}{10}$ (b) $\frac{3}{10}$ (c) $\frac{1}{10} + \frac{3}{10} = \frac{4}{10} = \frac{2}{5}$ (d) 0

2 (a) $\frac{3}{6} = \frac{1}{2}$ (b) $\frac{2}{6} = \frac{1}{3}$ (c) $\frac{1}{6}$ (d) 0

3 (a) (i) Blue
(ii) There are 7 blue sections out of the total 12 sections.
(b)

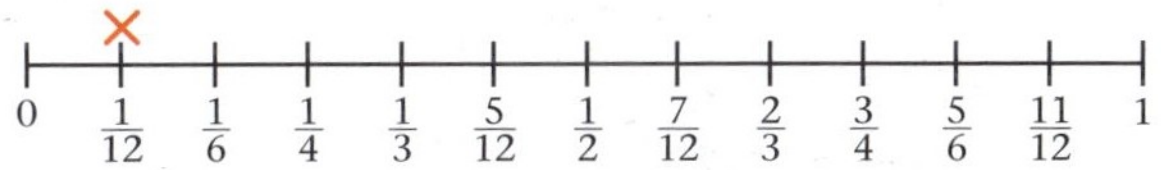

(c) $\frac{4}{12} = \frac{1}{3}$

4 0.28 + 0.31 + 0.26 + 0.23 = 1.08
But sum of probabilities = 1
So there must be an error.

5 0.09

6 (a) $\frac{4}{12} = \frac{1}{3}$ (b) $\frac{9}{12} = \frac{3}{4}$ (c) 0 (d) $\frac{7}{12}$

7 $\frac{997}{1000}$

8 (a) 0.998 (b) 60

9 4%

10 (a) 0.2 (b) 0.48 (c) 0.55

11 (a) (i) $\frac{1}{6}$ (ii) $\frac{1}{2}$ (iii) $\frac{1}{3}$ (iv) 0
(b) Ken's dice is biased. You would expect an unbiased dice to land with each face up ten times in sixty rolls. Ken's dice appears to be biased against 4 and towards 3.

12 They are not mutually exclusive events.

13 (win, win) (win, lose) (win, draw)
(lose, win) (lose, lose) (lose, draw)
(draw, win) (draw, lose) (draw, draw)

14 (a) (Red, 1) (Red, 2) (Red, 3) (Red, 4) (Red, 5)
(White, 1) (White, 2) (White, 3) (White, 4) (White, 5)
(Blue, 1) (Blue, 2) (Blue, 3) (Blue, 4) (Blue, 5)
(b) $\frac{1}{15}$

15 (wrap, chicken) (wrap, tuna) (wrap, cheese)
(wrap, ham) (wrap, hummus)
(baguette, chicken) (baguette, tuna) (baguette, cheese)
(baguette, ham) (baguette, hummus)
(bread, chicken) (bread, tuna) (bread, cheese)
(bread, ham) (bread, hummus)

16 (a)

1st spin \ 2nd spin	1	2	3
1	2	3	4
2	3	4	5
3	4	5	6

(b) (i) $\frac{1}{9}$ (ii) $\frac{2}{9}$ (iii) 0

17 (a) (i) 0.0375 (ii) 0.897 (3 s.f.)
(b) 276 500

18 (a) The outcome of the spinner is governed by the laws of chance, so it is likely that each time we spin it 100 times we will get a different set of outcomes. So it is unlikely Jenny will have twice the frequencies Michael had.
(b) (i) $P(B) = \frac{37}{150}$
(ii) $P(D) = \frac{1}{10}$
(iii) $P(\text{vowel}) = \frac{8}{25}$
(c) 100

19 If the spinner was not biased we would have $P(A) = P(B) = P(C) = P(D) = P(E) = 0.2$ i.e. we would expect each letter to come up about 2000 times. In fact, B came up 4009 times. A 593 times and C 1427 times, which suggests the spinner is biased in favour of B. It appears to be biased against A and, to a lesser degree, C.

Examination practice paper

Section A

1

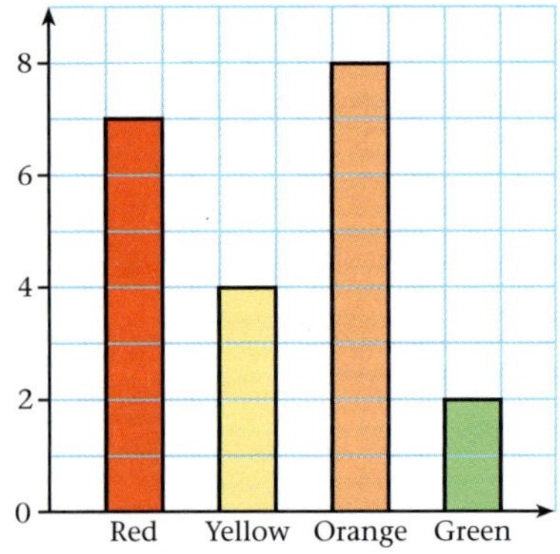

2 (a) 6 (b) 8 (c) 7

3

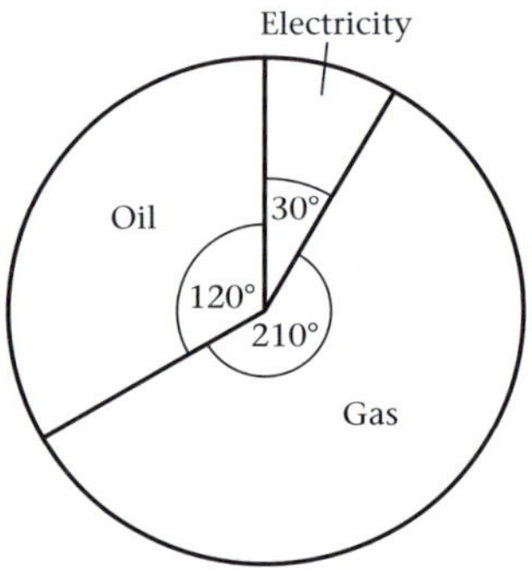

4 (a) 0.55 (b) 0.45

Section B

1 (a)

Flavour	Tally	Frequency
Salt and vinegar	𝍸	5
Cheese and onion	𝍸 |||	8
Plain	𝍸		6
Bacon	𝍸		6

(b) 6
(c) Cheese and onion

2 (a) B. There are more Bs than As or Cs
(b) $\frac{1}{6}$

3 The **mode** of a set of data is the value which occurs most often.
The **median** is the value in the middle when the values are listed in order of size.

4

	Badge	Flag	Sticker	Total
Male	27	**31**	**23**	81
Female	15	**37**	17	**69**
Total	**42**	68	**40**	150

5 (a), (c)

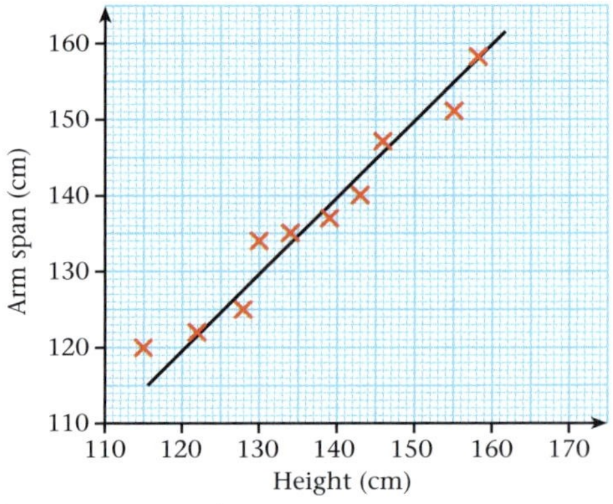

(b) Positive correlation
(d) About 150 cm

Foundations in Life Science
Second Edition

PEARSON
Custom Publishing

We work with leading authors to develop the strongest educational materials bringing cutting-edge thinking and best learning practice to a global market.

Under a range of well-known imprints, including Financial Times/Prentice Hall, Addison Wesley and Longman, we craft high quality print and electronic publications which help readers to understand and apply their content, whether studying or at work.

Pearson Custom Publishing enables our customers to access a wide and expanding range of market-leading content from world-renowned authors and develop their own tailor-made book. You choose the content that meets your needs and Pearson Custom Publishing produces a high-quality printed book.

To find out more about custom publishing, visit www.pearsoncustom.co.uk

A Pearson Custom Publication

Foundations in Life Science
Second Edition

Compiled from:

Science in Nursing and Health Care
Second Edition
by Mark Foss and Tony Farine

PEARSON
Custom Publishing

Pearson Education Limited
Edinburgh Gate
Harlow
Essex CM20 2JE

And associated companies throughout the world

Visit us on the World Wide Web at:
www.pearsoned.co.uk

First published 2008

Taken from:

Science in Nursing and Health Care Second Edition
by Mark Foss and Tony Farine
ISBN 978 0 131 86902 8

ISBN 978 1 84658 744 3

Printed and bound by in Great Britain by Ashford Colour Press, Gosport, Hampshire.

Contents

Chapter 1	Genetics in Health and Illness Chapter 15 in *Science in Nursing and Health Care* Second Edition Mark Foss and Tony Farine	1
Chapter 2	Microbiology Chapter 16 in *Science in Nursing and Health Care* Second Edition Mark Foss and Tony Farine	27
	Answers to Self-Test Questions 'Answers to Self-Test Questions in *Science in Nursing and Health Care* Second Edition Mark Foss and Tony Farine	77

15

Genetics in health and illness

After reading the following chapter and undertaking personal study, you should be able to:

1 Describe the structure of a nucleic acid.

2 Describe the structure of deoxyribonucleic acid (DNA) and compare it with that of ribonucleic acid (RNA).

3 Define the terms 'chromatin', 'chromosome', 'diploid', 'haploid' and 'gene' and relate these definitions to normal healthy cells.

4 In connection with the replication of normal healthy cells, describe the following:
   DNA replication.
   The cell cycle and mitosis.
   How meiosis differs from mitosis.

5 Describe briefly the three types of RNA – messenger RNA (mRNA), ribosomal RNA (rRNA) and transfer RNA (tRNA).

6 Differentiate between a codon and an anticodon.

7 Describe transcription and translation.

8 Explain the terms 'locus', 'allele', 'genotype', 'phenotype', 'homologous', 'homozygous' and 'heterozygous' and relate the explanations to genetic disease.

9 Identify normal traits that you might see in people that you meet each day and that are examples of simple autosomal inheritance (dominant and recessive), incomplete dominance (co-dominance), multiple alleles and polygenic inheritance.

10 Use a Punnett square in order to show the possible combination of alleles that may be inherited from parents and relate this to patients in clinical practice.

11 Give examples of the following patterns of genetic disease – simple autosomal inheritance (dominant and recessive), incomplete dominance (co-dominance) and sex-linked disorders – and give examples from clinical practice.

12 Describe briefly what is meant by a chromosomal aberration and give an example.

Introduction

When looking at photographs of people, have you ever noted similarities in the appearance of family members over several generations? If so, you were making an observation about **genetics**. The word 'genetics' is derived from '*genesis*' meaning creation, but really it is the study of **heredity**. Heredity is the transmission of physical characteristics (e.g. eye colour) from parents to children; it is also the study of diseases that have a genetic basis, e.g. **cystic fibrosis**. '*Genesis*' is also the origin of the word '**gene**', which is the name given to sections of **deoxyribonucleic acid (DNA)**. DNA is a large molecule that carries **genetic information** about such diverse things as eye colour, hair texture and which enzymes are made in the body. DNA is located in the **nucleus** of the cells of the body, and this is where we begin our study.

The nucleus of the cell

The cell (Figure 15.1) is the smallest living structure of an organism. The entire substance of a cell is referred to collectively as **protoplasm**, and it is separated from the outside environment by a membrane called the **cell membrane**. Most cells have an oval or spherical structure called the **nucleus** located within the protoplasm. The substance of the nucleus is collectively referred to as **nucleoplasm**, while the rest of the cell substance is called **cytoplasm**. Nucleoplasm is separated from cytoplasm by a membrane that forms the boundary of the nucleus; this membrane is called the **nuclear membrane**. This membrane contains pores (channels) through which molecules may enter or leave the nucleus.

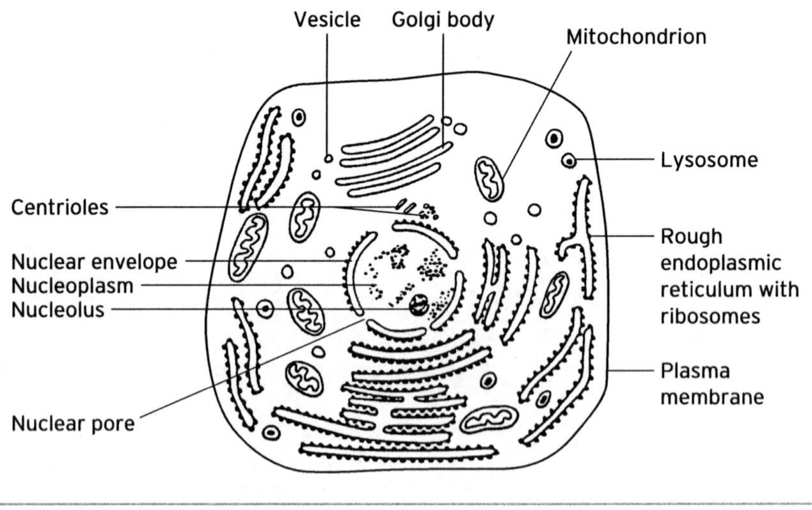

Figure 15.1

A typical animal cell. (From Cornwell A. and Miller R. (1997) *Longman Study Guides. A-Level and AS-Level Biology*. Harlow: Longman.)

Within the nucleus, **chromosomes** are found. These are important genetic structures made of DNA. Chromosomes can be seen with a light microscope, but they are visible only when the cell is actively dividing (reproducing).

- *How many chromosomes do human cells possess?*

To answer this question, it is important to explain that the body's cells form two groups – **gametes** and **somatic cells**. Gametes are the sex cells – **ova** (eggs) in females and **spermatozoa** (sperm) in males. All other cells are described as somatic. In somatic cells there are 23 pairs of chromosomes – the so-called **diploid number**. (The prefix 'diplo' means double, but here 'diploid' refers to the full number of chromosomes.)

- *Why do we say '23 pairs' and not simply '46'?*

Chromosomes are arranged in pairs according to their size and shape. Such pairs are referred to as **homologous chromosomes/homologous pairs**. One member of each homologous pair is derived from the mother and the other is from the father. One pair of chromosomes carries information about sex, and these are the **sex chromosomes**. The remaining 22 pairs do not carry information about sex and are called **autosomes**.

- *How many pairs of chromosomes do gametes possess?*

Gametes possess only 23 chromosomes – the so-called **haploid number**. (The prefix 'haplo' means single, but here 'haploid' refers to the reduced number of chromosomes.) Twenty-two of these chromosomes are autosomes, and one is a sex chromosome.

There are two types of sex chromosome; they are given the designation X and Y. Female somatic cells (non-sex cells) possess two X chromosomes, while ova (the female gamete/sex cell) possess a single X chromosome. (Remember somatic cells are diploid and gametes are haploid.) Male somatic cells possess one X chromosome and one Y chromosome; spermatozoa contain either one X chromosome or one Y chromosome. A new individual is formed when haploid gametes fuse in a process called **fertilisation**. This is the process that takes place after sexual intercourse, in which one of millions of male spermatozoa deposited in the reproductive system of the female penetrates a single ovum. The sex of the new individual is determined by which sex chromosome (X or Y) the spermatozoon is carrying, since the ova always carry an X chromosome. If the spermatozoon is carrying an X chromosome, then the new individual will be female (XX); if the spermatozoon is carrying a Y chromosome, then the new individual will be male (XY).

Chromosomes consist of deoxyribonucleic acid (DNA) and its associated proteins. Before cell division, DNA forms a mass of threads called **chromatin**. Electron micrographs (photographs taken with an electron microscope) show that chromatin resembles beads on a string. Each bead-like structure is called a **nucleosome** and consists of DNA wrapped twice around a core of eight proteins called **histones**. During the early stages of cell division, DNA is replicated (copied) and the chromatin coils to form the discrete structures that we call chromosomes. At this stage, it can be seen that each chromosome consists of two parts called **chromatids** joined by a structure called a **centromere** (Figure 15.2). Each pair of chromatids carries the same genetic information.

What is DNA made of?

Francis Crick and James Watson first described the structure of DNA in 1956. DNA is made of subunits (building blocks) called **nucleotides**. Each nucleotide has three components:

- a five-carbon atom sugar molecule
- a phosphate group
- An organic compound referred to as a **base** (the word 'base' refers here to 'foundation' and is used in reference to a major component of a molecule).

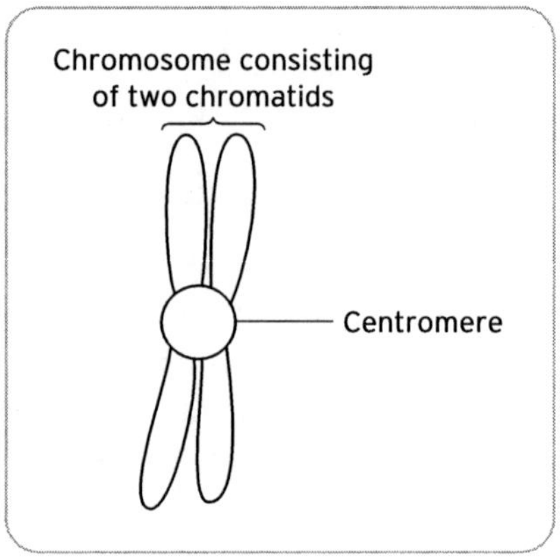

Figure 15.2
The structure of a chromosome.

The structure of a nucleotide is shown in Figure 15.3. Nucleotides that form DNA have the sugar **deoxyribose** and one of four bases - **adenine**, **thymine**, **guanine** or **cytosine**.

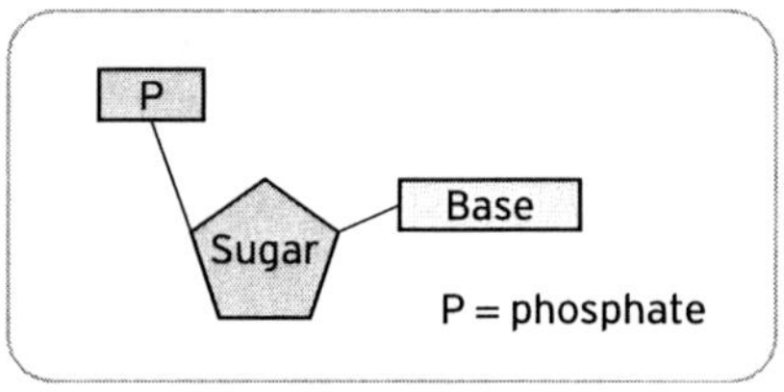

Figure 15.3
The structure of a nucleotide. (From Miller C. and Barber M. (1997) *Longman Study Guides. GCSE Biology*. Harlow: Longman.)

DNA possesses two chains that are formed from the bonding of the sugar of one nucleotide with the phosphate group of another. Consequently, these chains are sometimes referred to as **sugar-phosphate backbones**. Bonds formed between the bases then join these two chains. Adenine always bonds with thymine and guanine always bonds with cytosine. On first examination, this arrangement looks rather like a ladder, but actually the two sugar-phosphate chains spiral around each other. In fact, that is how the structure of DNA is described - as a double helix (Figure 15.4).

DNA is not the only nucleic acid - there is another called **ribonucleic acid** (**RNA**). RNA differs from DNA in three important ways:

- RNA consists of only a single strand of nucleotides.
- In the nucleotides that form RNA, the sugar is **ribose**, not deoxyribose.
- The base **uracil** is found instead of thymine.

DNA: the genetic code

DNA is often described as the body's genetic code. This is because DNA acts as the instructions for which proteins the body should make, and how the body should function.

How can a chemical act as a code?

To answer this question, let us think about codes in general. Codes are systems of characters (letters, numbers or symbols) that are used to represent words. Codes look mysterious

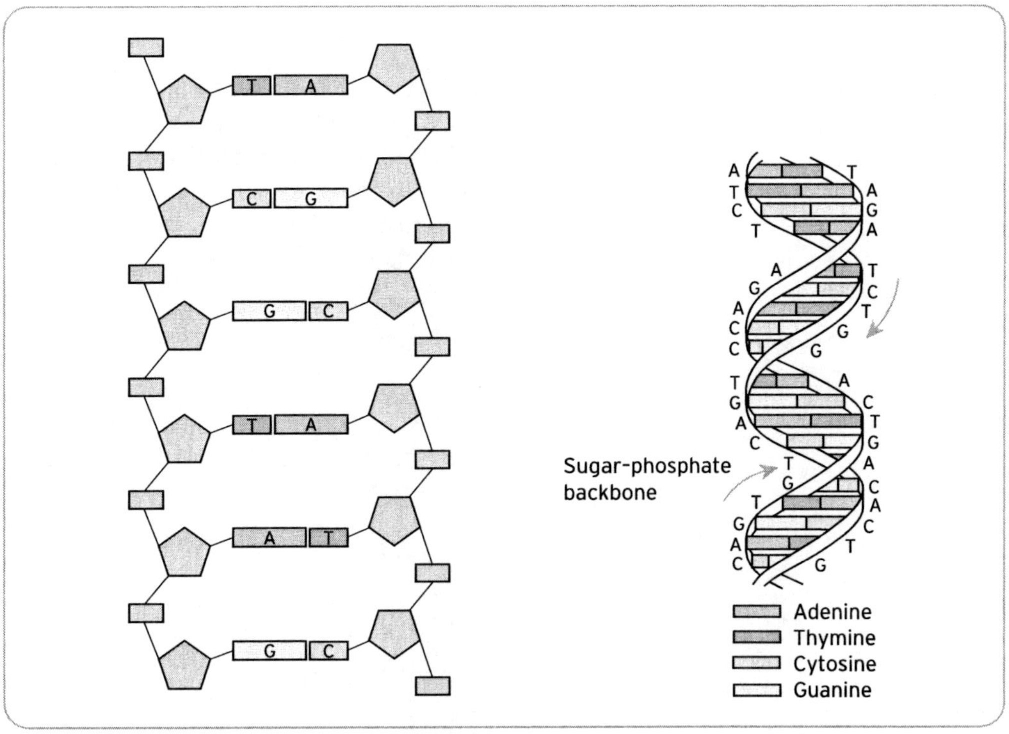

Figure 15.4

The structure of DNA. (From Miller C. and Barber M. (1997) *Longman Study Guides. GCSE Biology*. Harlow: Longman.)

until you know that the meaning of a word is determined by the sequence of characters in the code. It is similar with the genetic code - it appeared mysterious until it was discovered that its meaning is in the sequences of bases in DNA. These are arranged in triplets (groups of three), which are referred to as **codons**. Each codon acts as a code for a specific **amino acid** - there are 20 amino acids in nature.

- *How many codons would you expect?*

You might think that there should be 20 codons, but in fact there are 64. Some amino acids are specified by more than one codon - a condition referred to as **redundancy**. In addition, some codons have functions other than coding for specific amino acids. Some codons indicate the point at which a code for a particular protein begins; these are referred to as **start codons**. Other codons indicate the point at which the code for a particular protein ends and are referred to as **stop codons**.

At this point, it is probably worth returning to a term introduced earlier - **genes**. These are segments of DNA that code for a specific protein. Genes form a section of a strand of DNA located between a start codon and a stop codon. There are thousands of genes in human DNA. Later in this chapter, we shall explain how the body uses the genetic code, but before we do this we need to consider how DNA is replicated.

DNA replication

If a cell is to divide (reproduce), it must replicate its DNA so that 23 pairs of chromosomes can be passed on to each of the resulting new cells. New cells are always called **daughter cells**. The first process in DNA replication is the unwinding of the double helix, as shown in Figure 15.5. Next, newly synthesised bases pair with the bases of the two original strands. In this way, two DNA molecules result. Each DNA molecule consists of a strand of the original molecule and a new strand. Consequently, DNA replication is said to be semi-conservative, as it conserves one old strand as part of each new strand.

Once DNA has been replicated, the cell is able to divide to produce two new cells. This is what we consider next.

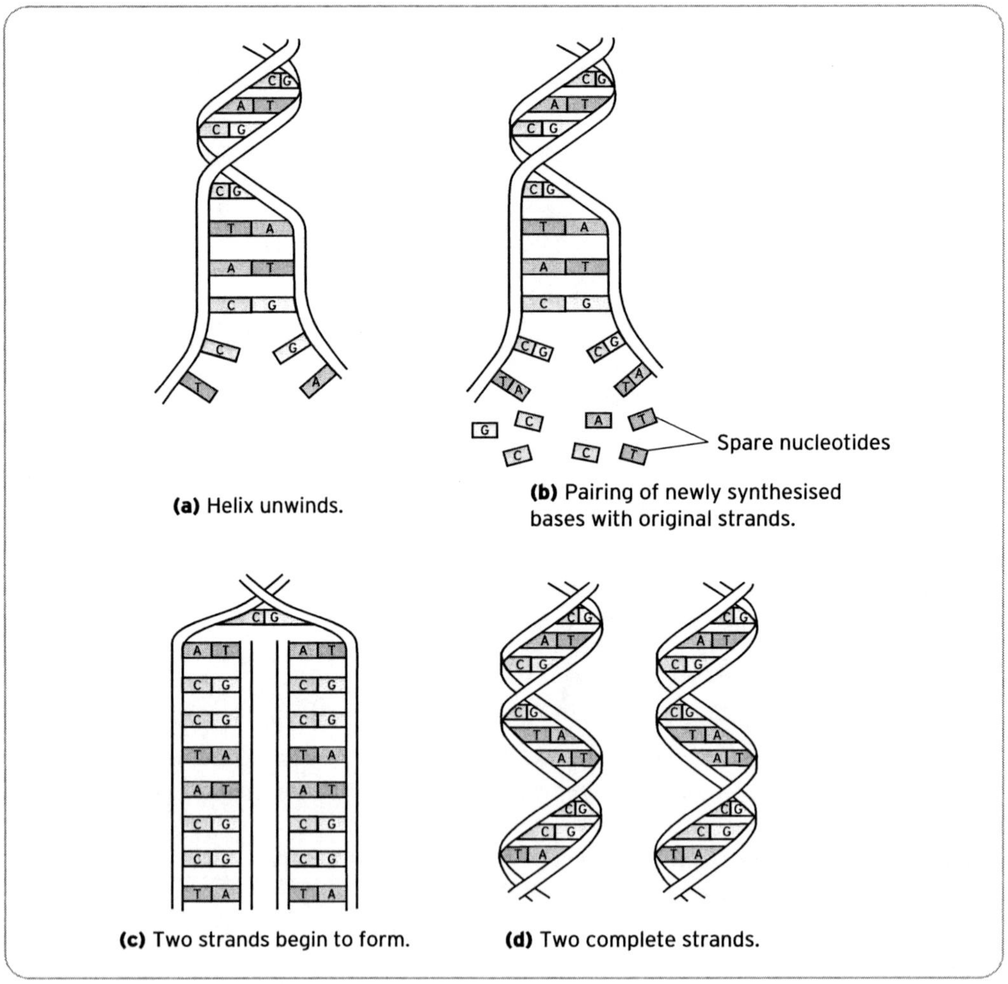

Figure 15.5
DNA replication. (From Miller C. and Barber M. (1997) *Longman Study Guides. GCSE Biology*. Harlow: Longman.)

Mitosis and the cell cycle

Cells need to reproduce so that damaged cells are replaced and growth takes place. Some cells, such as those of the basal layer of the skin, divide rapidly throughout life, while others, such as neurons in the brain, do not divide at all after birth. Figure 15.6 is a diagrammatic representation of the lifecycle of a somatic cell.

The cell cycle can be divided into two parts - **interphase** and **mitosis** (cell division). We consider each stage in turn.

Interphase

When a cell is not actively dividing, it is said to be in interphase. Interphase can itself be divided into distinct phases, which are represented in Figure 15.6. S stands for synthesis and refers to DNA synthesis (DNA replication); G_1 and G_2 are periods of growth, while G_0 is a period of rest. In G_0, the cell is actively metabolising but not growing or synthesising DNA.

Mitosis (cell division)

Cell division in somatic cells is referred to as **mitosis**, although strictly speaking this term refers only to the manner in which chromosomes are distributed between two newly forming cells (daughter cells). The division of the parent cell into two daughter cells is called **cytokinesis** (cytoplasmic division). Mitosis is divided into four stages called **prophase**, **metaphase**, **anaphase** and **telophase** (Figure 15.7). These are followed by cytokinesis. Each stage is described below.

Prophase: in this first stage of mitosis, chromosomes become visible and it can be seen that each is made of two chromatids. At the end of prophase, the nuclear membrane breaks down

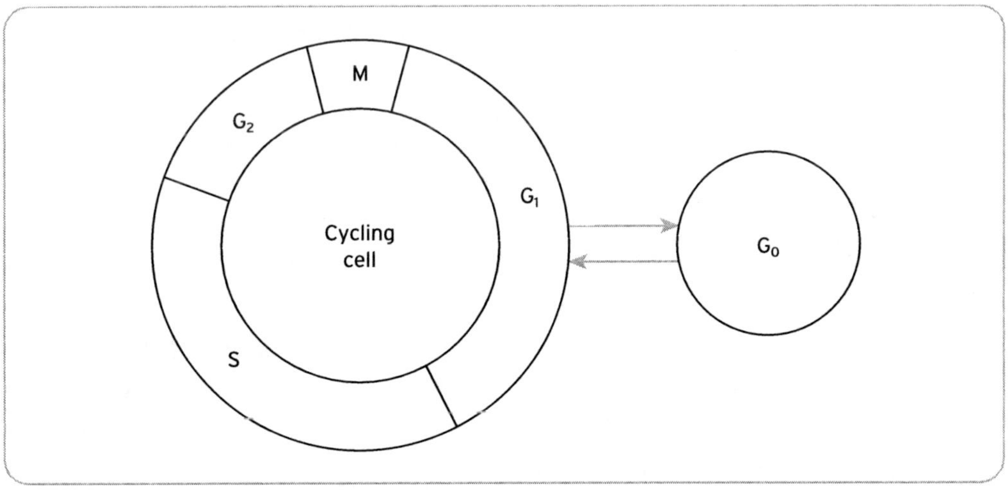

Figure 15.6
The cell cycle.

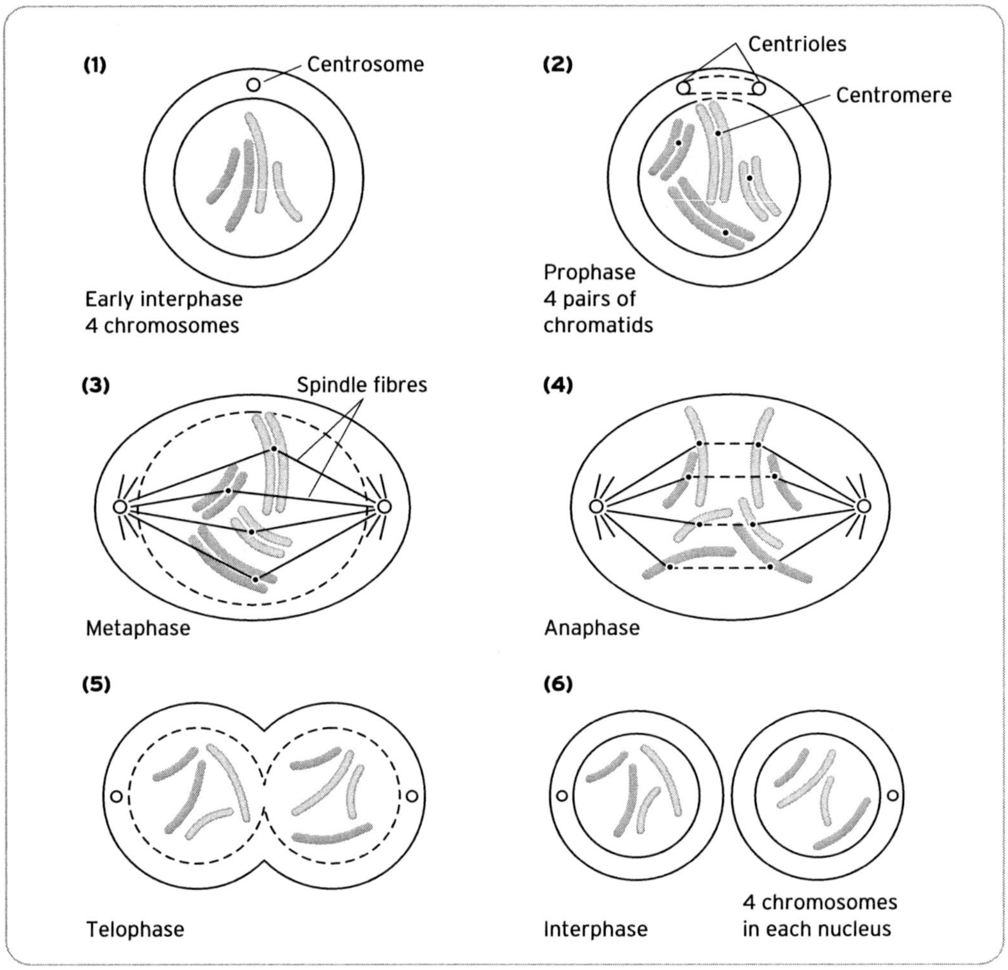

Figure 15.7

Mitosis. (From Sheeler P. (1996) *Essentials of Human Physiology*, 2nd edn. Dubuque: Wm. C. Brown.)

and fibres form between structures called **centrioles**. Centrioles are normally found adjacent to the nucleus in a region called the **centrosome**, but in prophase the centrioles move to opposite poles of the cell. The fibres that form between them are referred to as **spindle fibres**.

Metaphase: during this stage, chromosomes become attached along the centre of the spindle fibres at a position called the equatorial plate.

Anaphase: this stage is characterised by splitting of the centrosomes so that 'sister' chromatids separate and begin to move to opposite ends of the parent cell. From this point, each chromatid is regarded as a separate chromosome.

Telophase: in this stage, the DNA of both sets of chromosomes begins to uncoil and form thread-like chromatin again. The mitotic spindle disappears and a nuclear membrane forms around both sets of chromosomes.

Cytokinesis: cell division is completed when the cytoplasm of the parent cell is divided between the two newly forming cells.

In view of this sequence of events, we can summarise mitosis as the process of cell division that occurs in somatic cells and that leads to the production of two diploid daughter cells. Two important points about mitosis are that it is a controlled process and that only the right number of cells is produced for normal growth or replacement of dead cells. Sometimes, however, the process does not proceed normally, as Practice point 15.1 makes clear.

Practice point 15.1

Cancer

Cell division is normally a well-regulated process, so that the rate of production of new cells is adequate for the purposes of growth and repair. Sometimes, however, cells escape the normal controlling mechanisms, and a **neoplasm** (new growth) results. Neoplasms can produce unpleasant effects through a number of mechanisms, including the compression of vital structures such as nerves and blood vessels. Such effects are referred to as **space-occupying lesion effects**. Neoplasms are sometimes referred to as tumours, and they are of two kinds.

Benign neoplasms consist of cells that resemble those from which they arise, while the cells of **malignant neoplasms** are highly abnormal. As well as space-occupying lesion effects, malignant tumours spread out and invade adjacent structures in a way that resembles the spreading of a crab's legs. For this reason, malignant tumours are often referred to as **cancers**. You may wish to find out more about the difference between benign and malignant neoplasms.

We have seen that mitosis is the process of cell division that takes place in somatic cells. Gametes (sex cells) are produced in the gonads (reproductive organs) by a different process, which is explained below.

Meiosis

Cell division in the **gonads** (reproductive organs) takes place by **meiosis** - a different process from mitosis in somatic cells.

- *What is the reason for this difference?*

To answer this question, recall that gametes differ from somatic cells in having only 23 chromosomes rather than 23 pairs of chromosomes. Meiosis is a process whereby only one of each homologous pair is distributed to each gamete. For this reason, meiosis is said to be a reduction division. In fact, meiosis involves two divisions. Before the first division, DNA replication takes place in a similar way to mitosis. The first meiotic division results, therefore, in two diploid cells. The second meiotic division takes place without additional DNA replication, and so the final result is four haploid cells. Meiosis is clearly a more complicated process than mitosis, but each stage is given the same name as in mitosis; a Roman numeral is added in order to indicate whether the first or second division is being referred to (prophase I, prophase II, etc.). The details of meiotic division are not given here, but the key events that take place in prophase I are explained.

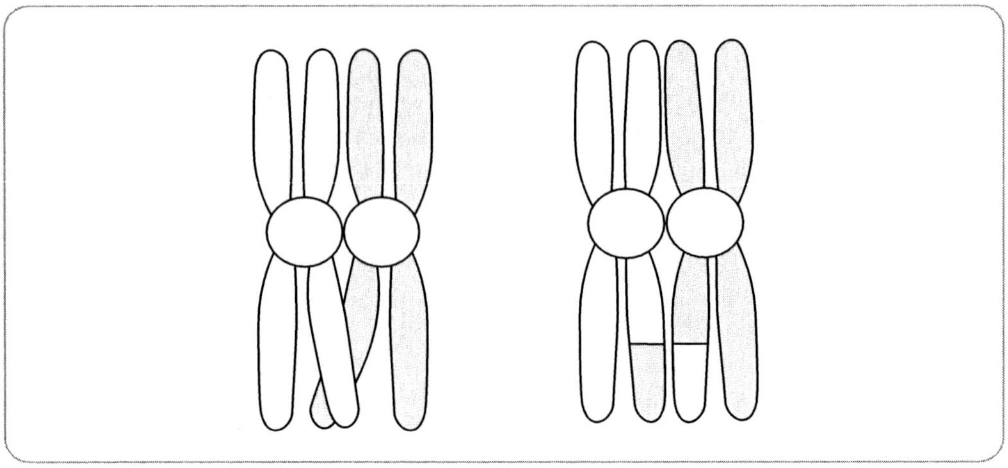

Figure 15.8
Crossing over.

Key events in prophase I

Certain events occur in prophase I that do not occur in prophase of mitosis. In prophase I, chromosomes thicken and shorten. They then arrange themselves in homologous pairs, each individual chromosome consisting of two chromatids. For this reason, when a homologous pair joins together, the structure that is formed is referred to as a **tetrad** (meaning four). It is worth remembering that one member of a homologous pair is derived from the mother and the other from the father. Following tetrad formation, pieces of DNA are exchanged between homologous pairs in a process referred to as crossing over (Figure 15.8).

- *What is the significance of crossing over?*

Remember that gametes possess only 23 chromosomes rather than 23 pairs. Crossing over ensures genetic variability by ensuring that each gamete receives chromosomes that contain a combination of maternal and paternal genetic information.

In-text review

- ✓ Genetics is the study of heredity.
- ✓ The genetic information of a cell is contained within its nucleus.
- ✓ Chromosomes are structures that are present in the nucleus and formed from tightly coiled deoxyribonucleic acid (DNA).
- ✓ The bases in DNA are arranged in triplets (codons) that form a code for protein synthesis.
- ✓ There are 23 pairs of chromosomes in human somatic cells and 23 chromosomes in human gametes.
- ✓ Somatic cells divide by mitosis, a process that leads to the formation of two diploid daughter cells.
- ✓ Gametes are the result of a meiotic division, a process that results in the formation of four haploid daughter cells.

Protein synthesis

No matter what job a protein does, all proteins are made up of chains of simple molecules called **amino acids** joined together by chemical bonds called **peptide bonds**. We have already noted that DNA is a code for protein synthesis, but you may wonder why this is important. Proteins form essential components of our body. Some proteins, such as **collagen**, are of structural importance; **actin** and **myosin** are the contractile proteins of muscle; and other proteins are referred to as functional and perform the roles of **enzymes**, **hormones** and **antibodies**. In essence, the way in which our bodies function is due to proteins of one kind or another. Consequently, whatever controls protein synthesis ultimately determines our physical characteristics and body function.

So, then, the code for protein synthesis is located within the nucleus; we consider next how it is employed to make protein. First, we return to RNA – in fact to three forms of this nucleic acid: ribosomal RNA (rRNA), messenger RNA (mRNA) and transfer RNA (tRNA).

Ribosomal RNA (rRNA)

Proteins are synthesised in cytoplasmic organelles called **ribosomes**. Ribosomes are made of **rRNA**, which is synthesised in the nucleus and enters the cytoplasm via nuclear pores. Ribosomes are made of two subunits (a large subunit and a small subunit), and these join together before protein synthesis takes place.

Messenger RNA (mRNA)

In essence, **mRNA** is a copy of a DNA gene that is made in the nucleus in a process referred to as **transcription** (literally, 'copying'). mRNA then leaves the nucleus via a nuclear pore and enters the cytoplasm. This copy of the genetic code forms the instruction for protein synthesis that is read by a ribosome. You probably now understand why this form of RNA is described as a 'messenger'. In effect, mRNA acts as a messenger from the nucleus to the ribosome.

Transfer RNA (tRNA)

tRNA molecules consist of three nucleotides, the base sequence of which is referred to as an anticodon. Each tRNA molecule picks up a specific amino acid and functions as a means of transferring it to a ribosome, where protein synthesis takes place in a process called **translation**.

In describing the three types of RNA, the processes of transcription and translation have been mentioned. We now move on to explain these processes in more detail.

Transcription

Remember that transcription is the process by which mRNA is synthesised in the nucleus. The first stage of this process is the separation of DNA base pairs so that the double helix unwinds, just as it does before replication. Only one of the strands of DNA is involved in mRNA synthesis, however, and this is referred to as the **sense strand**. The other strand is referred to as the **antisense strand**. As the DNA double helix unwinds, the bases of mRNA nucleotides pair with the corresponding DNA nucleotides in the manner shown in Figure 15.9. In this way, a single strand of mRNA is assembled alongside the sense strand.

The process does not begin and end at random. Remember that certain DNA codons perform the role of identifying the point at which a gene begins (start codons) and others the point at which it ends (stop codons). Consequently, mRNA synthesis begins with a start codon and ends with a stop codon. In addition, recall that although the bases adenine, guanine and cytosine are common to both DNA and RNA, DNA alone has thymine and RNA alone has uracil.

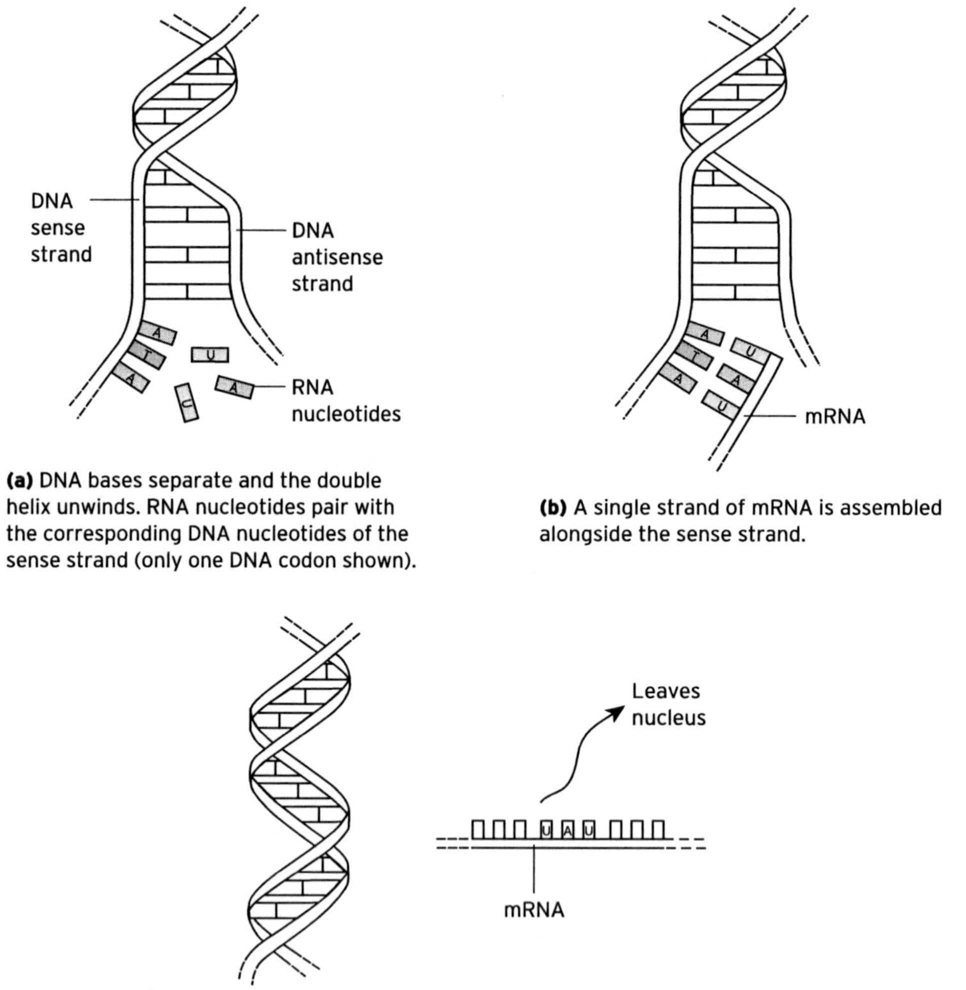

(a) DNA bases separate and the double helix unwinds. RNA nucleotides pair with the corresponding DNA nucleotides of the sense strand (only one DNA codon shown).

(b) A single strand of mRNA is assembled alongside the sense strand.

(c) An mRNA strand is completed and leaves the nucleus via a nuclear pore. The double helix of DNA is restored.

Figure 15.9
Transcription.

- *If a DNA codon contained the bases ATA, what would be the corresponding mRNA codon?*

The correct answer is UAU.

- *What now happens to the mRNA strand?*

Once an mRNA strand has been completed, it leaves the nucleus via a nuclear pore and enters the cytoplasm.

Translation

In the cytoplasm, a ribosome becomes attached to an mRNA strand at a start codon and the process of translation begins. We might summarise this process by saying that the code in the form of a sequence of bases in mRNA is translated into a sequence of amino acids in a protein chain. During translation, the ribosome moves along the length of the mRNA molecule from the start codon to the stop codon. This process is shown in Figure 15.10.

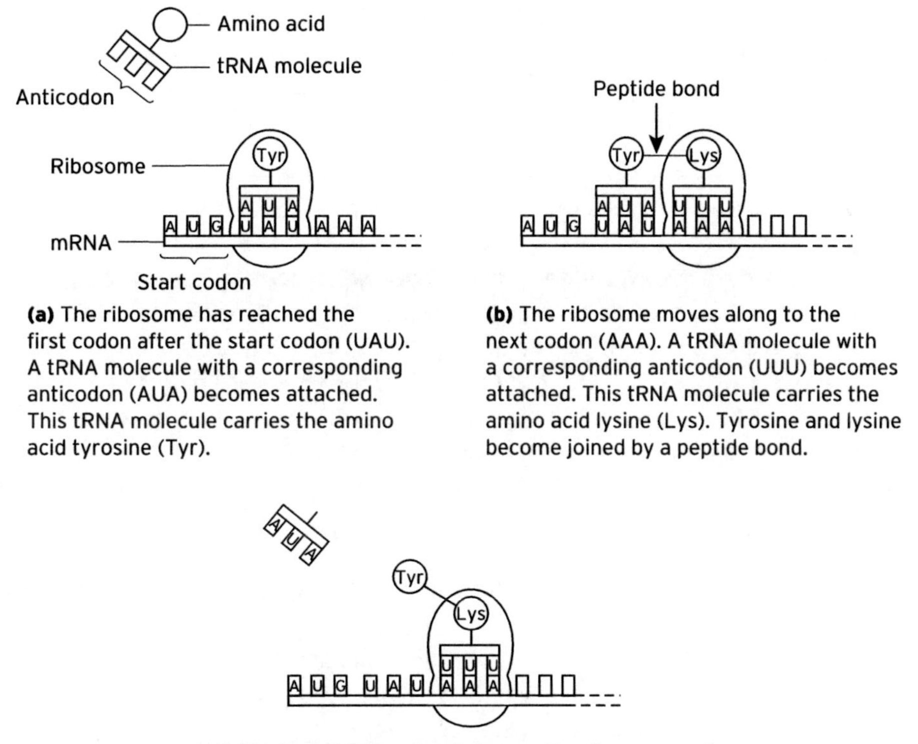

(a) The ribosome has reached the first codon after the start codon (UAU). A tRNA molecule with a corresponding anticodon (AUA) becomes attached. This tRNA molecule carries the amino acid tyrosine (Tyr).

(b) The ribosome moves along to the next codon (AAA). A tRNA molecule with a corresponding anticodon (UUU) becomes attached. This tRNA molecule carries the amino acid lysine (Lys). Tyrosine and lysine become joined by a peptide bond.

(c) The first tRNA molecule leaves the ribosome and becomes free to pick up another tyrosine molecule. The ribosome will now move on to the next codon.

Figure 15.10
Translation.

Let us imagine that the ribosome has reached the first codon after the start codon - UAU in Figure 15.10. At this point, a tRNA molecule with the corresponding anticodon (AUA) becomes attached to the mRNA molecule. Remember that each tRNA molecule carries a specific amino acid. The tRNA molecule with the anticodon AUA carries the amino acid tyrosine. The ribosome now moves along the mRNA strand and a second tRNA molecule becomes attached. At this point, the amino acids of the first and second tRNA molecules are joined by a peptide bond. The first tRNA molecule then leaves the ribosome and becomes free to pick up another amino acid, while the ribosome moves on to the third codon, where the process is repeated. In this way, the code for the synthesis of a specific amino acid is read by the ribosome until a stop codon is reached. At this point, the manufacture of the new protein is complete.

Thus far, we have been dealing with what might be termed the building blocks of genetics - nucleic acids. We have also examined processes such as translation that occur in the cell. We now move on to consider the impact of these processes on people - that is, inheritance.

Genetic inheritance

The nature of genetics is such that much of its study seems scientific and rather distanced from people. The reality is quite different, as you will see as we consider inheritance. Initially we do this using examples unrelated to illness, before proceeding to consider some common genetic diseases.

The position that a gene occupies on a chromosome is referred to as a **locus** (plural **loci** - the English word 'location' comes from the same origin). Genes that occupy the same loci on homologous chromosomes are said to be **alleles** or allelic genes. Alleles code for the same trait, such as eye colour; however, they do not necessarily code for the same expression of that trait. For example, one allele may code for blue eyes and the second allele for brown eyes. When both alleles code for the same expression of a trait, the individual is said to be **homozygous** for that trait. If alleles code for different expressions of a trait, then the individual is said to be **heterozygous**. The genetic makeup of an individual - that is, which genes are possessed - is termed the **genotype**, while the expression of the genes is termed the **phenotype**.

- *In the case of the heterozygous individual, which of the two alleles is expressed?*

When one allele is expressed fully over another, that allele is said to be **dominant**, while the allele that is not expressed at all is said to be **recessive**. Characteristics that are expressed by dominant genes can be observed in both the homozygous dominant state (possessing two dominant alleles) and the heterozygous state (possessing one dominant allele and one recessive allele), while characteristics that are expressed by recessive genes can be observed only when an individual is homozygous recessive (possessing two recessive alleles). When referring to genotypes, it is customary to identify each gene using a single letter. This is given as a capital letter in the case of a dominant gene and as a lower-case letter for a recessive gene. The simplest cases are those in which a characteristic is determined by only two alleles of a single gene present on an autosome (non-sex chromosome) – that is, simple autosomal inheritance.

Simple autosomal inheritance

Consider the example of dimples in cheeks, the presence of which is determined by a dominant gene. Let D stand for the dominant (dimples) gene and d the recessive (absence of dimples) gene. Table 15.1 gives the possible genotypes and phenotypes in this case.

Table 15.1 **The simple autosomal inheritance of the dimples in cheeks gene.**

Genotype	Phenotype
DD (homozygous dominant)	Dimples present
Dd (heterozygous)	Dimples present
dd (homozygous recessive)	Dimples absent

Recessive genes express certain traits – flat feet are an example. Let D stand for the dominant (normal arches) gene and d stand for the recessive (flat feet) gene.

- *What are the possible genotypes and phenotypes in this case?*

Check your answer against Table 15.2.

Table 15.2 **The simple autosomal inheritance of flat feet.**

Genotype	Phenotype
DD (homozygous dominant)	Normal arches
Dd (heterozygous)	Normal arches
dd (homozygous recessive)	Flat feet

In Table 15.3, a number of normal human traits and genetic diseases are listed according to whether the gene concerned is dominant or recessive.

The punnet square

If we had to work out which genes a child might inherit from two parents of known genotype, it would be rather easy to mix up in our minds the possible letter combinations. It is much easier if we write down the genotypes of the parents, but we can make matters simpler still

Table 15.3 **Phenotypes expressed by dominant and recessive genes.**

Phenotype due to the expression of dominant genes (DD or Dd)	Phenotype due to the expression of recessive genes (dd)
Normal skin pigment	Albinism
Freckles	Absence of freckles
Ability to roll tongue into a U shape	Inability to roll tongue into a U shape
Normal arches	Flat feet
Dimples in cheeks	Absence of dimples
Unattached earlobes	Attached earlobes

by using the Punnet square. This is a simple device consisting of a square divided into four boxes. The possible alleles derived from the father are placed to the left of the square and the possible alleles derived from the mother are placed above the square. In order to work out the possible genotypes of the parents' children, the alleles of the parents are combined in turn. Suppose we take the case of parents of whom both are heterozygous for the dimples gene (Dd). Remember that this gene is dominant, and so both parents have dimples. The use of the Punnet square in this case is demonstrated below:

	D	d
D	DD	Dd
d	Dd	dd

- *What are the possible genotypes and phenotypes of the children?*

They are DD (dimples present), Dd (dimples present) and dd (dimples absent).

- *What is the probability of the parents in the above example having a child with dimples?*

It is three out of four, or 75%. The probability of having a child without dimples is thus 25%.

Incomplete dominance

Incomplete dominance is the condition that exists when both alleles are expressed in the heterozygous state. The inheritance of hair texture is a good example. In this case, the individual who is homozygous for the curly hair gene has curly hair and the individual who is homozygous for the straight hair gene has straight hair.

- *What is the phenotype of the heterozygous individual?*

The heterozygous individual has an intermediate hair texture - that is, wavy hair.

Multiple allele inheritance

Although only two alleles are inherited for each gene, that does not necessarily mean that only two alleles exist. In some cases, there are multiple alleles, such as the ABO blood group system. Early attempts at blood transfusion were sometimes successful, but at other times they were disastrous and the recipient of the blood died. It was not until the ABO blood group system was discovered that it became possible to select only blood from individuals whose **erythrocytes** (red blood cells) were compatible with the proposed recipient. Compatibility depends upon the **antigens** (chemical groups on the surface of the erythrocyte) that an individual possesses. There are only two antigens - the alpha antigen (α) and the beta antigen (β).

Table 15.4 **Determination of ABO blood group.**

Alleles possessed		Antigens possessed	ABO blood group designation
I^A	I^A	α	A
I^A	i	α	A
I^B	I^B	β	B
I^B	i	β	B
I^A	I^B	α and β	AB
i	i	None	O

- *Is there an allele that codes for each of these antigens?*

Yes - one allele (I^A) codes for the alpha antigen and another allele (I^B) codes for the beta antigen. There is a third allele (i), however, that codes for 'no antigen'. The alleles I^A and I^B are co-dominant genes, while i is recessive.

- *Are we now in a position to work out the different antigen combinations?*

Yes - but remember that each individual will possess only two alleles - one on each homologous chromosome. The possible antigen combinations and blood group designations are given in Table 15.4.

Let us now use a Punnett square to answer a question.

- *What is the probability of a child of blood group O being born to heterozygous parents of blood group A?*

To answer this question, first note the genotypes of the parents. Since they are both heterozygous for the blood group A, they must have the genotype I^Ai. We can now use a Punnett square to work out the possible genotypes of the children, as shown below:

	I^A	i
I^A	I^AI^A	I^Ai
i	I^Ai	ii

There is a probability of one in four children (25%) born to the above parents having blood group O (ii).

Polygenic inheritance

When several genes control a trait, the term **polygenic inheritance** is used. Examples of polygenic inheritance traits include eye colour, hair colour and skin colour. In the case of skin colour, there are three separate genes involved, and each has two alleles: Aa, Bb and Cc. The genotype AA, BB, CC leads to a very dark-skinned phenotype and the genotype aa, bb, cc leads to a very light-skinned phenotype. Suppose two such individuals were to have children.

- *What would be the possible phenotypes?*

Once again we need to draw a Punnet square.

	abc	abc
ABC	Aa, Bb, Cc	Aa, Bb, Cc
ABC	Aa, Bb, Cc	Aa, Bb, Cc

In this case, all the children would have a skin tone of intermediate darkness.

Inheritance of sex

We have already seen that all ova and 50% of spermatozoa carry an X chromosome, while the remaining 50% of spermatozoa carry a Y chromosome. We can illustrate the inheritance of sex using a Punnett square.

	X	X
X	XX	XX
Y	XY	XY

On this basis, 50% of children should be male and 50% female. It is important to point out, however, that chromosomes determine genetic sex. Initially, both male and female embryos develop identically until about seven weeks after fertilisation. After this time, genes present on the sex-determining region of the Y chromosome (SRY) are responsible for initiating male development. When the SRY is absent, the embryo continues to develop physiologically as a female despite possessing a Y chromosome.

Thus far, we have considered examples of the genetics of physical features, such as eye colour and blood group. We next consider diseases that have a genetic basis.

Genetic disease

Cystic fibrosis (simple autosomal recessive)

Cystic fibrosis is often used as an example of an autosomal recessive disorder since it is relatively common, affecting about one in 2000 live births. It is not necessary to know a great deal about a genetic disorder in order to understand how it is transmitted. You may be interested to learn, however, that the gene of importance in this case codes for protein that regulates the movement of chloride ions (Cl^-) across epithelial membranes that line airways, ducts and hollow organs. On initial examination, this appears to be a rather insignificant function, but when the defective gene is present the affected individual has serious health problems, some of which are outlined in Practice point 15.2. For the time being, let us consider the case of a child with cystic fibrosis being born to parents, neither of whom has the disease. Let D stand for the (dominant) normal gene and d for the (recessive) cystic fibrosis gene.

Practice point 15.2

Cystic fibrosis

The gene of importance in this case codes for a protein that regulates the movement of chloride ions across epithelial membranes. These are the membranes that line airways, ducts and hollow organs. Patients with the abnormal gene produce thick mucus; an effect of this early in life is bowel obstruction. In the respiratory system, the mucus has the effect of making sputum difficult to cough up; people with cystic fibrosis require daily chest physiotherapy. Even when this is performed, they are predisposed to serious lung infections. Over a period of years, the lungs become damaged and the patient may experience heart failure. For this reason, people with cystic fibrosis may ultimately undergo combined heart and lung transplantation.

- *What are the genotypes of the parents?*

To answer this question, remember that since the defective gene is recessive, the disease is present only in homozygous recessive individuals (dd); the child in the above example must have inherited defective genes from both parents. Since neither parent has the disease, however, they must both be heterozygous (Dd).

- *What term is used to describe individuals who possess a single recessive gene for a disease?*

They are referred to as carriers. They possess the defective gene, but since the gene is recessive the disease is not expressed in the heterozygous state. Carriers can, of course, pass the gene on to their children, as the above case shows. The Punnet square helps us to explain the above example more fully:

	D	d
D	DD	Dd
d	Dd	dd

Parents who have a child with cystic fibrosis often ask the question 'What is the chance of having another child with the disease?'

- *What answer would you give?*

If you have checked the Punnett square, you should realise that it is 25%. There is the same probability of having a normal child and a 50% probability that a child will be a carrier.

Note that although cystic fibrosis is an autosomal recessive disease, it is relatively common. It is a common misconception that recessive traits are rare and dominant traits common, but this is not the case. In the section below, we briefly explain Huntington's disease as an example of an autosomal dominant disease. You might not have encountered this disease during your training - or even heard of it. There are two reasons for this. The disease is indeed uncommon, and most patients are encountered in the mental health context, since a major manifestation of Huntington's disease is dementia.

Huntington's disease (simple autosomal dominant)

This disease occurs even when a single defective gene is inherited - that is, it is an example of autosomal dominant inheritance. Huntington's disease involves a progressive degeneration of the nervous system, the symptoms of which include depression, chorea (involuntary dance-like movement) and dementia. Not all genetic diseases are evident at birth, and in the case of Huntington's disease the manifestations do not become evident until the third or fourth decade. You might like to imagine what you would feel like to discover that a loved one is developing dementia in his or her thirties or forties. What kind of support might the affected family require?

Having considered a recessive trait and a dominant trait, you have probably anticipated that the next section deals with a co-dominant trait - and indeed it does. Sickle cell anaemia is not included just to complete the picture, however. It has been chosen because it is a significant genetic disease affecting a particular ethnic group, and it is important in a study of genetics to reflect the multicultural nature of our society. You may be surprised to learn that up to 25% of Africans carry the sickling (abnormal) gene, but usually in the heterozygous (less serious) state.

Sickle cell anaemia (co-dominance)

Remember that co-dominance (incomplete dominance) is the condition that exists when both alleles are expressed in the heterozygous state. Sickle cell anaemia (sickle cell disease), which affects individuals of African and Caribbean descent, is a good example. This condition results from a gene defect that causes an abnormality of the red blood cell pigment **haemoglobin**. This molecule is important in oxygen transport, since oxygen binds to it to form **oxyhaemoglobin**. When the defective gene is present in the homozygous state, the abnormal haemoglobin produced precipitates within red blood cells, which, as a consequence, become sickle-shaped. Abnormally shaped red blood cells have a shorter lifespan than normal red blood cells, and **anaemia** (reduced number of red blood cells) results. In the heterozygous state, normal and abnormal haemoglobin is produced, and therefore the tendency for red blood cells to sickle is less. This leads to a milder form of the condition, referred to as **sickle cell trait**.

The normal gene is usually designated Hb and the sickling gene as Hb^S. Let us now consider the case of parents, both of whom have sickle cell trait and who are, therefore, heterozygous (Hb^AHb^S).

- *What are the probabilities of the following children being born?*
  (a) Unaffected child.
  (b) Child with sickle cell trait.
  (c) Child with sickle cell disease.

In order to answer this question, you will need to draw a Punnet square. If you have done this correctly, you will see that the answers are (a) 25%, (b) 50% and (c) 25%. If you are unsure about this, check your Punnet square against the one given below:

	Hb^A	Hb^S
Hb^A	Hb^AHb^A	Hb^AHb^S
Hb^S	Hb^AHb^S	Hb^SHb^S

Of course, such genetic considerations can appear removed from nursing, until one begins to think how genetic problems affect health. The effects of sickle cell anaemia are explained in Practice point 15.3.

Practice point 15.3

Sickle cell anaemia

For much of the time, the patient with sickle cell disease is quite well. The disease is characterised, however, by episodes of severe illness called **sickling crises**, especially in childhood. These episodes may be brought on by physical stressors such as dehydration, exposure to cold and infection, but sometimes they occur for no obvious reason. When a sickling crisis occurs, possible manifestations are pain, pyrexia (elevated temperature), **anaemia** and **jaundice**.

Pain

Sickle-shaped blood cells clump together and get stuck in small blood vessels, preventing normal blood flow, which causes pain. This occurs in the hands, arms, legs, back and abdomen and should be treated with **analgesics** (pain-relieving drugs). It is best, although not always possible, to avoid conditions that bring on a crisis.

Pyrexia

Infections often produce pyrexia, and the patient's temperature should be measured (see Chapter 9). A person with sickle cell disease is at risk of developing severe infections, especially pneumococcal pneumonia. For this reason, penicillin is taken **prophylactically** (preventatively).

Anaemia

Sickle-shaped erythrocytes are fragile and have a shortened lifespan. For this reason, the patient may be anaemic (reduced erythrocyte numbers/reduced amount of haemoglobin in the blood). It is especially important for the patient to maintain an adequate intake of the B group vitamin folic acid, found in leafy vegetables, which is required for the manufacture of erythrocytes (see Chapter 7). In a severe crisis, it may be necessary for the patient to receive a blood transfusion in order to restore the normal numbers of erythrocytes.

Jaundice

When damaged erythrocytes are destroyed in the body, a pigment called **billirubin** is released. This is quite normal, but the early death and destruction of sickle-shaped cells means that there is an excess of billirubin in the body, and the skin and **sclera** (white) of the eye take on a yellow tinge; this is called jaundice. Eventually, the body processes the excess pigment, but looking for yellowing of the skin and the sclera is an important assessment measure.

Sex-linked disorders

Thus far, the traits and disorders that we have considered have been the result of genes carried on autosomes. These traits and disorders affect males and females equally. We now turn to sex-linked disorders, which affect males rather than females and in which a defective recessive gene is carried on an X chromosome.

Sex-linked disorders are probably best demonstrated by **haemophilia** A. The term 'haemophilia' literally means 'blood love', and it is applied to conditions in which blood coagulation is impaired and there is a tendency to bleed severely following injury (or even spontaneously). Haemophilia is caused by the absence of one of a number of chemical substances called **clotting factors**. In the case of haemophilia A, clotting factor VIII is missing. The defective gene responsible is carried on the X chromosome and this is usually designated X′ in order to distinguish it from a normal X chromosome. The genotype of haemophiliac males is, therefore, X′Y.

- *Why, when the defective gene is recessive, do males with the genotype X′Y develop haemophilia?*

In order to answer this question, first note that X and Y chromosomes are not homologous in the true sense. The Y chromosome is only about a third of the size of the X chromosome and lacks some of the genes that are present on the X chromosome, including the gene for the production of factor VIII. Consequently, in the male with the X′Y genotype, the defective gene is not masked by a normal (dominant) gene on the Y chromosome. In contrast, females with the genotype X′X possess a normal (dominant) gene on the second X chromosome, and so the defective (recessive) gene is not expressed; such females are, however, able to pass on the defective gene and so are referred to as carriers.

- *What about females with the genotype X′X′?*

The X′X′ genotype usually results in spontaneous abortion early in pregnancy, and so affected individuals are not encountered.

- *Use a Punnett square to work out the possible genotypes and phenotypes of children born to parents of the genotypes XY and X′X.*

	X′	X
X	XX′	XX
Y	X′Y	XY

The possible genotypes and phenotypes are X′X (carrier female), XX (normal female), X′Y (haemophiliac male) and XY (normal male).

Chromosomal abnormalities

Thus far, we have considered abnormalities of specific genes. In contrast, chromosomal abnormalities (aberrations) affect the whole of a chromosome or a significant part of it. The most familiar is probably **Down's syndrome**, in which there are three copies of chromosome number 21 (**trisomy 21**). This defect results from either a failure of homologous chromosomes to separate in the first meiotic division or a failure of sister chromatids to separate in the second meiotic division. Such a failure is referred to as **non-disjunction** and results in a gamete that possesses both copies of chromosome number 21. The oocyte is most commonly affected. When fertilisation by a normal spermatozoon takes place, the child inherits three copies of the twenty-first chromosome. The characteristics of Down's syndrome include low IQ, poor muscle tone, short stature, protruding tongue and **epicanthal** folds (folds of skin over the inner junction of the eyelids).

In-text review

- ✓ Transcription is the synthesis of mRNA from the sense strand of DNA.
- ✓ Translation is the process by which proteins are synthesised.
- ✓ Translation occurs when anticodons of tRNA molecules pair with the codons of mRNA and amino acids carried by tRNA are joined together by peptide bonds.
- ✓ The patterns of genetic inheritance may be described as simple autosomal (dominant and recessive), co-dominance (incomplete dominance), multiple allele inheritance, polygenic inheritance and sex-linked inheritance. The following are examples:

Inheritance	**Example**
Simple autosomal (recessive)	Cystic fibrosis
Simple autosomal (dominant)	Huntington's disease
Co-dominance	Sickle cell anaemia
Multiple allele	ABO blood group
Polygenic	Colour of eyes, hair and skin
Sex linked	Haemophilia A

- ✓ The possible combinations of alleles inherited from parents of known genotype can be demonstrated using a Punnett square.

Summary

The early parts of this chapter dealt with the science of genetics, including the structure of the nucleic acids DNA and RNA. Covering such material is not an end in itself – the aim is to understand the genetic basis of disease. In a general science textbook such as this, only a few genetic conditions, such as cystic fibrosis, have been considered. Previously, these have been thought of as incurable and difficult to treat. In the working lives of you who use this book, however, there will be advances in the treatments available, particularly in genetic engineering (the science of altering the genotype of individuals). The gene responsible for cystic fibrosis was identified some years ago, and it is hoped that scientists will develop ways of incorporating normal genes into individuals with such genetic disease.

Summary points

- Chromosomes are structures that are present in the nucleus and formed from tightly coiled deoxyribonucleic acid (DNA).
- The bases in DNA are arranged in triplets (codons) that form a code for protein synthesis.
- There are 23 pairs of chromosomes in human somatic cells and 23 chromosomes in human gametes.
- Somatic cells divide by mitosis, a process that leads to the formation of two diploid daughter cells.
- Gametes are the result of a meiotic division, a process that results in the formation of four haploid daughter cells.
- The synthesis of mRNA from the sense strand of DNA is referred to as transcription.
- The synthesis of protein that occurs when the anticodons of tRNA molecules pair with the codons of mRNA is referred to as translation.
- The patterns of genetic inheritance may be described as simple autosomal (dominant and recessive), incomplete dominance (co-dominance), multiple allele inheritance, polygenic inheritance and sex-linked inheritance.
- The possible combinations of alleles inherited from parents of known genotype can be demonstrated using a Punnett square.

Self-test questions

1 Which of the following statements are true?
(a) Chromosomes are visible throughout the lifecycle of the cell.
(b) Chromatin is present within the cytoplasm of a cell.
(c) Chromosomes are formed from tightly coiled DNA.
(d) Histones are formed from DNA.

2 Which of the following statements are true?
(a) Gametes possess 23 pairs of chromosomes.
(b) Somatic cells possess 22 pairs of autosomes.
(c) Somatic cells possess one pair of sex chromosomes.
(d) Gametes possess one sex chromosome.

3 Which of the following statements are true?
(a) DNA consists of a single strand of nucleotides.
(b) RNA contains the base uracil.
(c) RNA consists of a single strand of nucleotides.
(d) DNA contains the base uracil.

4 Which of the following statements are true?
(a) Mitosis occurs in somatic cells.
(b) Meiosis leads to the formation of four haploid cells.
(c) Mitosis leads to the formation of two haploid cells.
(d) Tetrad formation occurs in prophase I of meiosis.

5 Which of the following statements are true?
(a) A triplet of DNA bases is referred to as a codon.
(b) A tRNA molecule contains three nucleotides.
(c) A triplet of mRNA bases is referred to as an anticodon.
(d) An mRNA molecule consists of three nucleotides.

6 Which of the following statements are true?
(a) Transcription is the process by which mRNA is synthesised.
(b) The DNA strand involved in mRNA synthesis is referred to as the antisense strand.
(c) The process that leads to the synthesis of protein is referred to as transformation.
(d) The nucleus is the site of protein synthesis.

7 Match the term on the left with the appropriate description on the right.

(a) Alleles	(i) Non-sex chromosomes
(b) Autosomes	(ii) Genes that code for the same trait
(c) Ribosomes	(iii) Proteins associated with DNA
(d) Histones	(iv) The sites of protein synthesis

8 What is the probability in simple autosomal recessive inheritance of the birth of a child with a trait when the parents are heterozygous for this trait?
(a) 25%.
(b) 50%.
(c) 75%.
(d) 100%.

9 What are the possible combinations of alleles of children born to parents with the blood groups AB and O? (Hint: use a Punnett square.)
(a) I^Ai, I^Ai, I^BI^B, I^BI^B.
(b) I^Ai, I^Ai, I^Bi, I^Bi.
(c) I^Ai, I^Ai, I^Ai, I^Ai.
(d) I^AI^A, I^BI^B, I^AI^B, ii.

10 Match the genetic diseases on the left with the appropriate descriptions on the right.

(a) Cystic fibrosis	(i) Simple autosomal dominant
(b) Haemophilia A	(ii) Simple autosomal recessive
(c) Huntington's disease	(iii) Incomplete dominance
(d) Sickle cell anaemia	(iv) Sex-linked

Further study/exercises

1 Describe the health problems experienced by individuals with cystic fibrosis and identify their nursing needs.

Madge S. (2002). Cystic fibrosis. *Professional Nurse*, 17(6), 343-4.
Ratjen F. and Doring G. (2003). Cystic fibrosis. *Lancet*, 361(9358), 681-9.
Cystic Fibrosis Trust website: www.cftrust.org.uk/index.jsp
NHS Direct: www.nhsdirect.nhs.uk/index.asp
Online Health Encyclopaedia Cystic Fibrosis: www.nhsdirect.nhs.uk/en.aspx?ArticleID=118

2 Outline the role of the genetic counsellor.

Crouch D. (2005). It's a bridge between science and people. *Nursing Times*, 101(7), 24-5.
Gulland A. (2001). Dealing with the facts of life. (Role of genetic counsellors.) *Nursing Times*, 97(36), 26-7.
Harrison S. (1995). Viewpoint. Practice tips: in the genes shop. *Nursing Standard*, 10(8), 50.
Visser A. and Bleiker E. (1997). Genetic education and counselling. *Patient Education and Counselling*, 32(1-2), 1-7.

16

Microbiology

After reading the following chapter and undertaking personal study, you should be able to:

1 Identify four types of microorganism and describe their characteristics.

2 Explain how bacteria are identified.

3 Describe various host-microorganism relationships and relate these to health and illness.

4 Identify the routes by which microorganisms enter the body and relate these to clinical practice.

5 Identify potential sources of infection and mechanisms of transmission of microorganisms with particular reference to clinical practice.

6 Describe how cross-infection can be prevented, especially in the health-care environment.

7 Describe the response of the body to infection.

8 Define immunity and distinguish between innate and acquired immune mechanisms.

9 Explain the process of immunisation and relate this to health.

10 Describe how in clinical practice samples of microorganisms are obtained for examination in the microbiology laboratory and outline the tests that are performed there.

11 Distinguish between cleaning, disinfection and sterilisation and describe the role played by each in the prevention of infection, with special reference to the hospital environment.

12 Describe how infections are managed and the role of antibiotics.

13 Explain antibiotic resistance and outline the ways in which it may be avoided.

Introduction

Microbiology is the study of organisms that are not visible to the naked eye (**microorganisms**) - that is, they can be examined only with the aid of a microscope or, in the case of the smallest microorganisms, with an electron microscope. When we think of microorganisms, we probably think of those that cause disease (**pathogens**). Indeed, as this chapter is being completed, the first UK bird death (a swan) caused by the H51N strain of bird flu has just been reported, and the British government has decided to continue culling badgers in an experiment to determine the effect of badgers on **tuberculosis** (TB) in cattle. Add to these examples the ongoing **AIDS** (acquired immune deficiency syndrome) **pandemic** (worldwide epidemic) and frequent reports of hospital superbugs, and one wonders whether there is space in the tabloids for any other news.

Many microorganisms, however, are not pathogens, and some microorganisms fulfil important roles in the environment. For example, many microorganisms live on dead and decaying matter (**saprophytes**) and fulfil an important recycling function in the environment; some soil bacteria produce nitrogen-containing compounds required by plants, while other microorganisms are involved in the production of foods such as cheese and yoghurt. Even our fight against pathogens depends upon microorganisms, since **antibiotics** are derived from them.

- *So where should our study begin?*

Perhaps we should describe how microorganisms are named.

Naming microorganisms

In most cases, a convention is followed in the naming of microorganisms. Before this is explained, perhaps we should point out that all life on earth is divided into five kingdoms.

- *Can you name any of the five kingdoms?*

You should have no difficulty naming the animal and plant kingdoms; you might also have given fungi too. The remaining two kingdoms are **monera** and **protista**. Each kingdom is subdivided into groups, until finally the name of the individual species is given. It is not necessary to learn the different subgroups, but it helps to understand the convention applied to the naming of species. This convention is referred to as **binomial nomenclature**, since two names are used to identify each organism. The names are given in Latin and understood by scientists the world over. For example, humans are *Homo sapiens* - which means 'wise man'. Whether the human race is wise is debatable - the point is that the names used in the binomial system do have a meaning that is an attempt to say something about the characteristics of the organism being referred to. Note that by convention, Latin is italicised and only the first name starts with a capital.

- *Not so difficult, then - have a go at* Felis domesticus. *What species is this?*

Did you work out that it is the domestic cat? Microorganisms are given their names in a similar way, for example *Streptococcus faecalis*. In this case, the first name tells you something about the shape of the organism - we explain this later.

* *So what does faecalis tell us?*

You should have no difficulty working out that it tells you that the organism is found in the faeces. This convention is followed in most but not all cases, as you will see later. In addition, the name is sometimes abbreviated, so that *Streptococcus faecalis* becomes *Strep. faecalis*. Although this is perfectly acceptable, in this introductory text abbreviated forms have been avoided in order not to be confusing. Having explained how microorganisms are named, we now introduce the four types of microorganism: **bacteria**, **viruses**, **fungi** and **protozoa**.

Bacteria

In Chapter 15, the structure of a typical animal cell was described. It was noted that the entire contents of the cell are collectively referred to as **protoplasm** and that this is separated from the outside by the **cell membrane**. Within the cell is located the **nucleus**, which contains the cell's genetic information. The contents of the nucleus (**nucleoplasm**) are separated from the rest of the cell contents (**cytoplasm**) by the **nuclear membrane**. Within the cytoplasm are a number of other structures that perform specific functions for the cell. For example, **mitochondria** generate energy and **ribosomes** make protein. These structures are referred to collectively as **organelles** - a term that means 'little organs'. We could say that just as organs such as the heart perform specific functions for the body, so organelles perform specific functions for the cell. This type of cell structure is described as **eukaryotic**.

* *So what about bacteria - are they similar?*

Bacteria are single-celled microorganisms, some of which are similar in size to human cells. For example, the bacterium that causes **anthrax** (*Bacillus anthracis*) is about 6 μm (6 microns - there are 1000 microns in a millimetre) in diameter and the **erythrocyte** (red blood cell) is about 8 μm (8 microns) in diameter. That is where the similarity ends, however. Bacteria have a cell structure that is unlike that of any other organism.

* *What are the differences between bacterial cells and eukaryotic cells?*

The cytoplasm of bacteria contains no compartments or distinct organelles, genetic material is not membrane-bound in a nucleus and the cell is bound by a special structure called the **cell wall**. This type of cell structure is described as **prokaryotic**. We are perhaps used to referring to the animal kingdom and the plant kingdom, but bacteria are so different that they have a kingdom of their own called monera - it means 'alone'.

Types of bacteria

* *So, bacteria are microscopic and difficult to see, but are they hard to find?*

Actually, no. Bacteria cover the surfaces of our bodies and are present in the food we eat; some bacteria are present in the high temperatures of sulphur springs and others deep within the polar ice. It is almost impossible to find a place where there are no bacteria, although the special measures taken in hospital operating theatres do limit their numbers somewhat.

If bacteria thrive in diverse environments, there must be different types.

Yes, this is certainly true, and we divide bacteria into a number of groups. The first divisions are the **archaebacteria** and **eubacteria**. Archaebacteria are distinct from all other types of bacteria, in terms of both their structure and the chemical processes that take place within them. Archaebacteria are found in some of the most hostile environments on earth, but they are not of medical significance, so we shall not consider them further. All other bacteria are classified as eubacteria, or true bacteria. This division is divided further into three groups based upon the mode of nutrition - this classification sounds strange, but we do the same with people when we ask 'Are you vegetarian?' **Photoautotrophs** (light self-feeders) contain **chlorophyll** (the green pigment found in plants) and use energy in the form of light to produce nutrients. **Chemoautotrophs** (chemical self-feeders) derive the energy they need from inorganic molecules, such as ammonia (NH_4); for example, nitrifying bacteria are found in root nodules of some plants (e.g. peas and beans) and convert ammonia into nitrates - a form of nitrogen that can be used by other plants. Organic gardeners make use of this by planting peas or beans in the season before other vegetables that require a lot of nitrogen. Finally, there are the **heterotrophs** (other feeders), which obtain their nutrients from organic molecules.

Is there a purpose to describing this classification?

First, it is probably helpful to understand that monera is a kingdom of diverse organisms that play important roles in the health of our planet. Not all bacteria cause disease; in fact, only some heterotrophs do so. Incidentally, you have probably also realised that, just like the bacteria that cause disease, humans are heterotrophs.

Identifying bacteria

A number of characteristics are used to identify bacteria, including appearance, staining reactions, metabolism and ability to form spores.

Appearance

The appearance of individual organisms is used as a means of identifying species. Four morphological (shape) forms exist (Figure 16.1) - **cocci**, **bacilli**, **vibrio** and **spirochaetes**.

Individual cocci are round, but groups occur together. In **diplococci**, the organisms are arranged in pairs. An example is *Neisseria gonorrhoeae* - the organism that causes **gonorrhoea**. Clusters of cocci are called **staphylocci** - an example is *Staphyloccus aureus*. This organism is part of the normal skin flora (organisms that normally live on the skin and cause no harm). Some members of this group, however, do also cause wound infections. In **streptococci**, the organisms are arranged in chains. Streptococci cause a wide range of infections, including sore throats.

Bacilli are rod-shaped organisms - the rods appear singly or in chains. A number of bacilli, such as *Salmonella enteritidis* and *Escherichia coli*, cause food poisoning.

Vibrio are curved bacteria - an example is *Vibrio cholerae*, which causes **cholera**.

Spirochaetes are spiral-shaped and include *Treponema pallidum* - the organism that causes **syphilis**.

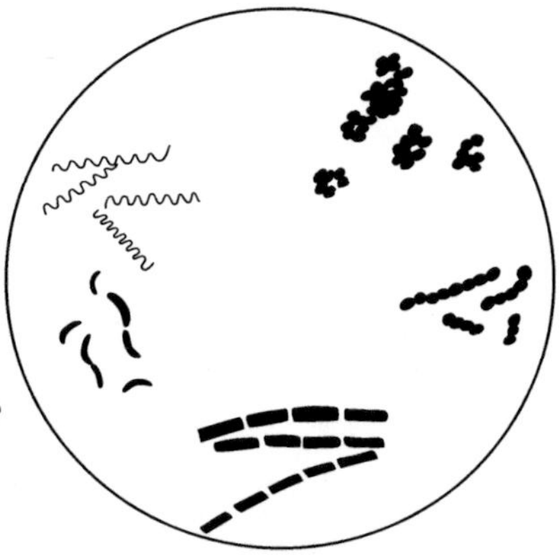

Figure 16.1
Four shapes of bacteria.

Staining reactions

The most important staining reaction is the **Gram stain**. A thin film of a specimen is smeared on to a glass microscope slide and stained with both violet and red dyes. Depending upon which dye is taken up, the organisms will appear purple (Gram-positive) or pink (Gram-negative). The difference in staining reactions reflects differences in the composition of the cell wall.

Metabolism

Like humans, some bacteria require the presence of oxygen in the environment. Such bacteria are called obligate **aerobes** - *Mycobacterium tuberculosis*, which causes tuberculosis (TB), is an example. Organisms that are unable to tolerate the presence of oxygen are called obligate **anaerobes** - *Clostridium tetani*, which causes **tetanus**, is an example. **Tetany** is a sustained muscular contraction that can have a number of causes. Since the toxins produced by *Clostridium tetani* cause tetany, the condition that results from infection by this organism is caused tetanus. If you have not heard of this condition, it is probably because immunisation against it is undertaken during childhood and it no longer causes the number of deaths that it once did.

Spore formation

Various Gram-positive species are able to form **spores**. In unfavourable conditions, the microorganism develops a protective capsule in which it lies in a dormant condition and is referred to as a **spore**. The spore is able to tolerate extremes of conditions, such as high temperatures, and is resistant to chemical disinfectants. The spore may remain dormant for many years, but when favourable conditions return it will 'germinate' and the organism will resume its active lifecycle. *Clostridium tetani* and *Bacillus anthracis* are examples of spore-forming organisms.

Reproduction of bacteria

The use of the term 'reproduction' here is a misnomer. Populations of bacteria increase when individual bacterial cells grow, duplicate their genetic material and divide into two in a process called **binary fission**.

- *So if the first generation consists of only a single cell, the next will consist of two, the next four, the next eight, and so on?*

Exactly so, and provided that there is a continuous supply of nutrients, the rate of growth can be very rapid indeed. A new generation may be produced every 5 minutes, but more commonly every 30 minutes - 'slow coaches' may take several days. In the space of a few hours, a small number of bacteria could become many millions.

Viruses

Perhaps the first thing we should note about viruses is that they are too small to be seen with a light microscope. You might wonder how they could have been discovered at the end of the nineteenth century, long before the invention of the electron microscope. Scientists realised that viruses existed when they were able to show that some infectious agents passed through filters designed to trap bacteria. It also became clear that these agents could multiply only inside living cells and, therefore, scientists concluded that they must lack some of the apparatus required for reproduction. In part, we can say that they were right. In reality, however, viruses are not living organisms at all. Viruses do not have a cellular structure but consist instead of a core of **nucleic acid** (either DNA or RNA) and a protein coat or **capsid**. Because viruses cannot replicate themselves, they are dependent on the host to do this for them. Consequently, they are **obligate parasites** - they can exist only at the expense of another organism. Viruses are responsible for disease in both plants and animals; they also infect bacteria. A specific virus can infect only a specific species of organism; in a limited number of cases, more than one species may be infected. An obvious example is **human immunodeficiency virus** (HIV), which is thought to have been introduced to humans from African monkeys. Although HIV infection is extremely serious, many viral illnesses are minor and self-limiting, as explained in Practice point 16.1.

Practice point 16.1

Self-limiting viral infections

We have already noted that viruses are not living organisms. There is a very important point to be made about treating viral infections - if viruses are not alive, they cannot be killed. In fact, there are very few effective **antiviral agents** (drugs used to treat viral infections). It is just as well that many viral infections are minor and self-limiting - after a short period of illness, the body deals with the infection without any specific treatment. Perhaps you have visited the doctor with a sore throat but been given no treatment. This is because most sore throats are viral in nature and the prescription of antibiotics is not required.

- *Couldn't the doctor prescribe antibiotics as a precaution?*

Since antibiotics do not shorten the length of a viral illness such as a sore throat, a cold or uncomplicated influenza (flu), it would serve no purpose to prescribe antibiotics. To do so would expose the patient to any complications that the antibiotics might cause. Excessive use of antibiotics may also lead to antibiotic resistance, as we discuss later.

- *So how are self-limiting viral illness managed?*

Since the illness will resolve spontaneously, any treatment is given purely to alleviate symptoms. Think about a severe cold or influenza.

- *What are the symptoms?*

Symptoms might include **pyrexia** (elevated temperature), discomfort such as headache or **myalgia** (muscle pain), lethargy, nasal congestion and cough.

- *What would you advise the patient to do?*

Lethargy is easy to deal with - just rest. Pyrexia and discomfort can be alleviated by an **analgesic** (pain-relieving drug) that also lowers the temperature; **aspirin** and **paracetamol** are both good examples. (It is important to note, however, that although these drugs are readily available over the counter, there are restrictions on their use. A pharmacist will be able to give advice about the most suitable over-the-counter medicine, and the information leaflet enclosed with each drug should always be read before taking the first dose.) Cold remedies often include a decongestant to help with nasal congestion, although these drugs can also be bought separately; **pseudoephedrine** is a common example. **Pholcodine** is an example of an **antitussive** (suppresses cough), but such drugs should be used only if the cough is not productive (coughing up sputum).

- *Think through why this is the case.*

If a patient is expectorating (coughing up sputum), the cough is serving a very important function - getting rid of the sputum. Suppressing the cough is clearly not a good idea in these circumstances - if sputum is not coughed up, then it may impair respiratory function, and congested respiratory passages are an environment in which bacteria can grow. Incidentally, secretions can be loosened and made easier to expectorate by old-fashioned steam inhalations.

- *'I went to the doctor with a cough and a cold and he didn't prescribe any treatment. I didn't get better - in fact, I got worse. When I went back a week later, he gave me antibiotics, which cleared it up in a week. Why didn't he give me them to start with?'*

Does this sound familiar? It is unfortunately true that some viral infections resolve only slowly; perhaps the patient fails to rest and the illness worsens. A virus may cause the initial infection, but following this the patient also succumbs to a bacterial infection. It is to treat this that antibiotics are prescribed.

Viral replication

Viruses are the ultimate parasite, being completely dependent on their host in order to replicate. Think about this for a moment: A virus enters the cell of a susceptible organism, where the viral nucleic acid acts as a code for the host cell to make more viral nucleic acid and protein coats that are assembled into new viruses. These leave the cell and move on to infect other cells, perhaps being transmitted to a second individual, before the process begins once more. If this did the cell no damage, then it would probably be unnecessary to include it in this textbook, but unfortunately the host cells may die as a consequence of infection.

In addition, infection by a virus sometimes transforms a normal host cell into a cancer cell, and this is more serious than the viral infection itself. For example, the Epstein-Barr virus causes the illness **glandular fever**, which produces flu-like symptoms. In some cases, the illness is severe and the individual experiences a prolonged period of weakness. A small number of sufferers, however, subsequently develop a form of lymphatic cancer (**Burkitt's lymphoma**/syndrome).

Fungi

When we think of fungi, we probably think of the multicellular organisms we also call mushrooms. Fungi, however, are a kingdom of eukaryotic organisms, most of which feed on dead or decaying organic material (**saprophytes**) and play an important role as recyclers in our environment. Most fungi are multicellular, but some, such as yeasts, are unicellular. Some fungi are also parasites and feed on living organisms. Examples of the latter include **ringworm** (not a worm at all) and athlete's foot. Fungi are composed of slender filaments called **hyphae** (singular = **hypha**). A mass of hyphae is called a **mycelium**. Hyphae grow into a food source and secrete enzymes to break it down and release nutrients. Hyphae often form fluffy masses that we see on top of spoilt food, but some species also produce large reproductive structures that we recognise as mushrooms.

Most fungi reproduce both sexually and asexually. The kingdom is classified into four divisions. The first three divisions are based upon the characteristics of the sexual stages of reproduction. Although fungi in these three groups are important in the environment, they do not cause disease and so are not dealt with here. The fourth division includes all the species that are unable to reproduce sexually and are referred to as **imperfect fungi**. These reproduce by the production of spores and they include some important disease-producing fungi.

Protozoa

We now come to the final kingdom of organisms important in the study of human disease - the kingdom Protista. Protists are eukaryotic organisms; most are single-celled, but some are multicellular. The kingdom is divided into groups based upon which other organisms the protists resemble. **Algae** are plant-like protists, **slime moulds** are fungus-like protists and **protozoans** are animal-like protists. Members of the latter group interest us here, since they cause disease in humans. Protozoa are grouped into four phyla (groups), depending on how the organism moves. They are the **amoebas**, **flagellates**, **ciliates** and **sporozoans**.

Amoebas

In physiology, the movement of certain **leukocytes** (white blood cells) is referred to as **amoeboid** - meaning 'like an amoeba'. That's fine if you know what an amoeba is but not very clear if you don't. Amoebas are often described as shapeless single-celled organisms - but clearly every organism has a shape, so what is meant by this term? Amoebas are able to move by pushing out cytoplasm in one area and retracting it from another. As cytoplasm is pushed outwards it is thought to resemble a foot, but as the cytoplasm continues to stream forward the foot disappears. For this reason, the term **pseudopods** (meaning 'false feet') is used. Pseudopodia are important in both the nutrition and movement of amoebas. Amoebas engulf their prey by forming pseudopodia around the prey. The prey is then contained in a **vacuole** (fluid-filled sac) within the amoeba, whereupon enzymes digest the prey. The process is referred to as **phagocytosis** - a term that means 'cell eating' (Figure 16.2).

Amoebas are abundant in both fresh and salt water. Some cause disease, such as *Entamoeba histolytica*, which is responsible for amoebic **dysentery**. This disease occurs mainly in tropical and subtropical countries, where it causes diarrhoea. The infection may be acute or chronic and is transmitted to others by the ingestion of contaminated fruit, vegetables and water. The use of human faeces as a fertiliser is responsible for a high incidence in some regions. Dysentery is further explained in Practice point 16.2, which deals with travel health.

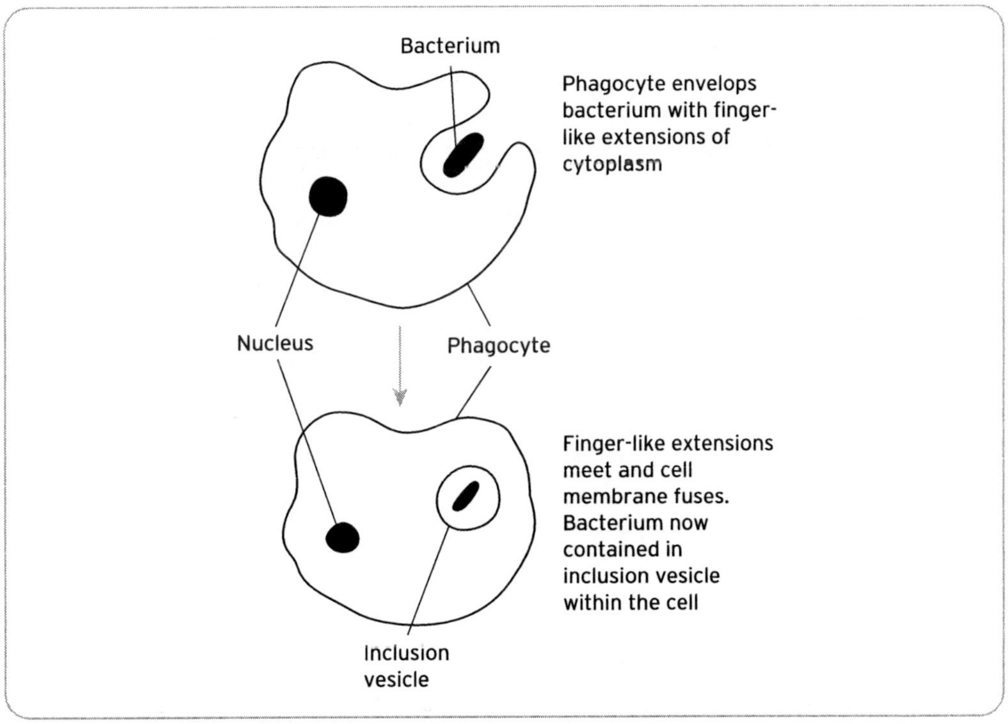

Figure 16.2
Phagocytosis.

Practice point 16.2

Travel health – dysentery

- *Someone asks you for health advice regarding a holiday in the tropics. What would you say about dysentery?*

You might want to explain how dysentery is transmitted. In addition, many good travel health practices are common to a variety of illnesses, including drinking only boiled or bottled water.

- *What about vegetables?*

You have probably worked out that you should avoid eating raw vegetables in the tropics, since they may have been grown in contaminated soil. You might think that fruit ought to be safe, but you cannot guarantee this. Fruit may have been washed in contaminated water, and there have even been cases of fruit being injected with water in order to make it look more appealing.

It would also be worth explaining what to do in the event of illness. The problem caused by diarrhoea is of fluid and electrolyte loss, and so the traveller should carry sachets of rehydration salts (available from a pharmacy).

Flagellates

This is a group of organisms characterised by the possession of at least one **flagellum** – a whip-like structure that is used for movement. The organism is propelled as the flagellum beats backwards and forwards. *Trypanosoma gambiense* and *Trypanosoma rhodesiense* are examples of flagellates that cause disease in humans – African **sleeping sickness**. The organism is transmitted by the tsetse fly after it has fed on the blood of an infected person. The symptoms caused by sleeping sickness include fever and skin eruptions, but in the longer term the blood-borne parasites may enter the **cerebrospinal fluid** of the brain, producing a chronic disease characterised by lethargy and drowsiness, hence its name. Eventually, sleeping sickness is fatal. Since insects transmit a number of tropical diseases, the use of insect repellents in tropical countries is important.

Ciliates

This group of protists gains its name from a Latin word meaning 'eyelash' – a reference to the hair-like **cilia** that cover the organism. Cilia beat in a coordinated way that enables movement. *Balantidium coli* is a ciliate that inhabits the intestinal tract of pigs and can cause dysentery in humans.

Sporozoans

Sporozoans are non-motile parasites with a complex lifecycle involving sexual and asexual phases and transmission from host to host by various species of insect. Of the diseases caused by sporozoans, **malaria** is the most important.

Malaria

Four members of the genus plasmodium cause malaria: *Plasmodium falciparum*, *Plasmodium vivax*, *Plasmodium malariae* and *Plasmodium ovale*. Malaria is characterised by intermittent pyrexia (raised temperature) with **anaemia** (reduced oxygen-carrying capacity of the blood) due to the destruction of erythrocytes (red blood cells). Symptoms can be diverse and severe, especially in malignant malaria (caused by *Plasmodium falciparum*), where capillaries can become obstructed by infected erythrocytes. Although the chances of dying from an attack of malaria are not large, the untreated disease is likely to take a chronic relapsing course. Malaria is a very widespread disease of the tropics, and as a consequence it accounts for the highest number of deaths worldwide of any single infectious disease.

The lifecycle of *Plasmodium*

Since malaria is so important worldwide, we spend some time describing the rather complicated lifecycle of the causative organism. In the first phase of infection (pre-erythrocytic phase - meaning that which occurs before erythrocytes are involved), the parasite is introduced into the blood through a bite by a female **Anopheles mosquito** (Figure 16.3). The sporozoans soon disappear from the blood, but they have not been killed. Instead, they have entered

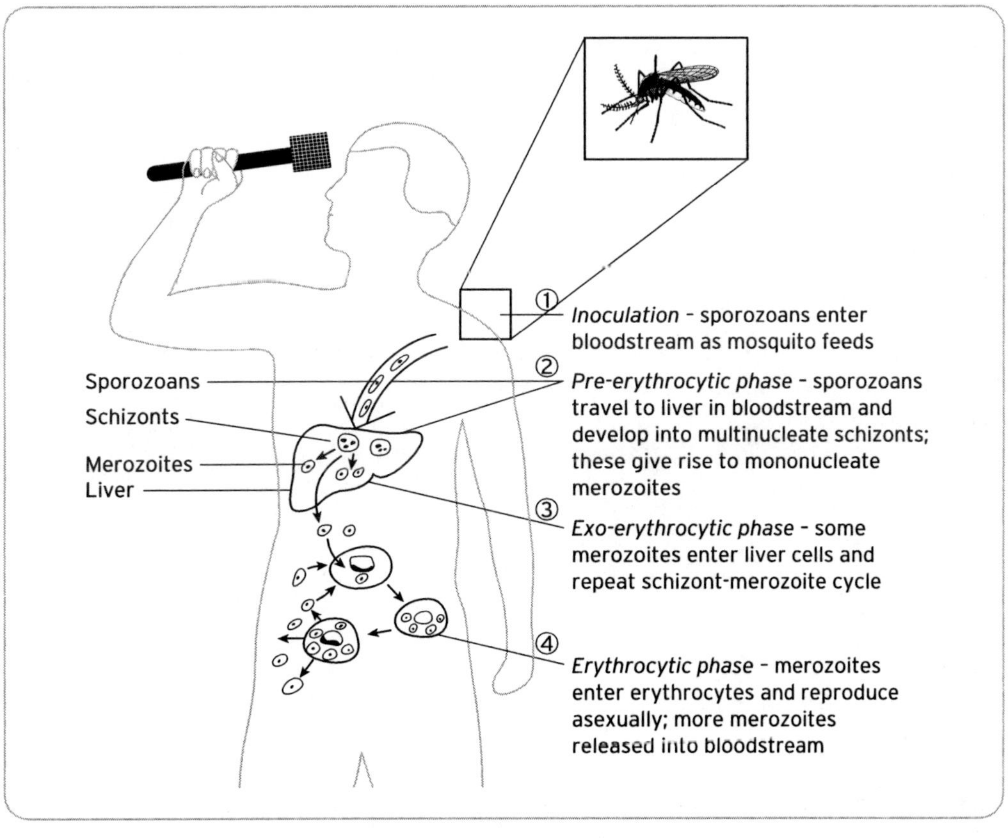

Figure 16.3
Lifecycle of the anopheles mosquito.

liver cells, where they develop into large multinucleate cells (cells with multiple nuclei) called **schizonts**, which give rise to small mononucleate (cells with a single nucleus) **merozoites**. In the next phase (exo-erythrocytic phase - meaning the phase that occurs outside erythrocytes), some merozoites enter other liver cells and repeat the schizont-merozoite cycle.

The main asexual phase is the erythrocytic phase, in which the merozoites enter erythrocytes and develop there. As you might expect, each stage of development through which the organism passes is given a further, difficult-to-pronounce name. It is sufficient to know, however, that the result of this development process is the release of even more merozoites into the blood, where they infect new cells.

- *Is there a purpose to learning about these stages?*

The disappearance from the blood of the parasites in the first stage helps us to understand why the patient has no symptoms early on.

- *So if someone has contracted malaria on holiday, when will they show symptoms?*

Unless the holiday is very long, the symptoms will probably not occur until they return home. A potential problem is that if health-care staff have not seen malaria before, a diagnosis may be delayed. For this reason, we have spent some time describing this disease.

- *So what actually causes the sudden severe pyrexia?*

This occurs when merozoites are released into the blood in the erythrocytic phase. Incidentally, the exo-erythrocytic phase persists for a long time in *Plasmodium vivax* infection and accounts for relapses after the parasite has been eradicated from the blood.

- *Why doesn't the body destroy the parasite?*

In its complex lifecycle, the parasite undergoes changes that enable it to repeatedly evade the immune system.

- *So is that the whole of the lifecycle of the malaria parasite?*

Not quite. Some merozoites develop into sexual cells (**gametocytes**), but sexual reproduction does not take place in the human. The lifecycle is completed only when a female Anophyles mosquito feeds on the human's infected blood. In view of the significance of mosquitoes in spreading malaria, these small creatures feature strongly in malaria prevention measures outlined in Practice point 16.3.

Host–microorganism relationships

Before we consider infectious disease further, we ought to clarify some important terms. The term '**symbiosis**' refers to the close living association of two different species of organism. Symbiosis takes a number of forms. In **commensalism**, one species benefits from the association while the other neither benefits nor is harmed. The surface of our skin supports the growth of a range of bacteria, sometimes described as skin commensals or normal skin flora. Our skin forms an environment on which the organisms grow, but we experience neither harm nor benefit as a consequence. **Mutualism** refers to a close relationship in which both organisms

Practice point 16.3

Malaria prevention

Since Anophyles mosquitoes are the sole carriers of malaria to humans, prevention depends on effective anti-mosquito measures. These include the use of insecticides in houses and insecticide-impregnated mosquito nets over beds. Insect repellents may also be applied to the body. Mosquitoes require water to breed, and so the risk of being bitten is greater near rivers and lakes. At these places, it is best to cover up as much of the skin as possible. Having said this, it is not possible to avoid sites where mosquitoes can breed - they actually need very little water, and you may have seen native British mosquitoes emerging from small pools of water, such as rain butts and puddles.

The mainstay of prevention measures is drug treatment. There are three problems, however. The first is that drug resistance is common and different drug regimes are required, depending upon which country, or even which area within a country, is visited. In the UK, practice nurses usually give travel advice, and you may be interested in this role. In view of the seriousness of malaria, considerable responsibility is borne by the nurse when planning a course of drugs.

- *Have you heard of any problems associated with malaria prophylaxis (prevention)?*

All drugs are capable of producing side effects, but some of the drugs used in malaria prophylaxis produce severe side effects. The side effects depend upon which drugs are used, but gastrointestinal disturbance is common.

- *What can be done about this?*

The worse thing that can happen is the patient stops taking the medication - after all, malaria is potentially fatal. Patients should be made aware of the side effects and of the importance of compliance with the regime. Gastrointestinal disturbance may be lessened if the drug is taken with food. If side effects are serious, it may be possible to take an alternative drug.

In order to be effective, malaria prophylaxis needs to be taken some weeks before and after the period spent in the high-risk area. Occasionally, patients leave the seeking of travel advice until late in their holiday plans, so that there is insufficient time to complete all the required preparation. Perhaps more often the patient returns home feeling well and then discontinues the prophylaxis prematurely.

benefit, but this kind of relationship does not exist in humans. The third type of relationship is **parasitism**, in which one organism benefits but the other is harmed. When the parasite is a microorganism, it is described as a pathogen and the harm done to the host is the disease.

It is probably worth pointing out that the above descriptions are not absolutely clear-cut. For example, the species *Staphylococcus aureus* is a skin commensal, but when a wound occurs *Staphlococcus aureus* may infect that wound. We could say that *Staphylococcus aureus* is taking the opportunity presented by the creation of the wound. In fact, that is the very expression used to describe what happens - we say that the organism is an **opportunist pathogen**. The important point here is that although *Staphylococcus aureus* is causing an illness (the wound infection), it does not need to do so in order to complete its lifecycle. It was already living and reproducing on the skin of the patient before the wound occurred, and at that point it was causing no harm. Compare this with a microorganism that cannot reproduce without causing disease; such organisms are called **obligate pathogens.** All viruses are obligate pathogens.

- *So, then, does the presence of an organism not always mean that there is an infection?*

That is correct. An **infection** occurs when an organism is living and reproducing in or on the host's tissues and causing damage (disease). The host's body will respond to this in a number of ways, and we discuss this later. If the presence of an organism produces no response and causes no damage, we simply refer to **colonisation**.

- *So colonisation is not a problem?*

Although colonisation may not be an immediate problem, it does result in a reservoir of microorganisms that may find their way to sites where they become opportunist pathogens. Consider a further example: Within our large intestines, we all carry *Escherichia coli*. At this location, it is a normal gut commensal, but *Escherichia coli* is capable of causing infection elsewhere. It may be transferred to the urinary tract and cause **cystitis** (infection of the bladder), or following ineffective handwashing it may be transferred to a wound or to food.

- *So are all pathogens equally capable of causing disease?*

No - the ability of a pathogen to cause disease depends upon its **virulence**. Virulence varies between species and even between strains of the same species.

In-text review

- ✔ Microbiology is the study of organisms that are not visible to the naked eye (microorganisms).
- ✔ Life on earth is divided into five kingdoms: animals, plants, fungi, monera and protista.
- ✔ Organisms are named using binomial nomenclature - so called since two names are used to identify each organism.
- ✔ Animal cells are characterised by a eukaryotic cell structure whilst microorganisms may be prokaryotic or eukaryotic.
- ✔ Four types of microorganism are important in disease: bacteria, viruses, fungi and protozoa.
- ✔ Bacteria are identified on the basis of their appearance, staining reactions, metabolism and ability to form spores.
- ✔ The term 'symbiosis' refers to the close living association of two different species of organism.
- ✔ In commensalism, one species benefits from the association while the other neither benefits nor is harmed, e.g. the normal skin flora.
- ✔ In parasitism, one organism benefits from the association but the other is harmed. When the parasite is a microorganism, it is described as a pathogen and the harm done to the host is a disease.

The response to infection

Immunity is the body's ability to resist infectious disease; the system that controls immunity is called the **immune system**. The immune system is also involved in other functions, including the detection and destruction of cancer, but this is not dealt with here.

The immune system

Think for a moment about one of the systems of the body - the respiratory system, perhaps.

- *What are its important structures?*

Your list probably includes the lungs and the upper and lower airways. It is not too difficult to think about the respiratory system, since the structures are large and easy to locate. The immune system is not so easy to picture. Its principal components are microscopic (e.g. cells in the blood) and it operates throughout the body - within structures of other systems, in fact. In order to explain how the body responds to an infection, some of the important components of the immune system are briefly described here.

Bone marrow

Blood-cell production (**haematopoiesis**) takes place in the red bone marrow of flat bones such as the sternum (breast bone). Among the cells produced are the **leukocytes** (white blood cells), which play an important role in immunity.

Leukocytes

Two groups of leukocyte exist: **Granulocytes** are so called because their cytoplasm has a granular appearance. The content of these granules determines the staining properties of three types of granulocyte. **Basophils** take up basic dyes ('phil' comes from *'philos'*, meaning to love), **eosinophils** take up the acidic dye eosin and **neutrophils** show no dye preference.

Agranulocytes are leukocytes that do not possess granules. There are two types - **lymphocytes** and **monocytes**.

- *What functions do the various leukocytes perform?*

Neutrophils are **phagocytes** that engulf microorganisms (phagocytosis) and destroy them with enzymes. Monocytes have the ability to be transformed into **macrophages** (literally, 'big eaters'), which have a considerable capacity for phagocytosis. There are a number of different types of lymphocytes, some of which are involved in the production of **antibodies** (**immunoglobulins** - an expression that means globular proteins of the immune system). Basophils produce **histamine** and eosinophils are involved in allergic reactions.

Thymus gland

The **thymus gland** develops beneath the sternum in foetal life and is involved in the development of a certain type of lymphocyte (**T lymphocyte** or T cell). Lymphocytes that are not processed in the thymus are referred to as **B lymphocytes** or B cells.

Immune mechanisms

Immune mechanisms are described as either **innate** or **acquired**.

Innate mechanims

The word 'innate' means 'inborn' or 'inbuilt', which is a very good description of a group of mechanisms that are the same in each member of a species. You might say that the body does not have to develop or 'learn' these defences. In addition, innate mechanisms do not adapt to the different microorganisms that the body encounters. For this reason, innate immunity is also referred to as non-adaptive. Innate immunity includes many different mechanisms - only some are described here, including physical barriers, chemical substances, **phagocytosis** and **inflammation**.

Physical barriers

The most obvious physical barrier is the skin on the outside of our body, which is several layers thick. The outer layer of skin is made up of tough dead cells, which are made waterproof by the substance **keratin**; this arrangement provides a barrier to the entry of microorganisms. After foetal life, we do not have to develop skin to protect us, and our skin does not change according to which microorganisms we encounter. The skin is then a good example of innate (non-adaptive) immunity.

Chemical substances

A number of chemical substances in the body help to prevent infection. One example is **hydrochloric acid** in the stomach - few microorganisms will survive this hostile environment. The skin is also acidic - **sebum**, which is secreted to keep the skin supple, contains **fatty acids**; the mildly acidic environment allows commensals to grow, but pathogens are inhibited. Not all protective chemicals are acidic, however - tears are protective of the eyes due to the presence of the enzyme **lysozyme**.

Phagocytosis

Neutrophils and macrophages are the body's phagocytes. The movement of these cells resembles that of an amoeba. When a microorganism is encountered, the cytoplasm is projected around it and the microorganism is engulfed (Figure 16.4). The microorganism is now contained within the phagocyte but surrounded by a section of the phagocyte cell membrane in a structure called a vacuole. Within the phagocyte cytoplasm are lysozomes that contain digestive enzymes. Lysozomes fuse with the vacuole and empty their contents into the vacuole. The microorganism within it is then digested before the vacuole moves to the edge of the cell and its contents are removed in a process called **exocytosis** (see Figure 16.4). Incidentally, pus is the accumulation of the end products of this microorganism-digesting process.

Inflammation

Think about what happens when a small wound occurs. Perhaps the wound is so small that you don't notice it at first. After a while, however, it starts to become more painful and the wound edges become red and swollen. If the wound is large enough, you might be able to feel that it is warmer than the undamaged tissue. We say that the wound is inflamed.

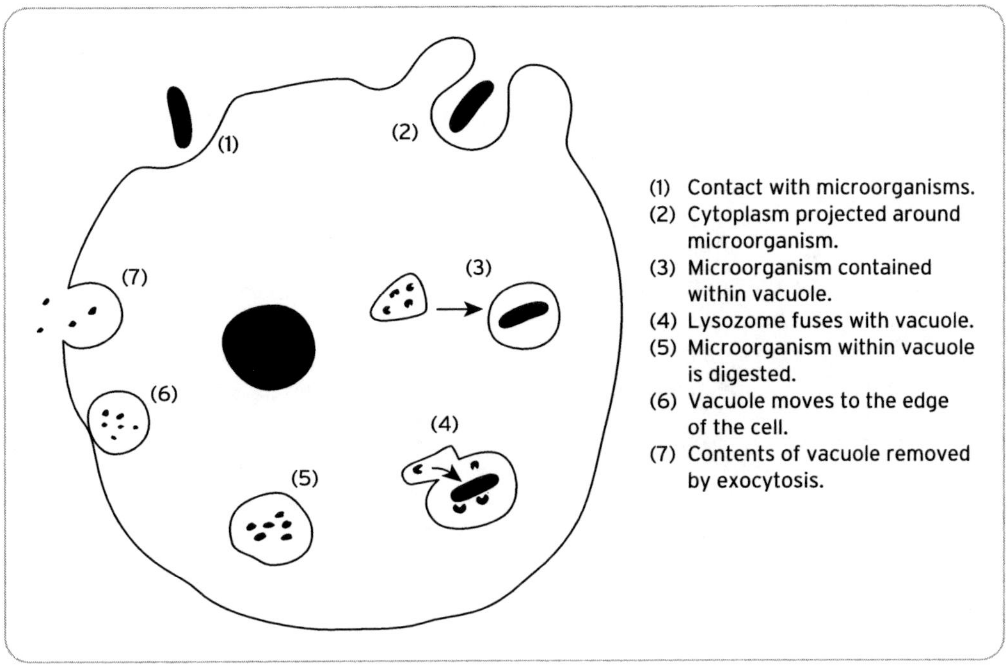

Figure 16.4
Stages of phagocytosis.

- *So to begin with the wound is not very sore, but then something happens to increase the pain and to cause redness, swelling and warmth?*

Yes, that is correct – these changes are the body's response to injury rather than part of the injury itself.

- *What purpose is served when the body's response to injury increases pain?*

One obvious effect is that the injured person starts to protect and guard the damaged tissue; if there was no pain, this would not occur. Inflammation is the response of the body to injury that serves to deliver important substances to the site of injury. When tissue is damaged, whether by a cut or damaged by a pathogen, substances are released from the affected cells. For example, **basophils** release **histamine**. These substances are **vasoactive**, meaning they have an effect on blood vessels – they cause the blood vessels to dilate.

- *Presumably the dilation accounts for the redness and warmth of the wound edges?*

Exactly so – this redness is referred to as **erythema**. The smallest blood vessels (capillaries) become leaky, and fluid and cells are lost from the blood, causing swelling.

- *Why is this important?*

It allows the phagocytes to appear in large numbers at the site of injury. In fact, phagocytes are attracted to move towards the chemical substances released at the site of injury in a process called **chemotaxis**.

Acquired immunity

- *Have you suffered from chickenpox?*

This is an infectious disease that is usually contracted in childhood - most people will have had the disease before adult life.

- *If you answered 'yes', do you worry about getting it again?*

The answer is almost certainly 'no'. You may have been so unconcerned that you have not thought to ask this question before. You are quite right to be unconcerned. The fact is that once people have had chickenpox, they become immune. This is clearly not because of some innate mechanism - after all, they did get the disease once. The immunity has been acquired - in fact, that is the name given to this type of immunity - **acquired immunity**.

- *Does immunity to chickenpox extend to other infectious diseases?*

No - when people become immune to chickenpox, they do not at the same time become immune to other infectious diseases. For this reason, acquired immunity is also referred to as **specific** immunity.

There are two aspects of acquired immunity - **humoral** and **cell-mediated**. Cell-mediated immunity refers to the activity of specialist types of T lymphocyte, while humoral immunity refers to the production of **antibodies** (immunoglobulins). The word 'humour' refers to body fluids, such as blood, breast milk and saliva, but it is antibodies present in body fluids that account for acquired immunity. These two aspects of acquired immunity are interrelated, but in this basic text only the production of antibodies is explained. For further details, you are advised to consult a physiology textbook.

Before antibody production is described, the term '**antigen**' needs to be explained. Antigens are large chemical groups that appear on the surface of cells. They act as a kind of code that the immune system uses to distinguish between **self** and **non-self**. B lymphocytes bind to antigens on the surface of microorganisms, after which they begin to grow and multiply, resulting in two populations of identical cells or clones (Figure 16.5). One population called **plasma cells** produce antibodies (immunoglobulins) in great numbers, but after some time they die. Consequently, the antibody level also begins to fall.

- *What do antibodies actually do?*

Antibodies inactivate antigens in a number of ways. For example, antibodies cause antigens to clump together to become more susceptible to phagocytosis.

- *But if the antibody level declines after the first infection, how is the body protected against further infections?*

Remember that the multiplication of B lymphocytes creates two populations. The second population consists of **memory cells**. These do not produce antibodies straight away but are able to do so if the antigen in encountered a second time. You could say that the body 'remembers' the infection and how to produce antibodies to fight it. This explains why a person becomes immune to chickenpox after the first infection. Of course, the process is a little more complex than the simplified picture presented here. For example, different

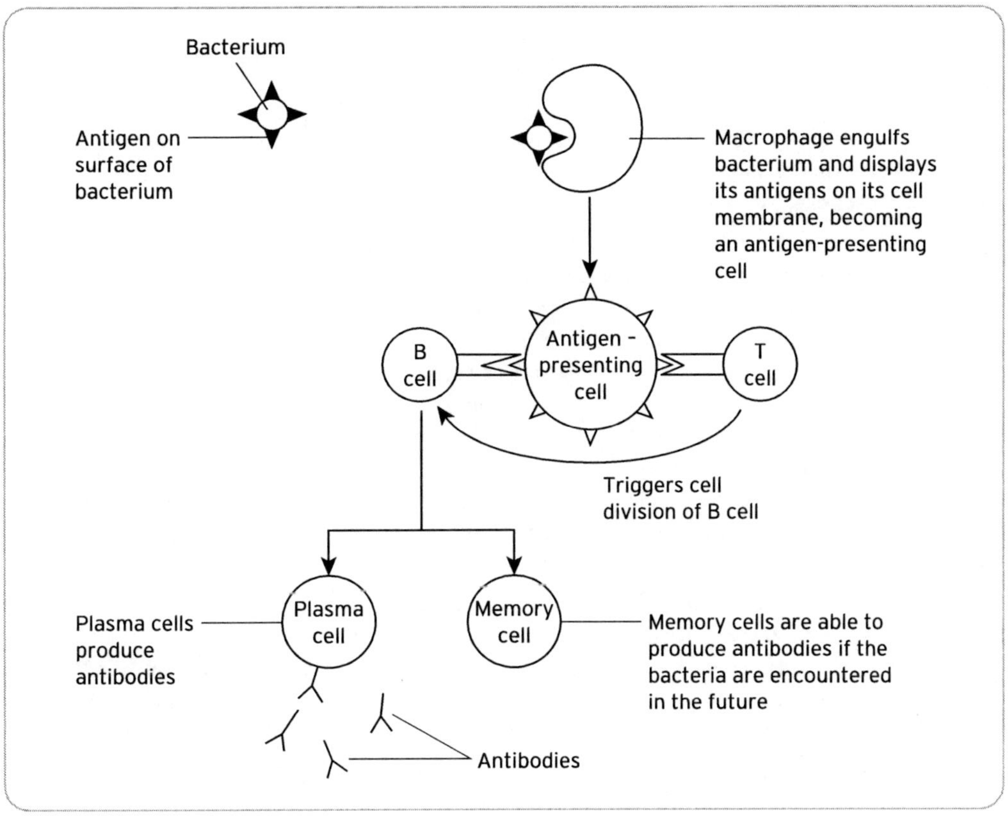

Figure 16.5
The production of antibodies.

types of T lymphocyte control the process. At this point in your studies, however, the above synopsis of acquired immunity will suffice.

- *Do health-care workers really need to know about acquired immunity?*

Perhaps we should ask some further questions. Recently, concerns about the safety of the MMR (measles, mumps and rubella) vaccination appeared in the media, with the result that many parents decided not to have their children immunised. Consequently, these children are exposed to the risks of some infectious diseases. You will not be able to answer questions about the safety concerns of MMR if scientists differ in their opinions, but could you explain what happens in the body following immunisation? In addition, on entering the health-care field, you were probably immunised against the serious blood-borne disease hepatitis B. Do you know what the risks of this disease are and why immunisation is effective? If not, how were you able to give consent to receive the immunisation? Whatever your answers to these questions, it is clearly important that all health-care workers have some level of understanding about acquired immunity for the reason that all are exposed to both the risks of infectious diseases and the immunisation against them. Immunisation is further explained in Practice point 16.4.

Practice point 16.4

Immunisation

In this section, we provide a brief explanation of immunisation so that you may have a basic understanding of how it is achieved. This understanding may help you to decide which immunisations you will consent to have yourself and give you the basis of a simple explanation for patients.

In the eighteenth century, people were highly anxious about contracting the infectious disease **smallpox**, since many people died from this. (The word 'pox' is the plural of 'pock', meaning pustule - a pus-filled skin lesion. Smallpox is a disease that produces small pustules - a descriptive name given at a time when the cause of infectious diseases was poorly understood.) Despite the fact that in the eighteenth century the cause of disease was not known, doctors did observe the effects of immunity - people who got smallpox and survived did not contract it again. Doctors made crude attempts at immunisation involving the inoculation of material taken from the skin lesions (pox) of sufferers. Here, the word 'inoculation' masks a rather unpleasant procedure - a knife deliberately contaminated with pus from a patient with smallpox was used to open a wound in the hitherto healthy subject. The obvious problem with this approach was that the inoculated person might very well contract smallpox and die.

If antigens of the causative organism of an infectious disease could be administered without the risk of the disease, then the recipient would develop immunity safely. You may be surprised to learn that some modern immunisations actually contain live organisms, but these have been cultured in such a way as to weaken them (**attenuated**). Other immunisations contain killed organisms or an altered form of the toxin produced by a microorganism called **toxiod** (tetanus).

Immunisations are usually administered by **intramuscular** (into muscle) or **intradermal** (into the dermis of the skin) injection. At some point, you might find it helpful to consult a nursing textbook to learn about correct injection techniques.

Virulence

Virulence is the name given to the characteristics of a microorganism that favour its survival in or on the host and its ability to cause disease. The factors that influence virulence include the ability to grow in or on the host, to evade host defences and to damage the host.

Ability to grow in or on the host

Nutrition

Some pathogens are able to synthesise certain nutrients, but to the greatest extent they obtain them from the tissues in which they live. The availability of nutrients may be one factor that determines whether an organism is able to live at a particular site. The **exudate** of a wound and an excess of pulmonary secretions both provide nutritious environments for bacterial growth.

Temperature

An organism is more likely to cause an infection if the host temperature is within its own optimal temperature range. Host susceptibility also varies with temperature. In everyday language, we recognise this by referring to upper respiratory tract infections as 'colds'.

pH

Most organisms grow within the pH range of the body's tissues. The slight acidity of the skin surface, however, deters some organisms, and the strongly acidic stomach contents offer some protection against swallowed organisms.

Other factors

There are a number of diverse examples that are not easy to fit into any classification. Consequently, a number of examples are given:

- Projections (**pili**) on the surface of *Neisseria gonorrhoea* enable the organism to adhere to the lining of the cervix and urethra.
- *Staphylococcus aureus* and *Streptococcus pyogenes* have receptors for **fibronectin**, a **glycoprotein** (molecule made up of a sugar and a protein) found on the surface of cells.
- *Staphylococcus epidermidis* produces a slime that enables it to stick to plastic such as intravenous **canulae** and giving sets.

Ability to evade host defences

The ability to evade host defences depends on many complex properties and so we deal with this only superficially. Some bacteria are able to resist phagocytosis (being engulfed by the body's defensive white blood cells), while others are engulfed but not subsequently destroyed. Resistance to phagocytosis is dependent upon the surface characteristics of the microorganism, such as the possession of a polysaccharide (type of carbohydrate) capsule.

Ability to damage the host

Occasionally, pathogens structurally damage the tissue that they infect. In most cases, however, damage is the result of the microorganism's biochemical activity - specifically, the production of toxins and enzymes. Toxins are bacterial products or constituents of the micro-organism itself that fall into one of two groups - **exotoxins** and **endotoxins**. Living bacteria (mainly Gram-positive organisms) produce exotoxins. Exotoxins diffuse into the surrounding tissue and are circulated in the bloodstream. They are highly toxic proteins that produce specific effects. Nonetheless, they are inactivated by heat and neutralised by specific antibodies. Endotoxins form part of the bacterial cell wall (typically of Gram-negative organisms) and are released only when the organism dies. They are non-specific in their action and are relatively heat-stable. Examples of toxin-producing organisms are given in Table 16.1. It should be borne in mind that some organisms that do not produce toxins nonetheless cause disease.

Table 16.1 **Toxin-forming bacteria.**

Exotoxin-forming organisms		Endotoxin-forming organisms	
Organism	**Disease**	**Organism**	**Disease**
Clostridium botulinum	Botulism	*Salmonella typhi*	Typhoid fever
Clostridium tetani	Tetanus	*Neisseria meningitidis*	Meningococcal meningitis
Corynebacterium diptheriae	Diptheria	*Shigella sonnei*	Dysentery

Table 16.2 **Enzymes produced by bacteria.**

Type of enzyme	Action	Example
Coagulase	Leads to formation of fibrin clot that protects organism from phagocytosis	*Staphylococcus aureus*
Fibrinolysin	Destruction of fibrin - assists in spread of microorganism	*Streptococcus pyogenes*
Hyaluronidase	Destroys hyaluronic acid that joins cells together - assists spread of microorganism	*Clostridium perfringens*
Collagenase	Breaks down collagen and destroys muscle	*Clostridium perfringens*
Lecithinase	Destroys lecithin, a component of cell membranes	*Clostridium perfringens*
Deoxyribonuclease	Breaks down DNA	*Clostridium perfringens, Streptococcus pyogenes*

Many pathogens produce disease by releasing enzymes that damage the body in some way. Table 16.2 gives some examples of enzyme-producing bacteria.

In-text review

- ✔ Immunity is the body's ability to resist infectious disease; the system that controls immunity is called the immune system.
- ✔ The immune system operates throughout the body within structures of other systems. Its principal components are microscopic (e.g. leukocytes/white cells in the blood).
- ✔ Immune mechanisms are described as either innate or acquired.
- ✔ Innate mechanisms are inbuilt and include physical barriers, chemical substances, phagocytosis and inflammation.
- ✔ Acquired mechanisms involve development of the ability to resist specific diseases following exposure to them.
- ✔ There are two aspects of acquired immunity - humoral and cell-mediated.
- ✔ Humoral immunity refers to the production of antibodies.

Sources of infection

Let us think back for a moment to the example of *Staphylococcus aureus*. Suppose a patient with this skin commensal is admitted to hospital after sustaining a serious wound - perhaps they have been in a road traffic accident. Subsequently, the wound becomes infected with *Staphylococcus aureus*. Let us now ask a rather obvious question.

- *From where did the infecting organism come?*

It came from the patient's own skin – this is an example of **endogenous infection** (self-infection). Now imagine that the staff in the hospital ward wash their hands ineffectively and transfer the organism to another patient, who then develops a wound infection. This is an example of **exogenous infection**.

- *In everyday language, we use an alternative term for 'exogenous infection'. What is it?*

Perhaps you know that we normally speak of cross-infection. Sources of cross-infection can be objects in the environment, members of staff and other patients. For example, organisms may be spread by a bar of soap or on dust particles floating in the air. Incidentally, we also refer to hospital-acquired (**nosocomial**) infection.

Routes of entry

- *So how do organisms enter the body?*

Even if you have not studied science before, you should be able to come up with some good answers to this question. Depending on how you classify them, there are four routes of entry: inhalation, ingestion, inoculation and congenital transmission.

Inhalation

Perhaps it is not surprising that the organisms that enter the body via inhalation tend to cause illnesses of the respiratory tract – think about coughs and colds. **Tuberculosis** is another, much more serious respiratory disease. In addition, many childhood illnesses enter the body via inhalation, including measles.

- *So what is actually inhaled?*

If an individual exhales forcibly or coughs, they will release droplets of respiratory secretions into the air. We do not mean visible droplets – these are far too large to travel far or be inhaled. In addition, large droplets will be readily filtered in the nose and airways. Large droplets may fall to the ground, however, and the organism subsequently may be circulated in the air on small dust particles. In contrast, droplets less than about 5 µm (5 microns) in diameter can travel in the air and may reach the lower airways when inhaled.

- *So how might droplet inhalation be prevented?*

It is good practice to provide a patient with a respiratory tract infection with tissues and a disposal bag to place them in when used. The bag should be changed regularly. If a patient is expectorating (coughing up) sputum, then a sputum pot with a lid should be provided. This should be labelled with the patient's name and date – then it will not be given to another patient by mistake and can be replaced daily.

Ingestion

Organisms that cause infection of the gastrointestinal tract enter the body by being ingested in contaminated food or water. Examples include *Salmonella enteritidis*, which causes salmonella food poisoning. The common term 'food poisoning' is something of a misnomer, since 'poisoning' implies toxins but no toxin is involved in this case (a better term would be **salmonellosis**). *Salmonella enteritidis*, present in contaminated food, is ingested; the organisms multiply in the body, causing dairrhoea, vomiting and fever. Salmonellosis is an example of a **zoonotic infection** - zoonoses are diseases that are transmitted from animals to humans. *Salmonella enteritidis* is found in domestic livestock, although it often fails to give rise to any symptoms in its animal hosts. It may also be present in eggs.

- *How could salmonellosis be prevented?*

Salmonella enteritidis grows readily at room temperature and will survive light cooking. Consequently, meat (especially chicken) and eggs should be cooked thoroughly. The organism survives freezing, although refrigerator temperatures will slow the growth rate. Cross-contamination is possible, and so cooked food and raw meat should be kept separately. Some people become asymptomatic carriers - that is, they carry the organism but they have no symptoms. The danger then is that inadequate handwashing during food preparation may result in the organism being transferred to previously uncontaminated food.

Inoculation

In this context, the term **inoculation** refers to transmission across a breech in the skin or mucous membranes. Sometimes, the term 'injection' is used instead, and indeed needles are often involved. Two examples are infection of an intravenous cannula site (drip site) by *Staphylococcus epidermidis* and transmission of hepatitis B virus through needle-sharing by drug addicts. A wound, including a surgical incision, is another example, as is inoculation by the mouth parts of biting insects. A mosquito transmits the plasmodium that causes malaria, while the trypanosome that causes African sleeping sickness is transmitted by the tsetse fly. Perhaps a less obvious example is anal intercourse and the transmission of human immunodeficiency virus (HIV); the recipient of secretions from an infected individual is at great risk because of trauma to the anal mucosa.

In the above cases, it is not possible to make general comments about prevention of infection - specific interventions are required. Hospital policies specify the frequency with which intravenous cannulae and giving sets should be changed, and staff should always wash their hands before attending to such therapies. Needle-exchange programmes, where drug addicts can replace used needles with sterile needles, are an attempt to reduce the incidence of blood-borne cross-infection in this group of people. The use of condoms helps to reduce the likelihood of transmission of HIV, and there are specific drug regimes for malaria prevention.

Congenital transmission

Although the placenta has features that help to prevent microorganisms from crossing it, some microorganisms are passed from mother to foetus. This type of transmission is sometimes referred to as 'vertical'. Examples include transmission of *Treponema pallidum*, the spirochaete that causes syphilis, and rubella virus, which causes German measles. Human immunodeficiency virus (HIV) may be contracted in this way, but transmission is more likely by contact between the foetus and maternal blood at birth.

Methods of transmission

Airborne spread

Inhalation has already been described as a possible route of entry for respiratory organisms that cause respiratory illness. Other organisms, however, are also airborne. Think about the following question:

- *Why were nurses traditionally taught to make beds?*

It is certainly true that some patients spend a good deal of time in bed, and comfort measures such as clean and unwrinkled sheets are important. But when changing sheets, why were nurses taught to loosen a dirty sheet, fold it carefully and drop it into a linen skip without letting it touch the uniform or bed curtains?

- *Why not pull it from the bed and carry it down the ward?*

Have you worked out that the purpose of the rather old-fashioned, formalised way of making a bed was to prevent shed skin cells from being shaken into the atmosphere or deposited on the uniform or bed curtains? Although these precautions were directed at airborne spread, they were not aimed at respiratory illness.

- *So what organism were they directed against?*

The above precautions were meant to reduce the spread of skin commensals such as *Staphylococcus aureus*. Such traditional nursing tasks have rather gone out of fashion, but there is a sound rationale for them. The emergence of resistant strains of *Staphylococcus aureus* means that measures to prevent transmission should be emphasised once again.

Under the heading of airborne spread, we should mention the organism that causes Legionnaire's disease – *Legionella pneumophila*. This organism is a problem in contaminated water, but it is dealt with here since ingestion is not a problem. Look at the name of the organism.

- *What does 'pneumophil' tell us?*

'Pneumo' refers to the lungs and 'phila' is derived from '*philos*', meaning to love. So *Legionella pneumophila* is an organism that loves the lungs – that is, it causes **pneumonia** (infection of the lung tissue). The organism enters the lungs via droplets of contaminated water – like those created by air-conditioning units and showers.

- *How can infection be prevented?*

The key to the prevention of infection by any microorganism is to identify the kind of environment it likes and then change the environment so that it cannot grow or break the chain of its transmission. In this case, person-to-person transmission does not occur, but we do know that *Legionella pneumophila* likes stagnant water at a temperature of up to 45 °C.

- *So the answer is simple – just keep water temperatures high.*

Exactly so, which is why we often see warnings about water temperatures above the taps in public buildings – the water is stored at a high temperature. Cold water comes direct from the water mains, and so organism growth in storage is not then a problem.

Contaminated food and water

We have previously considered ingestion as one means by which organisms enter the body, and we gave *Salmonella enteritidis* as an example. We now consider further cases of food and water contamination, while Practice point 16.5 deals with basic food hygiene.

Escherichia coli

This is a Gram-negative bacillus, of which a great many strains exist. Some of these strains are normal gut commensals, but others cause gastroenteritis in which diarrhoea and vomiting lead to dehydration. Laboratory tests are used to identify the different stains.

Escherichia coli 0157 has been responsible for a small number of very serious outbreaks. One of the most serious outbreaks took place in Lanarkshire in 1996. The outbreak was eventually traced to a single butcher's shop, but not until 20 people had died.

Listeria monocytogenes

This Gram-positive bacillus may cause serious illness such as **meningitis** (infection of the meninges - the membranes covering the brain). The ability of the organism to cross the placenta means that it is a particular problem during pregnancy. A pregnant woman who becomes infected with *Listeria monocytogenes* may have mild flu-like symptoms or be asymptomatic. Unfortunately, the consequences for the foetus are more serious and include spontaneous abortion. Infection has sometimes been attributed to unpasteurised milk and cheese made from it; consequently, pregnant women are advised to avoid these foods.

Contact

Contact with a source of infection is the main route by which organisms are spread. Sometimes a distinction is made between **direct** contact and **indirect** contact. Direct contact refers to contact between a person with an infection or carrying a microorganism and others who are not infected.

- *Which microorganisms are involved in transmission by direct contact?*

You probably will not be surprised to learn that skin commensals (e.g. *Staphylococcus aureus*), organisms infecting intravenous infusion equipment (e.g. *Staphylococcus epidermidis*) and any organism infecting a wound are transmitted readily by direct contact. You may be more surprised, however, to learn that organisms causing upper respiratory tract infection are often spread in this way rather than by being airborne.

- *What is the best way to prevent spread by direct contact?*

You might suggest that we need to break the contact, and you would be right. But think about this a little more. Let us take the example of a typical hospital ward - perhaps it has four bays, each with six patients.

- *This doesn't seem to be a good idea - we take 24 sick people and put them all together.*

Yes, that is exactly what we do and you are right - it is not a very good idea. Worse still, the same nurses care for all the patients. You might describe this as a recipe for cross-infection. This is not the end, however: some health-care workers, e.g. doctors and physiotherapists, also have contact with patients in other wards and departments - there might be several hundred patients in a regional hospital in the UK, and the opportunities for cross-infection are great indeed.

- *How, then, do we break the contact?*

The most significant practice that health-care workers can undertake to stop the spread of microorganisms is to wash their hands between touching each patient.

- *So then the problem is solved?*

Not exactly - think about it for a moment. Imagine that you are working in a hospital ward and a patient in the toilet uses the call buzzer. The patient needs your help to clean himself

Practice point 16.5

Food hygiene

When nursing physically ill patients, it is important to monitor the nutritional state of the patients, and thus nurses often have to deal with patients' food. Nurses are rarely involved in actually preparing food, but they may be involved in helping patients to eat or simply in taking food to patients. The following lists some important points regarding basic food hygiene measures, but insufficient information is provided for formal training in food handling.

General points

- The kitchen should be clean.
- Hands should be washed before food is handled.
- In the home, kitchen towels should be changed regularly.
- In institutions, paper towels should be used instead of fabric towels.
- Refrigerator temperatures should be monitored.
- People with gastrointestinal symptoms should not prepare food.

Safe storage

- Food should be stored in a refrigerator.
- Raw meat and cooked foods should be kept separately - the raw food should be on the bottom shelf so that it does not drip on to cooked food.
- Food in damaged containers (e.g. bulging tins) should not be consumed.
- Sell-by dates should be observed - but note that it is still possible for food to spoil before the sell-by date.

Preparing food

- Hands should be washed before preparing food and after preparing raw meat and eggs.
- Wounds on the hand should be covered with an appropriate waterproof dressing.
- Utensils should be kept clean, and separate chopping boards should be used for raw meat and other food.
- Fruit and vegetables should be washed in running water.

Cooking food

- Allow adequate thawing times before frozen food is cooked. Once thawed, food should not be refrozen without cooking if first.
- Ensure that the oven is at the correct temperature before cooking begins.
- Ensure food is cooked thoroughly - if necessary, use a food thermometer.
- If there is a delay before serving, cooked food should be kept hot - do not allow it to remain warm for a prolonged period.
- If food is to be stored after cooking, it should be cooled rapidly and placed in the refrigerator. Once again, it should not be allowed to remain warm.

after having a bowel movement. You are certainly going to wash your hands after that. After helping the patient back to his bed, another patient asks you to check the intravenous infusion site (drip site) on the back of her hand because it has become painful. Before you do this, you need to wash your hands. Having dealt with this, a colleague asks for your help repositioning an immobile patient in the next bay.

- *What do you need to do first?*

Yes, wash your hands. Are you starting to get the point? Washing your hands between direct contact with each patient is very inconvenient and time-consuming. It is never going to be easy to break the contact, but no matter how inconvenient or difficult, your hands must be washed between contact with each patient.

- *Is there no alternative to handwashing?*

When handwashing is done properly, it is very effective, but when entering and leaving a ward or when moving from one person to another after normal social contact, an antiseptic hand rub may be used instead. Next time you undertake a clinical placement in a hospital, check out the handwashing policy and other requirements for prevention of cross-infection. In the meantime, read Practice point 16.6, which describes typical handwashing practice.

Practice point 16.6

Social handwashing technique

The following description explains important points that might form part of a typical hospital procedure for social handwashing - that is, before normal social contact with a patient. More thorough handwashing is required before invasive procedures.

Hands should be washed in the following circumstances:

- As soon as the hands are visibly soiled.
- Between contact with different patients.
- After handling any items that are soiled or contaminated. Note that certain items, such as a sputum pot, may not be visibly soiled but may well be contaminated with microorganisms.
- Before handling food or food-related items, such as cutlery.

Liquid soap is satisfactory for a normal social handwash. Antiseptic solutions must be used before undertaking clinical procedures, when a more lengthy handwash is required. Soap dispensers should be used until completely empty and then replenished. Bar soap should be avoided, since it can itself be contaminated.

Elbow-operated mixer taps should be used and the temperature of the water temperature adjusted so that it is quite warm but not hot enough to cause discomfort or scalding.

Adequate liquid soap is applied to the hands so that lather can be created. The hands are rubbed together for approximately 30 seconds in the following way (Figure 16.6):

1. Palm to palm.
2. Palm of one hand over back of other, then alternate.
3. Between fingers - fingers interlocked and rubbed back and forth.

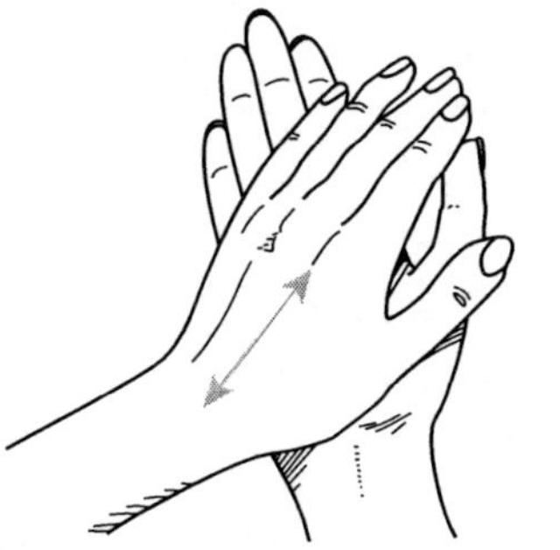

(1) Palm to palm.

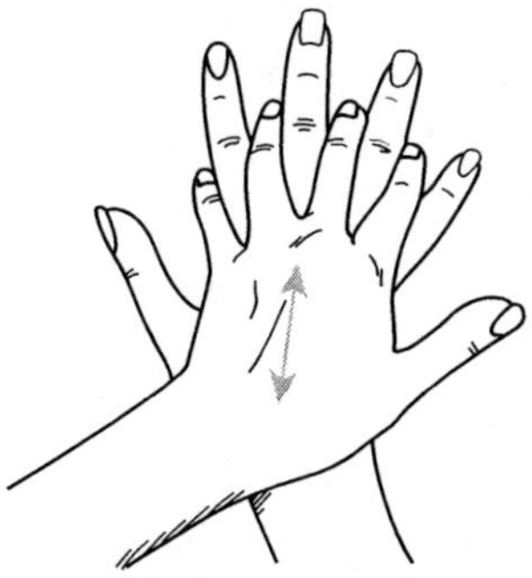

(2) Left palm over back of right hand, then reverse hands.

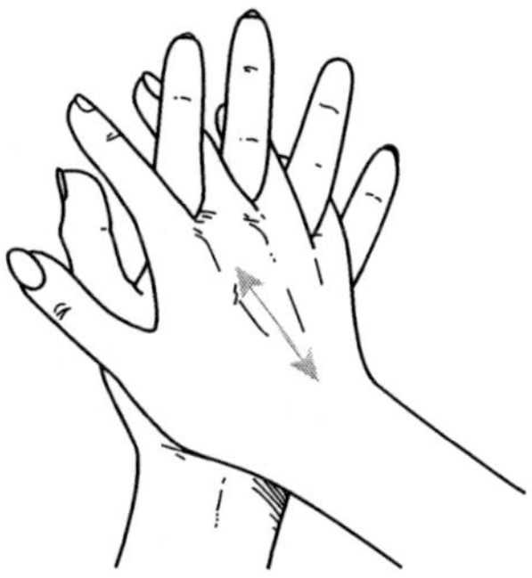

(3) Palm to palm with fingers in between each other.

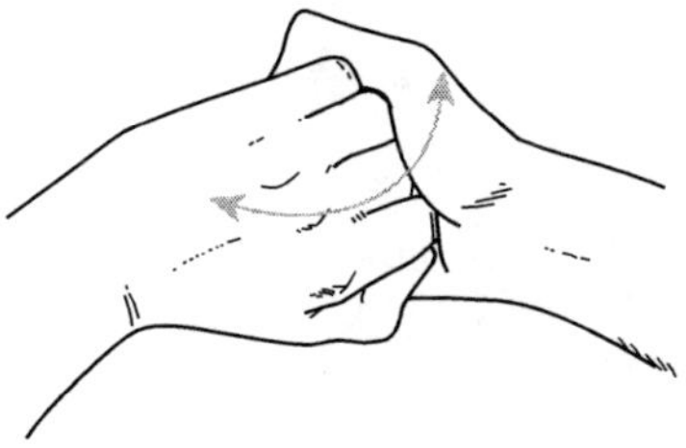

(4) Back of left fingers in palm of right hand, then reverse hands.

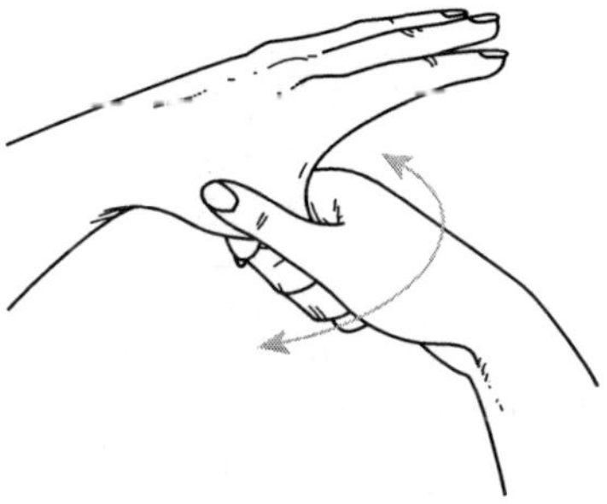

(5) Clasp left thumb in palm of right hand and rotate, then reverse hands.

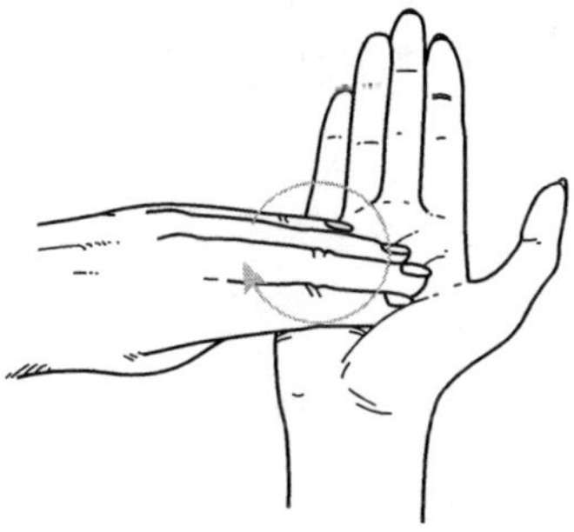

(6) Rotate fingers of left hand in palm of right hand, then reverse hands.

Figure 16.6
The procedure of handwashing.

4 Fingers of one hand to palm of other, then alternate.

5 One hand clasps thumb of the other and rotated back and forth, then alternate hand and thumb.

6 Fingers of one hand rubbed in palm of the other, then alternate.

7 One hand rubs wrists of the other arm, then alternate.

It is important to note that the physical action of rubbing removes soiling and transient microorganisms. Antiseptics have an additional chemical effect, but frequent use may cause irritation or soreness. This may lead to reluctance to wash the hands and cause small breaks in the skin, which can become a source of microorganisms. Consequently, it is preferable to reserve antiseptics for clinical procedures and to use liquid soap for normal social handwashing.

Cuts and abrasions should be covered with a waterproof dressing.

If hands are physically clean - that is, not soiled with dirt - then a hand rub may be used as an alternative to handwashing. Note that hand rubs do not contain detergents - the active component is alcohol. This means that they are ineffective at removing physical soiling of the hands. Hand rubs are ideal for use on entering a clinical area and between normal social contact with patients. Sufficient rub is applied to the hands so that the entire skin surface is covered. The hands are rubbed together until dry. The alcohol will not take long to evaporate, so if too little is applied the hands may have dried before all areas are covered.

- *What, then, is indirect contact?*

This refers to the transmission of microorganisms from one person to another via an object of some kind. Such objects are sometimes described as **fomites**. The object may be moveable and used by more than one person; crockery and cutlery are obvious examples - and most of us would not wish to share such objects without them being washed thoroughly first.

- *Can you think of objects that we sometimes share and that are actually involved in personal hygiene?*

Perhaps you have worked out that bars of soap and domestic towels are examples. For this reason, you should not see these used in hospitals, except for personal use by a single patient. For some years, the authors of this book conducted with student nurses experiments in handwashing. Bacteria would be taken from the unwashed and washed hands of students and grown in a hospital laboratory. Different types of soap and handwashing solution were used. Many students were surprised to see that after washing with used bar soap, the number of bacterial colonies grown actually increased. The used soap was acting as a fomite.

Other fomites are static and it is the people who move. For example, you might wash your hands very well after using the toilet and then unknowingly open the toilet door with a handle that has been touched by someone who did not wash their hands.

Insect vectors

The term 'vector' is derived from a Latin word meaning 'to carry' and is used here since insects do not function simply as a kind of fomite - they actually move about and carry microorganisms from one person to another. Indeed, the microorganism might complete part of its lifecycle within the insect - we have already mentioned malaria and African sleeping sickness in this context. In both these cases, the organism enters the body by inoculation - a bite. Insect vectors do not always function in this way, however. For example, flies transmit the Gram-negative bacillus *Shigella sonnei*, which causes bacillary dysentery, from faeces to food; the organism then enters the body by ingestion. Nonetheless, the number of cases caused by faecal contamination of the hands is probably very many times greater than that caused by flies.

In-text review

- The term 'endogenous infection' (self-infection) is used when an infection occurs because of the transfer of microorganisms from one part of a person's body, e.g. the skin, to another, e.g. a wound.
- The term 'exogenous infection' (cross-infection) is used when an infection occurs because of the transfer of microorganisms from one person to another.
- The term 'nosocomial' refers to hospital-acquired infection.
- There are four possible routes of entry of microorganisms into the body: inhalation, ingestion, inoculation and congenital transmission.
- There are four possible methods of transmission of microorganisms: airborne spread, contaminated water, contact (direct or indirect) and insect vectors.
- Removing a reservoir of microorganisms or preventing their transmission can prevent cross-infection.
- The single most effective means of preventing cross-infection in health care is effective handwashing.

Microbiology samples

Since microorganisms are not visible with the naked eye, laboratory tests are required for their identification.

- *What is it that is actually tested?*

For a microbiological test to be performed, some kind of sample is required – of body fluid, for example. Certain body fluids, such as **cerebrospinal fluid** (CSF – a fluid that cushions the brain and spinal cord), can be obtained only during specialised procedures. Others, such as urine, are obtained easily, and it is these that we concentrate on here. Practice point 16.7 provides general advice concerning obtaining specimens for microbiological examination.

Urine specimens

A specimen of urine for microbiological examination is obtained when the patient has symptoms of **cystitis** (infection of the urinary bladder). Symptoms include **frequency** (passing urine frequently), **urgency** (urgent need to void) and, sometimes, pain on passing urine. In addition, infected urine often has an unpleasant smell. Nurses often perform a quick test for the presence of Gram-negative organism using nitrite urinalysis strips. The reagent strip is dipped into a specimen of urine and the presence of nitrites confirmed by a change in colour of the reagent pad.

Practice point 16.7

Obtaining specimens for microbiological examination

Important general points common to obtaining various types of specimen include identification, container, collection and transport.

Specimen identification

Identify the type of specimen required from the microbiology laboratory request card. Next, check the identity of the patient concerned. Ensure that the patient details are correct on both the card and the specimen container. Patients are identified by four items of information: full name, date of birth, address and hospital unit number.

Specimen container

Ensure that the specimen container is the correct type. For example, a simple urinalysis does not require a sterile container, but a urine specimen for microbiological examination does.

Specimen collection

Ensure that the specimen is collected with regard to proper sampling technique. For example, urine specimens need to be collected without contamination by skin commensals. Note that when specimens are being collected, there may be a threat of cross-infection, and so precautions are required. For example, when obtaining a stool specimen, disposable gloves and an apron should be worn.

Specimen transport

Specimen collection should be timed so that the specimen arrives quickly at the laboratory. Little purpose is served by obtaining a specimen at night if it is not examined until the following morning. A delay gives time for contaminating organisms to multiply and produce confusing results. All specimens of body fluids should be transported in containers with tightly fastened lids. They should then be placed upright in racks or sealed plastic bags.

- *If a positive nitrite test confirms the presence of Gram-negative bacteria, why is a sample of urine required for the microbiology laboratory?*

Treatment could be commenced on the basis of the nitrite test alone. The specific organism causing the infection would not have been identified, however, and the antimicrobial drug to which the organism is sensitive would not be known. For this reason, it is preferable to obtain a urine specimen for the microbiology laboratory before any drug therapy is commenced.

- *If the nitrite test is negative, is a urine specimen for the laboratory not required?*

Remember that a positive nitrite test only confirms the presence of a Gram-negative organism. If the test is negative, there might still be an infection caused by another type of organism. Consequently, a urine specimen for microbiological examination is obtained on the basis of the symptoms alone.

- *Can the same urine specimen be used for urinalysis and microbiological examination?*

Certainly not - the sample that has had the reagent strip dipped into it has been contaminated. The problem with collecting urine samples is that it is far too easy to contaminate the sample. First, the correct sterile container needs to be obtained. Once the top has been removed, care must be taken to avoid touching the inside of the top or the container. The patient is then asked to urinate into the container. This is not as easy as it sounds, since skin commensals are easily washed into the sample as urination commences. This is particularly the case in women; to avoid contamination, the **labia** should be separated and the middle of the stream collected. It is a little easier in men, since the foreskin is usually easily retracted, although once again the middle of the stream is collected. Incidentally, if you see the abbreviation MSU (sometimes MSSU), this refers to a **mid-stream specimen of urine**.

Some patients who are unable to pass urine normally have a urinary **catheter** (a type of long tube) passed into the urinary bladder via the urethra (the tube that leads from the bladder to the outside). Urinary catheters are invariably problematic, for a number of reasons, including increased incidence of infection. One way to reduce the incidence of catheter-related cystitis is to avoid disconnecting the catheter from the drainage bag. Each time the tubing is disconnected, there is the opportunity for microorganisms to enter. Instead, the bag is emptied via a tap at its base.

- *If a specimen of urine is required, how is it obtained?*

If you check along the length of the catheter, you will find a self-sealing sleeve. A sterile needle can be inserted here and a sample of urine withdrawn into a syringe.

Stool specimens

Stool (faecal) specimens are obtained easily using a container in which a spoon is incorporated into the lid. The patient is asked to pass a stool into a container (a card bedpan liner) without passing urine too. A scoop of faeces can then be placed in the container and the lid sealed.

Sputum specimens

Sputum is part of an important mechanism for trapping microorganisms before they reach the lowest airways. When an infection of the lungs or lower airways is present, it may be possible to identify the organism in the sputum.

- *How is a specimen of sputum obtained?*

The patient is asked to spit into a sterile container, but there is a problem here. If you use the word 'spit', that is exactly what you will get - spit (saliva) rather than secretions from the lungs.

- *Could you ask the patient to cough instead?*

Indeed, you could - try for a moment by giving a cough yourself.

- *Where did the noise of the cough come from?*

From the throat - that is still not good enough - we need sputum from the lungs. One way to ensure that the secretions collected come from the lower airways and lungs is to begin by asking the patient to slowly and deeply breathe in and out three times. If there is an excess of pulmonary secretions, this simple exercise may trigger an episode of effective coughing, so have the specimen container ready. If not, at the end of the third inhalation encourage the patient to give a 'huff' - that is, to breathe out forcibly through the mouth (you might need to demonstrate this first). The aim of this exercise is not to create a noise from the throat but to forcibly exhale sputum from the lungs.

Wound specimens

A sample of microorganisms from a wound can be obtained using a sterile wound swab - this looks rather like a large cotton bud in a sealed container. The seal is broken and the swab removed without allowing it to become contaminated. The wound is wiped gently with the sterile end; the swab is then returned to its container. If a wound is exuding or pus is present, a specimen should be obtained on the swab. In large wounds, parts may show signs of healing but other areas may be infected: Ensure you do not drag pus from the infected area on to parts of the wound that are healing.

Blood cultures

Two important terms must be distinguished at this point. **Bacteraemia** is a transient condition in which bacteria are present in the blood but the host's defences then destroy them. This can occur after insertion of a urinary catheter or following wounding with a dirty object. When microorganisms are actively reproducing in the bloodstream, the patient becomes gravely ill and the term **septicaemia** is used. The patient urgently requires an intravenous (into a vein) course of antibiotics.

- *Which antibiotics?*

In order to identify the causative bacteria and discover which antibiotics the organism is sensitive to, two samples of blood are required. From these, the organism can be cultured (grown). Strict aseptic technique is used to obtain the blood from a patient's vein.

- *Can you work out why two samples are needed?*

One is used to grow aerobic bacteria and the other to grow anaerobic bacteria.

Other specimens

There are many other types of specimen for microbiological examination that are beyond the scope of a basic science book. Nonetheless, you might be interested to find out about them. Two examples are listed below:

- When bacterial meningitis is suspected, a sample of cerebrospinal fluid (CSF) is obtained during a procedure called **lumbar puncture** (a needle is passed between the lumbar vertebrae in order to aspirate CSF from around the spinal cord).
- Sexually transmitted diseases are increasing in prevalence in the UK. Swabs may be taken from the urethra in men and the vagina and cervix in women.

Microbiological tests

It is worth pointing out that once appropriate specimens have been obtained, laboratory tests are undertaken on the specimens rather than on the patient. Such tests are described as 'direct' - the tests are performed directly on the microorganisms.

- *What, then, are 'indirect' test?*

In contrast to direct tests, indirect tests are not performed on the microorganisms but on the patient in an attempt to identify some form of response to infection. Two examples are given below:

Serological tests

The word '**serological**' is derived from the word '**serum**' and refers to the fluid components of blood (meaning not the cells). In the present context, serological tests are those performed on a sample of the patient's blood.

Venereal disease research laboratory test

This test is used to quantify antibodies to the organism *Treponema pallidum*, which causes the venereal disease syphilis. The test is used as a screening tool to confirm a diagnosis and also to monitor the progress of the patient under treatment.

Hypersensitivity tests

Heaf test

This test employs a **Heaf gun** - an injection device that delivers purified protein derivative (PPD) to multiple punctures of the dermis of the skin. PPD is a protein derivative of *Mycobacterium tuberculosis*, the organism that causes tuberculosis (TB). If the patient is suffering from tuberculosis, has had the disease or has been immunised against it, the patient will develop an allergic (hypersensitivity) reaction to PPD and the puncture sites will become red and inflamed.

- *What use is this test of allergy?*

In developed countries, where immunisation against tuberculosis is routine, the Heaf test is used to confirm that a child has responded to immunisation and has become immune to the disease. Antibodies confer immunity; the presence of antibodies is confirmed by allergic reaction to PPD. You may remember having a Heaf test performed or the site being examined some time afterwards. If you look carefully on your upper arm, you might still be able to see the faint circular scar left by the test. In contrast, when tuberculosis immunisation has not taken place, the Heaf test can be used in the diagnosis of the disease.

The microbiology laboratory

This section provides a basic introduction to some of the tests performed in the microbiology laboratory. A detailed description is beyond the scope of this book, but the reader will gain an appreciation of some of the main techniques employed once a specimen has left the patient.

Cultivation of microorganisms

Unless you have studied microbiology before, the expression 'cultivation' probably sounds rather strange. After all, it refers to nurturing – the expression is often used of gardeners caring for prized plant specimens, but here we are talking about disease-causing organisms.

- *Do we really mean that the organisms are nurtured in the microbiology laboratory?*

Yes, that is what occurs: Microorganisms present in a specimen are given ideal conditions in which to grow. If microorganisms are to be identified and various tests performed upon them, then the microbiologist requires a supply in pure culture – that means each species grown separately and not mixed up together.

Cultivation of bacteria

The classical way to grow bacteria is referred to as **plating out**, since the growth medium is contained in special shallow culture plates with overlapping lids. The plates are sometimes called **Petri dishes** after a German bacteriologist. A wire loop is sterilised by passing it through a flame and then allowed to cool.

- *Why does the wire loop need to be sterilised?*

When obtaining a specimen, you will have taken care to prevent contamination – the intention is to grow the bacteria present in the specimen rather than bacteria from the nurse's hands or the environment. Contamination must also be avoided in the microbiology laboratory, and so the wire loop is sterilised each time before it is used. Next, a small quantity of the specimen (e.g. sputum, pus, etc.) is picked up and streaked across the culture medium. The wire loop is allowed to cool first after sterilisation in order to not kill the bacteria in the specimen.

- *What would happen if bacteria were now simply allowed to grow in this dish?*

A great many microorganisms would grow very close together. Instead, the first streaks are confined to a segment of the Petri dish; then the wire loop is sterilised again and a second segment of the dish is streaked. This segment overlaps with the first so that microorganisms from the first segment are deposited on a fresh area of the medium. The process is repeated several times so that each newly streaked segment has fewer and fewer microorganisms deposited upon it (Figure 16.7).

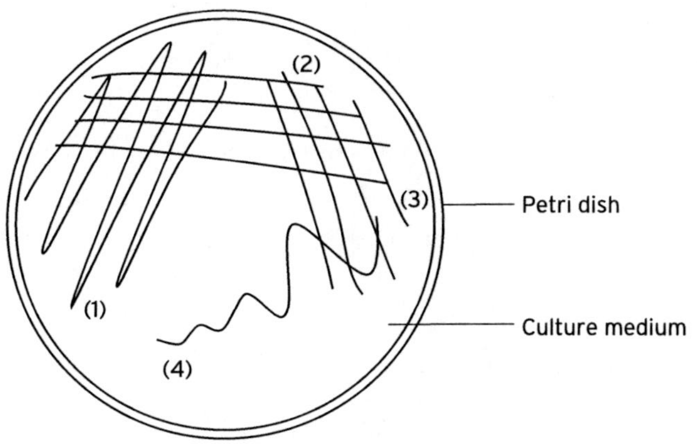

Figure 16.7
Growing bacteria on a Petri dish.
(1) Small amount of material (e.g. pus) is streaked over solid culture medium (e.g. agar). (2), (3), (4) Wire loop is sterilised in a flame and streaked on to uninoculated areas before incubation.

- *What happens next?*

Petri dishes are loaded into an incubator, which maintains the warm conditions ideal for bacterial growth. The result is that bacteria grow and form colonies. These are recognised as clumps on the surface of the medium. The size, shape and colour of the colonies vary according to the species of bacteria that has grown; for example, colonies of *Pseudomonas aeruginosa* are green. If growth on the first segment to be streaked is very heavy, then it will be possible to distinguish individual colonies from other segments. Each colony represents the offspring of a small number of microorganisms deposited there. Once this crop of micro-organisms has been obtained, a pure culture of each type can be grown.

- *Can you think how this might be done?*

We start with a fresh batch of Petri dishes and our wire loop once again. The loop is sterilised and material from a single colony is picked up and streaked across the medium in one of the dishes. Just as before, the dish is streaked in segments. The same is done for each different type of colony. The dishes are incubated and the result is a number of dishes, each containing colonies of a single species.

- *What is the medium on which the bacteria are grown?*

The medium is called **agar** - a jelly obtained from seaweed. (Agar was used by the Victorians to make desserts.) Agar consists of polysaccharides (complex sugars), which bacteria cannot use as a nutrient. Thus, the agar is simply a medium on which the bacteria grow. Of course, if microorganisms are to be cultured, they need nutrients, and these are added, mostly in the form of meat extract. The exact makeup of the medium can be adjusted so that different types of bacteria can be grown.

Cultivation of other microorganisms

In the above description, only the cultivation of bacteria has been described. Other types of organism require different cultural techniques that are beyond the scope of this book. It is worth asking one important question, however.

- *What are the particular problems in cultivating viruses?*

Do you remember that viruses are obligates parasites? That is, they require living cells in which to complete their 'lifecycle'. Consequently, viruses are grown in special preparations of living cells, called **tissue cultures**.

Identifying bacteria

- *Thus far, we have described how a pure culture is obtained, but how are bacteria identified?*

There are a number of techniques, including microscopy, staining techniques and biochemical tests.

Microscopy

We have previously described that bacteria are initially identified by their shape and consequently examination using the light microscope is performed. When material containing bacteria is smeared on to a glass slide and covered with a thin glass cover slip before examination, the term '**wet film**' is applied. It is more common, however, to use a **dry film** - that is, the slide is passed through a flame. Using a staining technique facilitates visualisation of bacteria. There are a number of staining techniques, and two are described here:

Gram stain

The dry film is stained purple (crystal violet or methyl violet) before being flooded in turn with iodine and acetone. The film is then washed with water. The film is then stained with red carbol fuchsin, washed with water and blotted dry. Some bacteria take up the purple dye, but in some the dye is successfully washed out. These then take up the red stain and appear pink under the microscope - they are referred to as Gram-negative. Gram-positive bacteria are those that appear purple - it has not been possible to wash out the dye. Differences in the structure of the cell wall account for the different staining properties. The Gram stain can help to identify bacteria. For example, the genus *Neisseria* is one of few Gram-negative cocci.

Ziehl-Neelsson stain

The film is stained with hot carbol fuchsin before being washed with water and then flooded with an acid and alcohol solution. The film is stained with methylene blue or malachite green and then washed with water and blotted dry. In most organisms, the acid and alcohol solution will wash out carbol fuchsin. The genus *Mycobacterium* (e.g. *Mycobacterium tuberculosis* - the organism that causes tuberculosis), however, is acid-fast - that is, the acid does not wash out the carbol fuchsin and the bacteria appear red/yellow. This test is performed because

Mycobacteria have thick cell walls that are difficult to stain using Gram's method. Once stained with hot carbol fuchsin, however, they resist decolouration.

Biochemical tests

Metabolic products of bacteria may be demonstrated by the use of specially prepared media. For example, the medium may undergo a colour change when certain substances are present.

Antibiotic sensitivity

The sensitivity of bacteria can be demonstrated by applying an antibiotic-impregnated paper disc to a pure culture of organisms. Where bacteria are sensitive to a particular antibiotic, growth will be inhibited around the paper disc.

Cleaning, disinfection and sterilisation

Cleaning

Think for a moment about a typical hospital ward.

- *Identify objects that several patients use in the course of a day.*

Perhaps your list includes furniture, toilets, baths, showers, wheelchairs, trolleys and aids for moving and handling. When we think of hospital hygiene, we often think of specialist procedures such as **autoclaving** (more about this later). It is sobering, however, to contemplate that objects used by the greatest number of people are not subject to specialist cleaning or sterilisation. They do not need to be - they simply need to be physically cleaned. Nonetheless, the process of cleaning makes a significant contribution to preventing cross-infection. It is unfortunate, then, that we often think of cleaning as a rather menial task. Worse still, cleaning is often subject to the severest cost-saving measures in health care.

A clinical colleague of the authors visited a hospital in a developing country and commented on how clean it was compared with a UK hospital. It had to be: The staff had no other way of preventing cross-infection and no antibiotics to treat infection if it occurred. Perhaps in the developed world we have become so confident in our ability to deal with infection that we place inadequate emphasis on simple preventive measures. Of course, cleaners are employed to perform most of the cleaning that takes place in care settings, but nurses and other care workers are also involved, and for this reason some important points about cleaning are included in Practice point 16.8.

Disinfection and sterilisation

Disinfection refers to processes that render an object non-infective. It does not mean that there are no organisms remaining but means that the number of microorganisms has been reduced greatly. Spores remain following disinfection. In contrast, **sterilisation** refers to the destruction of all living organisms, including spores. A number of methods are employed, including dry and moist heat, electromagnetic radiation and chemical methods.

Practice point 16.8

Cleaning

- Objects that are used by more than one patient should be cleaned adequately. An appropriate cleaning agent is required. For example, a table on which food is served simply needs to be cleaned with a detergent in order to remove dried spilt food. In contrast, a toilet requires a toilet-cleaning fluid. Just because an object is located in a hospital does not necessarily mean that it requires specialist cleaning, although some objects require more frequent cleaning - just imagine how many times a ward toilet is used in a 24-hour period.
- Cleaning solutions should be changed regularly. Do not carry on 'cleaning' if the solution has become soiled.
- Keep dedicated items (e.g. bowls) for cleaning purposes.
- Use sinks for dedicated purposes. For example, sinks in patient areas may be used for hand-washing, but the kitchen sink should not be used for this purpose. Soiled cleaning solutions should be disposed of in the sluice sink.
- Although cleaners undertake most of the cleaning in care settings, do not be reluctant to get your hands dirty. For example, if a patient soils a commode seat, the seat needs to be cleaned immediately after use.
- Disposable cloths are used for cleaning. Wet non-disposable items are an ideal environment for microorganisms to grow.
- Items that are not disposable should be stored dry. For example, mops should not be allowed to stand in buckets of water but should be wrung dry. Patient washing bowls should be cleaned after use, rinsed and dried with paper towels. They should be stored upside-down, with airflow around them.
- Clean surfaces should be wiped regularly with a fresh damp disposable cloth in order to remove dust. Dust is composed of a number of different materials, including skin cells - not the kind of thing you want to have floating around and landing in someone's wound. A surface that has been damp-dusted should then be dried.
- Clinical procedures, such as wound dressing, should not be performed during or immediately after cleaning. Cleaning may cause dust to circulate. It is always preferable to have a room set aside for clinical procedures. This room should not double-up as an office or storeroom where dust collects and that is difficult to clean because of the volume of stock.
- Take care to avoid solutions seeping into electrical equipment or being spilled and thus creating a danger to others.

Physical methods

Heat

Dry heat: this is used occasionally, for example in sterilising wire loops in the microbiology laboratory and in the burning of infected waste and Petri dishes. Methods that use moist heat are more common, however.

Pasteurisation: this is the process of heating milk in order to kill common bacterial pathogens. Louis Pasteur developed the process as a way to destroy *Brucella abortus* - the bacteria that causes **brucellosis**. One of a number of regimes is used, e.g. heating at 65 °C for 10 minutes.

Autoclaving: the autoclave is a device that employs steam under pressure and is used to sterilise surgical instruments and operating gowns. Heat-sensitive tape with stripes that darken in the autoclave are used so that it is possible to see which materials have been sterilised.

Electromagnetic radiation

You can read about electromagnetic radiation in Chapter 14. Various forms of radiation are effective, including ultraviolet (UV) light. In a primitive way, when hospital staff in developing countries hang out theatre gowns to dry in the sun, they are making use of UV light. Intense, artificially generated UV light is even more effective on the surface of objects, but penetration is poor and therefore it has limited use. Water from wells or boreholes may be treated with UV light in order to make it safe to drink. In health care, **ionising radiation** (e.g. gamma rays) is used to sterilise heat-sensitive objects such as plastic syringes and latex gloves.

Chemical methods

A large number of chemical solutions are available; some are more suitable for particular purposes than others. Suitability is dependent partly upon the ability of the solution to kill specific organisms and partly on the nature of object to be treated. For example, not all solutions are suitable for application on the skin. Chemical solutions rarely destroy spores, and some microorganisms will survive treatment. Consequently, chemical methods cause disinfection rather than sterilisation, and thus such solutions are referred to as **disinfectants**. If a chemical solution is safe to be applied to the skin, then the term '**antiseptic**' is often used instead of 'disinfectant'. Having noted this, strong solutions of antiseptics can cause damage if applied to the skin. Commonly used disinfectants are listed in Table 16.3.

Table 16.3 Common disinfectants.

Type of solution	Examples	Use
Halogens - hypochlorites	Hypochlorite solutions (e.g. Milton - sodium hypochlorite), bleach	Weak solutions are used to clean baby feeding bottles; strong solutions (bleach) are surface disinfectants
Halogens - iodine	Solution of iodine in water or alcohol and iodophors (combination of iodine and surface active agents)	Skin disinfectants, e.g. before surgery
Alcohol	Ethanol, isopropyl alcohol	Variety of uses, e.g. surface disinfection, skin cleansing, hand rubs
Chlorhexidine	Chlorhexidine gluconate (e.g. Hibitane)	Skin disinfection, e.g. as a solution for cleansing wounds, component of hand rubs
Phenols	Phenolic solutions (e.g. Hycolin)	Surface disinfectants

Treating infections

Even if we take the most careful precautions in order to avoid pathogenic microorganisms, our nature as social beings still results in the contraction of infectious diseases. The question that then arises is how to treat infections. Perhaps the immediate response to this question is 'With antibiotics.'

- *Name an antibiotic.*

You have probably given **penicillin**, the very first antibiotic, as your answer. If you have already gained experience in practice placements, however, you may be able to name some other antibiotics too. It is a sobering thought that until penicillin became widely available, there were few effective treatments for infections, and many people died as a consequence. Scientists had been searching for antimicrobial drugs for a long time, and one of the earliest successes was a compound of arsenic made by Ehrlich in the first decade of the twentieth century. A long course of this drug was successful in killing *Treponema pallidum* - the organism that causes syphilis. In the 1930s, Dogmagk successfully used the dye prontosil to treat animal infections and subsequently antimicrobial drugs called **sulphonamides** were developed.

- *We began by referring to antibiotics and then antimicrobials. Is there a difference?*

An **antimicrobial** is a drug that is effective in killing microorganisms or preventing their growth. Strictly speaking, antibiotics are antimicrobials that are produced naturally by microorganisms. Perhaps it helps to think of this as a microscopic example of survival of the fittest - one microorganism reducing competition from another by producing chemicals harmful to its competitor. On the basis of these definitions, arsenical compounds and sulphonamides are antimicrobials, and penicillin is an antibiotic. In this book, however, we follow common practice and use the terms 'antimicrobial' and 'antibiotic' synonymously. In addition, we ought also to clarify the proper use of another term - 'chemotherapy'. You have probably heard this used of the drug treatment of cancers. You need to be aware, however, that the term is also used of drug treatment of infections.

The account of the discovery of penicillin in 1929 is worth repeating. In Alexander Fleming's laboratory at St Mary's Hospital in Paddington, London, the fungus *Penicillium notatum* contaminated a culture of *Staphylococcus aureus*. Fleming noticed that the fungus inhibited the growth of the bacteria, but he was unable to isolate the substance responsible (penicillin). Consequently, although Fleming was the first to observe the effects of penicillin, there was no immediate therapeutic benefit from his observations. In 1940, two scientists, Chain and Florey, finally isolated the first penicillin (there are many closely related compounds), but penicillin was not widely available until after the Second World War. The development of other antibiotics was subsequently rapid - **streptomycin**, **chloramphenicol** and **tetracylines** were all identified before the end of the 1940s.

Action of antibiotics

Antibiotics are sometimes distinguished as **bactericidal** (kill bacteria) or **bacteristatic** (inhibit the growth of bacteria). The distinction is not clear cut, however. A number of different mechanisms account for the action of antibiotics.

Prevention of cell-wall formation

The bacterial cell wall is a unique structure – an animal cell does not possess one. Consequently, a selective drug attack on the cell wall is a good way of causing the bacteria to burst while leaving host cells unharmed. Penicillins, **cephalosporins** and **vancomycin** work in this way.

Inhibition of protein synthesis

Bacteria need to synthesise protein, just as animals do. Certain antibiotics, including tetracyclines and **erythromycin**, inhibit bacterial protein synthesis without harming the host's mechanisms.

Enzyme inhibition

Enzymes control the metabolism of bacteria, just as they do in animals. Drugs that interfere with bacterial but not human enzymes function as antibiotics, such as **sulphonamides** and **trimethoprim**.

Blocking DNA replication

Before bacteria divide, they replicate their genetic material (deoxyribonucleic acid/DNA). **Quinolones**, e.g. ciprofloxacin, are antibiotics that interfere with enzymes involved in this process.

Range of action of antibiotics

Certain antibiotics are effective mainly against Gram-positive bacteria (e.g. penicillins and erythromycin). Others are effective mainly against Gram-negative bacteria (e.g. **nalidixic acid**). The expression '**broad-spectrum**' is used of antibiotics that are effective against both Gram-positive and Gram-negative bacteria (e.g. tetracyclines, chloramphenicol, **cephalosporins** and **ampicillin**).

Adverse effects of antibiotics

Pharmacologists describe different types of adverse drug effect. A number of adverse effects are considered here, including toxicity, side effects and secondary effects.

Toxicity

All drugs produce toxic effects if given in high enough doses. The safe effective dose is determined in an extensive research programme before the drug is marketed. Toxicity is largely a problem of administration – that is, giving too much drug. Needless to say, care must be taken to ensure that the correct dose is prescribed, dispensed and administered. Prescription is normally the role of the doctor, but there are increasing numbers of non-medical prescribers, including nurses. Nurses normally dispense drugs – that is, take out the correct number of tablets or pour the correct volume of liquid. Three aspects are important here: identification of the correct patient, identification of the correct drug and calculation of the correct dose. You may find it helpful to review drug administration procedures in a nursing textbook and check the hospital policy in your next clinical placement.

Side effects

A side effect is an adverse effect of a drug that is unrelated to its primary action. For example, the antibiotic **gentamicin** may damage the eighth cranial nerve. (A cranial nerve is a nerve that arises from the brain rather than the spinal cord. The eighth cranial nerve conveys impulses to the brain from the ear.) This damage may result in deafness or **tinnitus** (ringing in the ears).

- *When you are next with a patient for whom antibiotics are prescribed, find out what the possible side effects are.*

You can do this by consulting the *British National Formulary* (**BNF**). There should be a copy of the BNF in each clinical placement where drugs are administered. Sometimes it is possible to minimise the risk of side effects. For example, in the case of gentamicin, which has to be given by intravenous injection, the dose should be administered slowly so that it becomes diluted in the bloodstream.

Secondary effects

Secondary effects are adverse effects related to the drug's primary action. For example, antibiotics are given for the purpose of treating infection, but the causative organism may be destroyed only to be replaced by another. The expression '**superinfection**' is sometimes used of this phenomenon.

- *Has this got anything to do with 'superbugs'?*

The expression '**superbug**' is commonly used in the media in a way that is misleading; we shall return to this point later. In common usage, 'super' refers to strength, but in this case it means 'on top of'.

- *So superinfection is where an infection is treated successfully but the patient contracts a second infection on top of the first?*

Yes, that is correct. One common example of this is oral **thrush** - infection of the oral mucosa by the fungus *Candida albicans*. Thrush is visible as white plaques that cause soreness of the tongue and mouth. Thrush takes hold once the normal bacterial flora of the mouth has been destroyed by a course of antibiotics. This is not the intended effect of the antibiotics - they are used to treat pathogens. It is simply that chemotherapy does not distinguish between harmful bacteria causing an illness and harmless bacteria inhabiting the mouth. You should always look for signs of thrush in any patient who has taken a long course of antibiotics.

- *How is thrush treated?*

Normally, *Candida albicans* is eradicated by the antifungal drug **nystatin**, although more serious and widespread infection can occur and the second infection is not necessarily a fungus: It might instead be a different species of bacteria or a resistant form of the same species.

In view of the number and potentially serious nature of adverse effects to antibiotics, their prescription and administration thus needs to be undertaken with care, as described in Practice point 16.9. Following this, the problem of antibiotic resistance is explained in Practice point 16.10.

Practice point 16.9

The use of antibiotics

The aim of antibiotic treatment is to eradicate infection while causing the fewest adverse effects as possible. With this in mind, the following points serve as guidance:

- Antibiotics are not prescribed for viral infections and minor self-limiting infections.
- Antibiotics have a limited role in the prevention of infection, for example following surgery.
- The main means by which transmission of infection is prevented are physical measures (e.g. patient isolation) and good hygiene (e.g. washing hands).
- Antibiotic treatment is based both on the patient's condition and on microbiology laboratory reports. It may be necessary for chemotherapy to commence before a laboratory report is available, but ideally suitable specimens are collected before antibiotic treatment begins.
- Chemotherapy is under the control of suitably qualified practitioners and antibiotics are not normally available over the counter.
- A course of antibiotics should always be completed, but sometimes patients stop taking drugs once symptoms have subsided; if the organisms have not been eradicated, the infection may then return. In addition, resistance may develop in microorganisms exposed to antibiotics but not killed. If the reason for non-compliance is unwanted effects, then an alternative drug may be substituted.

In-text review

- Since microorganisms are not visible with the unaided eye, laboratory tests are required for their identification.
- Important general points regarding specimens include identification, container, collection and transport.
- Common microbiology specimens are urine, stools, sputum, wound swabs and blood cultures.
- Direct tests are those performed on microorganisms, while indirect tests are those performed on patients with diseases.
- Microorganisms are cultivated in the microbiology laboratory and subjected to a number of tests, including microscopy, staining techniques and biochemical tests.
- Disinfection refers to processes that render an object non-infective, while sterilisation refers to the destruction of all living organisms, including spores.
- A number of methods of sterilisation are employed, including dry and moist heat, electromagnetic radiation and chemical methods.
- An antimicrobial is a drug that is effective in killing microorganisms or preventing their growth.
- Antibiotics are antimicrobials that are produced naturally by microorganisms.

Practice point 16.10

Antibiotic resistance

The term '**antibiotic resistance**' is probably self-explanatory - it refers to the condition that exists when a microorganism is not susceptible to an antibiotic.

- *That is quite straightforward - so a particular antibiotic is effective only against certain bacteria?*

This is certainly true. For example, the complex cell wall of Gram-negative bacteria makes these bacteria more difficult to destroy than Gram-positive bacteria. We refer to this type of resistance as 'innate' - meaning inbuilt. It is acquired resistance, however, that is most often referred to. This is the term used when bacteria that are initially sensitive to an antibiotic subsequently become resistant to that antibiotic. This can be observed in the laboratory when bacteria are cultured in the presence of sublethal doses of antibiotics.

Resistance was recognised as a problem very early in the history of the development of antibiotics. Penicillin-resistant strains of bacteria were reported in the 1950s, but newer drugs temporarily proved effective. Certain strains of *Staphylococcus aureus* became resistant to **methicillin** (a type of penicillin), and the expression '**methicillin-resistant *Staphylococcus aureus***' (MRSA) came into being. Methicillin-resistant strains are also resistant to a variety of other antibiotics, and infection by MRSA is particularly difficult to treat. The expression 'superbug' is misused, however, since the organisms are no more virulent than sensitive strains - they are simply resistant to many antibiotics.

Resistant strains of *Staphylococcus aureus* may be carried as skin commensals, just as sensitive strains are. The carrier experiences no ill effects as a result. If the carrier develops a wound, however, MRSA may opportunistically infect that wound. In addition, MRSA can be transmitted from a healthy carrier to other people.

- *So what should we learn from this?*

The early successes of antibiotic therapy resulted in a degree of complacency concerning infection-control procedures. The current high incidence of infection by resistant forms means that health-care workers are again emphasising the importance of preventing cross-infection rather than relying upon the ability to treat infection once it has occurred.

Summary

This has been a long chapter, with quite a lot of science, including the classification of microorganisms and how they are identified. At times, however, topics related closely to physical health, such as immunity and immunisation, have been explained, and some of the content, such as the prevention of spread of microorganisms, has been highly practical. Despite massive technological advances in the twentieth century, people in modern society experience significant threats to health from microorganisms, including HIV and MRSA, and new threats such as H15N bird flu emerge all the time. The optimism that followed the development of the first antibiotics has given way to an uneasy suspicion that 'out there somewhere' are further organisms ready to cause infections that we shall find very difficult to treat. At present, the role of the nurse in preventing cross-infection and in the care of patients with infections has again become very important indeed.

Summary points

- **Four types of microorganism are important in disease: bacteria, viruses, fungi and protozoa.**
- **Bacteria are identified on the basis of their appearance, staining reactions, metabolism and ability to form spores.**
- **Various forms of host-microorganism relationship exist, including commensalism and parasitism.**
- **Various mechanisms exist to resist infectious disease. Immunity may be described as innate or acquired.**
- **Microorganisms enter the body by inhalation, ingestion, inoculation and congenital routes.**
- **The means of transmission of microorganism are airborne, contaminated food and water, contact and by insect vectors.**
- **Microorganisms are identified largely by tests performed in the microbiology laboratory on specimens taken from the patient. These specimens must be obtained without contamination.**
- **Cleaning, disinfection and sterilisation are important techniques used to reduce the risk of transmission of infection.**
- **Proper handwashing is the most important single action performed to reduce cross-infection.**
- **Antimicrobial drugs kill or inhibit the growth of bacteria, but in view of the possible development of resistance their prescription and administration should be controlled carefully.**

Self-test questions

1 Match the term on the left with the most appropriate description on the right:

(a) Saprophyte	(i) A microorganism that can complete its lifecycle only at the expense of another organism, in which it causes disease
(b) Obligate pathogen	(ii) A microorganism that lives on dead or decaying matter
(c) Commensal	(iii) A microorganism that has a close relationship with a host on which it confers no benefit or harm
(d) Heterotroph	(iv) A microorganism that obtains its nutrients from organic matter

2 Match the disease on the left with the most appropriate type of microorganism on the right:

(a) AIDS	(i) Bacteria
(b) Ringworm	(ii) Virus
(c) Malaria	(iii) Fungus
(d) Tuberculosis	(iv) Protozoa

3 Match the term on the left with the most appropriate shape description on the right:

(a) Cocci	(i) Curved
(b) Vibrio	(ii) Round
(c) Bacilli	(iii) Rod-shaped
(d) Spirochaetes	(iv) Spiral-shaped

4 Which one of the following is an example of a zoonotic infection?
(a) Cystitis.
(b) Salmonellosis.
(c) Glandular fever.
(d) Chickenpox.

5 Match the type of microorganism on the left with the most appropriate description on the right:

(a) Bacteria	(i) Microorganisms that consists of nucleic acid surrounded by a protein coat (capsid)
(b) Protozoa	(ii) Microorganisms characterised by hyphae
(c) Viruses	(iii) Microorganisms with a prokaryotic cell structure, some forms of which produce resistant spores
(d) Fungi	(iv) Animal-like protists

6 Which one of the following diseases do insect vectors **not** spread?
(a) African sleeping sickness.
(b) Bacillary dysentery.
(c) Malaria.
(d) Tuberculosis.

7 Which one of the following terms best describes the situation characterised by the presence of microorganisms but that produces no response from the host and that does not benefit or harm the host?
(a) Colonisation.
(b) Parasitism.
(c) Mutualism.
(d) Infection.

8 Which one of the following are cells of the immune system that are responsible for antibody production?
(a) Neutrophils.
(b) Macrophages.
(c) Monocytes.
(d) B lymphocytes.

9 Match the organism on the left with the most appropriate description on the right:

(a) *Clostridium tetani*
(b) *Mycobacterium tuberculosis*
(c) *Staphylococcus aureus*
(d) *Salmonella enteritidis*

(i) A microorganism that is an obligate aerobe that infects the lungs
(ii) A microorganism that produces an exotoxin with powerful effects on muscle
(iii) A microorganism that causes food poisoning
(iv) A microorganism that is a skin commensal capable of opportunistic wound infection

10 Match the items on the left with the most appropriate form of treatment to kill microorganisms on the right:

(a) Milk
(b) Operating theatre gowns
(c) Plastic injection syringes
(d) Microbiology wire loops

(i) Autoclaving
(ii) Pasteurisation
(iii) Dry heat
(iv) Ionising radiation

Further study/exercises

1 How is MRSA prevented and treated?

Bissett L. (2006). Reducing the risk of acquiring antimicrobial resistant bacteria. *British Journal of Nursing*, 15(2), 68-71.

Collins F. and Hampton S. (2005). Handwashing and methicillin resistant *Staphylococcus aureus*. *British Journal of Nursing*, 14(13), 703-7.

Fairclough S. (2005). Hand hygiene: a simple way to stem the tide of MRSA. *Nursing and Residential Care*, 7(12), 554-6.

Fairclough S. (2006). Why tackling MRSA needs a comprehensive approach. *British Journal of Nursing*, 15(2), 72-5.

NHS Direct Online Health Encyclopedia - MRSA: www.nhsdirect.nhs.uk/articles/article.aspx?articleId=252

Department of Health: www.dh.gov.uk/Home/fs/en

A simple guide to MRSA:_www.dh.gov.uk/PolicyAndGuidance/HealthAndSocialCareTopics/HealthcareAcquiredInfection/HealthcareAcquiredGeneralInformation/HealthcareAcquiredGeneralArticle/fs/en?CONTENT_ID=4093113&chk=7/XgcQ

2 Identify how, as a student nurse, you can help to reduce cross-infection during placements in clinical practice.

Candlin J. and Stark S. (2005). Plastic apron wear during direct patient care. *Nursing Standard*, 20(2), 41-6.

Chalmers C. and Straub M. (2006). Standard principles for preventing and controlling infection. *Nursing Standard*, 20(23), 57-65.

Jeanes A. (2005). Keeping hospitals clean: how nurses can reduce health care associated infection. *Professional Nurse*, 20(5), 35-7.

Johnson D. (2004). Infection thrives when basic cleanliness is ignored. *Nursing Times*, 100(13), 18.

Patel S. (2005). Minimising cross-infection risks associated with beds and mattresses. *Nursing Times*, 101(8), 52-3.

Patel S., Murray-Leonard J. and Wilson A. (2006). Laundering of hospital staff uniforms at home. *Journal of Hospital Infection*, 62(1), 89-93.

Rickard N. (2004). Hand hygiene: promoting compliance among nurses and health workers. *British Journal of Nursing*, 13(7), 404-10.

Answers to Self-Test Questions

Chapter 15

1.	c
2.	b c d
3.	b c
4.	a b d
5.	a b
6.	a
7.	(a) → (ii) (b) → (i) (c) → (iv) (d) → (iii)
8.	a
9.	b
10.	(a) → (ii) (b) → (iv) (c) → (i) (d) → (iii)

Chapter 16

1.	(a) → (ii) (b) → (i) (c) → (iii) (d) → (iv)
2.	(a) → (ii) (b) → (iii) (c) → (iv) (d) → (i)
3.	(a) → (ii) (b) → (i) (c) → (iii) (d) → (iv)
4.	b
5.	(a) → (iii) (b) → (iv) (c) → (i) (d) → (ii)
6.	d
7.	a
8.	d
9.	(a) → (ii) (b) → (i) (c) → (iv) (d) → (iii)
10.	(a) → (ii) (b) → (i) (c) → (iv) (d) → (iii)